THE FINE PRINT
— of Self-Publishing —

3ᴿᴰ EDITION

THE FINE PRINT
— of Self-Publishing —

The Contracts & Services of 45 Major
Self-Publishing Companies—Analyzed,
Ranked & Exposed

Mark Levine

Bascom Hill
Publishing Group

Third Edition

Bascom Hill Publishing Group
212 3rd Avenue North, Suite 570
Minneapolis, MN 55401
1.612.455.2293
www.bascomhillpublishing.com

ISBN - 0-9802455-7-5
ISBN - 978-0-9802455-7-8
LCCN - 2008925944

Printed in the United States of America

DEDICATION

This book is dedicated to every author who knew there was a book inside of them and did something about it. One of the most amazing publishing experiences you will have is when you hold an actual printed and bound copy of your book for the first time. My goal with this book is to help you find the right publisher so that the first time you lay eyes on your book, it will be with great pride and happiness.

Table of Contents

Introduction xi

Chapter 1
Don't Wait Any Longer To Publish Your Book—Make Your Own Big Break 5

Chapter 2
Why You Need To Read This Book 8

Chapter 3
The Nine Qualities of a Good Self-Publishing Company 10

Chapter 4
The Fine Print of Publishing Contracts 31

Chapter 5
Analyzing the Fine Print of Each Publisher's Contract and Service 46

Chapter 6
Outstanding Self-Publishing Companies 50

    AVENTINE PRESS 51

    BOOKLOCKER 54

    BOOKPROS 60

    COLD TREE PRESS 70

    DOG EAR PUBLISHING 76

    INFINITY PUBLISHING 82

    RJ COMMUNICATIONS 89

    XULON PRESS 92

CHAPTER 7

Some Pretty Good Self-Publishing Companies 99

    BLITZPRINT 99

    FOREMOST PRESS 105

    LULU 110

    MAGIC VALLEY PUBLISHING 117

    OUTSKIRTS PRESS 121

    UNIVERSAL PUBLISHERS 129

    THIRD MILLENNIUM PUBLISHING 133

    WAHMPRENEUR BOOKS 137

    WASTELAND PRESS 142

CHAPTER 8

Publishers Who Are Just OK 149

    BLOOMING TWIG BOOKS 149

    BOOKSURGE PUBLISHING 155

    BOOKSTAND PUBLISHING 163

    CREATESPACE 169

    LLUMINA PRESS 176

    VIRTUALBOOKWORM.COM 181

    WHEATMARK PUBLISHING 188

CHAPTER 9

Publishers to Avoid 197

    ARBOR BOOKS INC. 198

    AUTHORHOUSE 203

    THE BECKHAM PUBLICATIONS GROUP 211

    DORRANCE PUBLISHING 219

    E-BOOKTIME 225

    HOLY FIRE PUBLISHING 229

    INDYPUBLISH 234

    INKWATER PRESS 239

    ITHACA PRESS 244

    iUNIVERSE 246

    LITERARY ARCHITECTS 256

    PAGEFREE PUBLISHING, INC. 259

PLEASANT WORD 265

PUBLISHAMERICA 273

PUBLISH TO GO. 281

SIRIUS PUBLICATIONS 285

TATE PUBLISHING 290

TRAFFORD PUBLISHING 294

WINGS PRESS 298

WORDCLAY 302

XLIBRIS 308

CONCLUSION

You Found a Publisher, Now What? 319

ACKNOWLEDGMENTS

ACKNOWLEDGMENTS 323

INTRODUCTION

The publishing world is changing. If you're reading this book, you probably already know that. Most traditional publishers—those who front all the costs associated with publishing—are no longer risking dollars on new authors the way they did even five years ago. In 2005, traditional publishers offered 18,000 fewer new titles than they did in 2004, and the gap is only widening.[1] If you have a shoebox full of rejection letters from publishers and agents, you're living this statistic.

Luckily, thanks to advances in digital printing and the Internet, new authors are realizing that they don't really need traditional publishers. The publishing industry is going the way of the music industry—individual artists are bypassing the middleman (the publisher) and going straight to the consumer.

Writing a book is an amazing accomplishment. I've published three books (six if you count the editions of this book), and every time I finish the process and hold that book in my hand, I'm still amazed that I actually did it. With the exception of my first novel, all of my books have been self-published. If you do it right and make smart decisions, you will produce something you're proud of, make sales and have a pretty good time along the way.

Once you've decided that you are going to self-publish your book, your next decision will be whether or not you want to take on every step of the publishing process, including finding a printer, book formatter, cover designer, obtaining an International Standard Book Number

---

1 "U.S. Book Production Plummets 18K in 2005; Smaller Publishers Show the Largest Drop in New Titles," Bowker, http://bowker.com/press/bowker/2006_0509_bowker.htm.

(ISBN) and UPC bar code, locating sales and distribution avenues, filing for a copyright registration and all the other details associated with self publishing a book. If you determine that handling every aspect of the publishing process on your own is a ton of work and that your time is better spent devising a plan to promote and market your book, you'll want to let a competent and ethical self-publishing company handle the process for you.

The Fine Print of Self-Publishing reviews only self-publishing companies that provide the full range of book publishing services and not those that simply provide book printing services. All of the publishers featured in this book have these common characteristics:

- Accept submissions from new or inexperienced writers without requiring the writer to have an agent
- Publish the book in six months or less (in most cases 60 to 90 days)
- Don't pay an advance
- Offer little or no marketing budget for the author's book but sometimes provide these services for a fee
- Pay higher royalties than traditional publishers
- Charge up-front publishing fees.

I am proud to say that *The Fine Print of Self-Publishing* has been well received in the self-publishing community, especially by the ethical companies whose reputations have been unfairly soiled because of the actions of the "Publishers to Avoid" listed in Chapter 9. In the last edition, I sent out questions to all the publishers listed in this book. Many cooperated, some threatened to sue me, and some just ignored my requests altogether. I put all of that into the book. Eight of the publishers even agreed to remove language from their contracts that I deemed to be unfair for authors.

This time around, my editor contacted each publishing company discussed in this book as a prospective author—just like any of you would. The difference between you and her is that I armed her with the tough questions to ask, regarding justifications for 50%–200% printing markups, excessive publisher royalties, and more. You will be amazed at how some of these publishers treated a prospective author, and how they lied when we started asking the tough questions. We even submitted a book of poetry by a Jack Russell Terrier (yes, a dog) to some of the publishers who claimed they were "selective"—almost every "selective" publisher accepted it.

So, as you read this book, know that I've asked the questions you might not know to ask and, for the most part, got the answers—good or bad.

Note: After the second edition of this book was published, I realized that some of the issues I feel strongest about (like some publishers taking excessive royalties when they do nothing for your book and outrageous printing markups) were never going to be addressed. In late 2006, my company, Click Industries, invested in a new type of self-publishing company that agreed to try doing things the way that I believed they should be done. Mill City Press (http://www.millcitypress.net) is not reviewed in this book and will not be mentioned again. The publishers covered in this book that are ranked "Outstanding" and "Pretty Good" are solid choices. You may want to compare their services to those of Mill City Press when evaluating your options. Click Industries' investment in this new venture has given me insight into the publishing business that I would not otherwise have had.

CHAPTER 1

Don't Wait Any Longer to Publish Your Book—Make Your Own Big Break

Whether your idea of a big break is to have your book published so your story can be read by family and friends or to become the next writer on the best-seller lists, you have some decisions to make. You can polish your query-letter-writing skills and spend the time it takes to get your manuscript into the hands of an agent or traditional publisher. You can also attend writers' conferences to network with agents and publishing executives. Regardless of your talent, the odds will be stacked against you.

Or, you can take control of your writing career and spend a little money to publish your book.

Yes, it would be awesome to tell your friends that Random House just signed you. But, even if that happened, you'd still be a small fish in an ocean and likely worse off than if you'd published your book through one of the ethical self-publishing companies discussed in this book. Forget the agents and the publishers—you don't need them.

How can that be? Simple.

If Random House publishes Joe Nobody's book, it probably won't dump a bunch of money into marketing. If Joe's lucky, he'll get $5,000 to $10,000 in marketing efforts from the publisher, but Joe still has to do all the real marketing on his own. And, if the book takes off through Joe's efforts, Random House takes all the credit, and Joe only makes a 5%–10% royalty. Then again, if Joe's book doesn't sell, that's the end of Joe and his book with the big-time publisher. The only benefit to Joe, in this scenario, is that Random House foots the bill for costs such as printing, editing, and cover design.

If you believe in your book, then publish it. Period.

If you have unrealistic expectations (e.g., "My book is the next Harry Potter" or "Everyone will want to read this!") self-publishing will not be a pleasant experience. Set publishing goals that you can achieve, like selling 1,000 books in one year. It's good to dream big, but when you're paying to publish it's smarter to live in the real world. Don't mortgage your house to publish your book. Spend only what you can afford to lose. If you are calculating to the penny how many books you need to sell to recoup a $2,000 investment, don't self-publish your book. Whatever you spend is an investment in you as an author. Please look at it that way. It might be book number two is the one that turns you into a star, but until you get into the game, you'll never be discovered.

As you'll learn from reading about the companies listed in this book, publishing fees range from $299 to $40,000. A lot of companies have bait-and-switch packages, luring writers with no-frills $299 packages and then up-charging them for the additional services they need, such as cover design. To get a quality product (a custom cover design, professional layout, etc.) you'll need to spend $1,000 to $2,000, at least. You'll also need to budget some money for marketing.

Yes, you pay the up-front costs of design and layout, but you own the book outright, and if you choose the right publisher, your royalties will amount to at least three to four times more than what Joe Nobody's contract with Random House would have paid. Plus, if you follow the tips in this book, and your book takes off through your marketing efforts, you can pull it from the self-publishing company and publish it on your own (and keep 100% of the profits) or shop it around to agents and traditional publishers. Once you've sold several thousand copies and proven your marketing ability, Publisher X and Agent Y, who previously rejected your book, may suddenly be clamoring to get it.

Publishing your book with one of the recommended publishers in this book is by no means a second-class way to become a published author. It is an opportunity to make your book available, garner the attention you deserve and tell your story. If you are a talented writer, readers, agents and big-time publishers will find you.

It took me six years to become proactive about publishing my first novel, *I Will Faithfully Execute*, through a small self-publishing company. In 1994, when I finished the novel, I put it into the hands of a few big-time publishing houses. They all told me the same thing, "We like the writing, but in order for us to sell it, you have to rewrite this and rewrite that, then send it back to us."

I wasn't about to start rewriting my book so that maybe some traditional publisher would take it. I didn't have the time to invest in that gamble. My manuscript languished in my computer's hard drive for six more years.

In 2000, I founded Click&Copyright (www.clickandcopyright. com), an online copyright registration service, and discovered the whole world of self-publishing companies. Back then, many of the self-publishing companies had business models that couldn't work. They believed that they could make money solely on the printing and royalties, without charging up-front fees. My first publisher, Bookbooters Press, was one of them. I ultimately chose Bookbooters because they charged no publishing fees, offered free editing services, paid decent royalties, agreed to a nonexclusive contract, and expressed genuine interest in my manuscript. As you'll soon learn, if you don't know already, that business model no longer exists (neither does Bookbooters).

I Will Faithfully Execute was named Bookbooters Book of the Year for 2000–2001 and remained on its best-seller list until 2005, when the company went out of business. The novel is a political thriller that takes place inside a presidential campaign. In fact, it was one of the first books former President Clinton read when he left office (I have a handwritten letter in which President Clinton details his favorite parts about book).

My second novel, *Saturn Return*, a story about two 30-year-olds who discover themselves and who they're meant to be with, was published in 2006. My company published it, arranged for distribution and used the Internet to generate buzz for the book.

Most everyone who reads *The Fine Print* has a completed manuscript and is wondering, "What do I do now?" Many of you probably have queried traditional publishers and agents, only to end up asking the same question. The answer is easy. Publish your book.

CHAPTER 2

WHY YOU NEED TO READ THIS BOOK

If you decided to buy a television or a car, you might read Consumer Reports to find the best price and highest quality. Spending hard-earned money to publish your book should be approached with the same care. But, unlike buying a car, your book is an extension of you. If you choose any publisher ranked "Outstanding" or "Pretty Good" in this book, you won't get stuck with a Lemon. This book is all about helping authors find and choose a publisher that offers a superior product at a fair price.

Here are a few reasons why you need to read this book:

- To know what you need to look and watch out for when choosing a self-publishing company

- To understand what these self-publishing contracts really say and how to negotiate better terms with a publisher
- To get the most value for your money by not overpaying for services or book printing and by getting the highest royalties

I got the idea for the first edition of this book because a fellow author at Bookbooters contacted me about a shady publishing contract he had signed with another publisher. The contract gave the publisher the exclusive right to publish the book through the expiration of the copyright term (which is 70 years past the copyright holder's life). My fellow author was a professor at a prestigious West Coast university. I figured that if this guy wasn't reading the fine print of publishing contracts, there were probably thousands of other writers who weren't either. This book makes sure that you understand what the fine print says and the ramifications of signing a contract that may contain unfavorable language.

If you were signing a contract with Random House, you'd hire a lawyer, right? But when you sign with a self-publishing company, your legal fees could exceed all the money you hope to make from the sales of your book. That's why I wrote *The Fine Print of Self-Publishing*: to help writers understand self-publishing contracts and enable them to find the best publishing situations to fit their goals and expectations.

I can't give you legal advice, but what I can do is use my legal training, knowledge and experience to show you what these contracts really say and which publishers provide the best service for the best price.

The reason I keep putting out new editions of this book is because, now that I speak to writers' groups and at writers' conferences all over the country, I always meet people who got scammed—really scammed. In May 2007, I met a nice man who had been conned out of $35,000 to publish his book. His $35,000 got him 3,000 hardcover copies of his book that he couldn't sell, a lot of debt, and a series of lies from an unscrupulous publisher.

I can promise you that, if you follow the advice in this book, you won't get ripped off by any self-publishing company and that you may, in fact, negotiate a better deal. If you don't follow the advice here you may find yourself out a lot of money and involved with an unethical publisher.

CHAPTER 3

THE NINE QUALITIES OF A GOOD
SELF-PUBLISHING COMPANY

Choosing the right self-publishing company comes down to finding one that offers the best mix of price, low printing markups, high royalties, and favorable contract terms. The publishers rated "Outstanding" in this book come closest to meeting all of the must-have qualities in the list below. If you're already considering a specific publisher, go through this list of qualities and make sure your publisher matches up to it. If the publisher you're considering doesn't have most of these qualities, you'd be better off finding a different publisher.

An excellent self-publishing company should have the following:

1. A good reputation among writers
2. Fair publishing fees
3. Generous royalties without any fuzzy math
4. Low printing costs and high production value
5. Favorable contract terms
6. Fair policy regarding the return of your book's original production files
7. Fairly priced add-on services, such as marketing and copyright registration
8. A standard offering of an ISBN, UPC bar code, and LCCN (Library of Congress Control Number) as part of any basic publishing package
9. Registration of an author's book with R.R. Bowker's Books In Print; availability through a distributor (e.g., Baker & Taylor or Ingram); and a listing it on Amazon.com and other online retailers

A Good Reputation Among Writers

Every self-publishing company has some disgruntled authors, even the good ones. Let's face it, authors can be hard to please, and we often demand more from our publishers than we have a right to. So, while it's important to see what some of the company's authors are saying about them, you need to speak to more than one. If you find mostly satisfied people, you'll likely have a good publishing experience.

I talk to a lot of authors, and some of the gripes that I hear are unfair to the publishers. If you spend a few hundred or even a few thousand dollars to publish your book, don't expect to be treated the way that Scholastic treats J.K. Rowling. Again, it's about living in the real world. So long as the publisher provides what its contract agrees to provide, and does so within the time frame set forth in the contract, an author has no real complaint. If the publisher lied to an author to get him or her into the contract (and the author can prove it—keep your e-mails), then complaints carry more weight. You don't have a right to have your e-mail returned 20 minutes after you send it or to call your publisher 15 times a day. When you start making the publisher millions of dollars, then you've earned those rights.

Remember, self-publishing companies are really acting as general contractors with regard to publishing your book. When considering a publisher, talk to authors who've already published with the company. Most publisher websites provide author pages or links to authors' websites, which provide contact information. Do not pay too much attention to authors who complain that a self-publishing company didn't help them sell books. Remember, some of these people have done nothing to promote their own books, and their disappointment in their sales may get turned into disappointment in the publisher. This is still self-publishing, and the author is ultimately responsible for making his or her book sell.

You can also contact the Better Business Bureau (BBB) in the state or city in which the publisher is located. Even if the publisher isn't a member, if people have complained about the publisher, the BBB will have a record of it. If you see dozens of unresolved complaints, that's a problem. If you see a few complaints and they have been resolved, don't be alarmed. Anyone can file any type of claim with the BBB, and these often get stuck on a publisher's record even if they are bogus. I know of a case where an author filed a BBB report accusing her publisher of stealing her books and selling them on the black market (trust me, it was a book that wouldn't have sold in any market). The report was so outrageous that the BBB actually threw it out, but that's a rarity. All that aside, the BBB is a good first step in checking out a publisher you're considering.

There are some websites that do the sleuthing for you and provide warnings about shady publishers. While these sites can be helpful, they don't often check out whether the information posted is true or not, allowing authors to complain about issues that either they caused or aren't accurate. And, even when publishers provide documents to prove otherwise, some of these sites refuse to remove or modify a posting. Thus, some good publishers get an unfair rap on these sites. However, these sites can provide some guidance and should be consulted without accepting them as the gospel:

- Google Groups (http://groups.google.com). This is my personal favorite. Just type in the name of the publisher, and you'll get links to each posting in which someone has discussed it.
- Writer Beware (http://www.sfwa.org/beware).
- Writers Weekly Warnings (http://www.writersweekly.com /whispers_and_warnings.php).

Fair Publishing Fees

Choosing a publisher involves more than price comparisons. You get what you pay for in self-publishing, just like with anything else. If all you have is $500 to spend, I would save up until you can afford a publishing package that includes a custom-designed book cover and interior, not templates. Your book will scream "self-published" if you don't pay for real design work. If your goal is to be discovered as an author, pay to do it right. If your goal is to provide a book for friends and family only, then one of these cheap packages may work for you.

Don't be fooled by the "Publish for $299" offers. Like any other bait-and-switch offer, it's just to get you in the door. Be wary of the "Free Self-Publishing" offers from sites like Lulu.com and CreateSpace. com. It might technically be "free," but the markup on printing is so astronomical, as are the add-on services, that these offers don't turn out to be free at all. If you're committed to publishing your book, then spend the money it takes to create something you can be proud to give people to read. A book is more than just the story.

Once you get past the "bait-and-switch" packages, you'll find that most publishers offer a complete solution for between $1,000 and $2,000. No matter what package you choose, a quality publishing package should include:

- A high-quality, custom-designed book cover (Don't use any publisher's template—covers sell books.)
- Professional layout of the book
- Registration with Ingram or Baker & Taylor and listing the book on Amazon.com, BarnesandNoble.com and other online retailers
- A page on the publisher's website or some other online venue (other than a third-party online retailer), where you can sell your book
- The ability to purchase your own books for a reasonable price
- A contract that you can cancel anytime
- The return of the original production files, or at least a press-ready PDF, of your interior and cover[2]

When you find a company that meets these criteria, don't submit your book without having it professionally edited. Publishing an unedited book is a waste of money. If you're serious about your book, you will need to have it edited, and not by a friend or your old English teacher, but by a real editor. Many publishers provide this service for an additional fee: editing costs should be around $.01 per word for standard copyediting (spelling, grammar and punctuation) and $.02–$.04 per word for more substantive editing. Most self-publishing companies charge more than $.01 per word for standard copyediting.

In chapters 6–9, the publishing packages and fees of each publisher are discussed in detail.

Generous Royalties without Any Fuzzy Math

One of the highly touted benefits of self-publishing is that the author's percentage of royalties is much greater than what a traditional

---

2 A press-ready PDF file of your interior and cover can sometimes be manipulated to remove an old copyright page (one that has the publisher's name, ISBN number, etc., on it), to cover up a publisher logo, and to place a new bar code on the back cover. However, it is best to get the original production files.

publisher offers. Unless you're lucky or famous, traditional publishers offer royalties between 2.5% and 12%. Self-publishing companies offer royalties from 20% to 80% (a few even offer 100%). The way the publisher calculates this percentage, and what costs are built into it, is the most important and often the most deceiving aspect of self-publishing.

Publishers calculate the author's royalty percentage in a few different ways. In many cases, 15% of the gross and 30% of the net may end up to be the same amount. If the publisher you choose pays royalties based on the net sales price of your book, you must closely examine how it's calculated. Net sales figures can be manipulated by, for example, hiding inflated printing costs within the actual printing cost, which is backed out before a royalty is paid.

All publishers that pay a royalty on net sales prices subtract the cost of the book before calculating the royalty. Most self-publishing companies use the same printer to print their books and pay approximately $.015 per page and $.90 per cover for a standard paperback book. So, a 200-page book costs a publisher $3.90. Knowing this information might be the most important thing in my book; it will help you see not only which publishers lie to you about their production costs, but also whether or not the price you're paying for copies of your own book is reasonable.

When querying a publisher about its royalty calculation, the first thing you must ask is if it uses the actual print cost in that calculation or a higher cost (generally based on the marked-up price the author pays for copies of his or her book). Always ask a publisher to give you, in writing, the cost to print a single copy of your book. If it's more than $.015 per page and $.90 they are marking it up—no publisher pays more than that—and you should demand justification for the increase. Many self-publishing companies build extra profits into the "cost" of producing each book. Until now, they knew you had no way of figuring out what they were actually paying for each book. Now you do.

Most publishers covered in this book have two ways in which they sell your book: through their website or through online retailers, like Amazon.com and BarnesandNoble.com. What follows is a general overview of how royalties are calculated through these various sales channels. Each publisher review includes a breakdown and examples of how the publisher calculates royalties.

Net vs. Gross Royalty Percentages from Book Sales through the Publisher's Online Store

You want to find a publisher that pays a royalty based either on a fixed percent of the retail sales price or on retail sales price less the printing cost. Period. Let's say your royalty is based on net sales. If your book sells for $15 through your publisher's website and the cost of printing the book is $6, you should make $4.50 on each book sale if you've negotiated a 50% royalty.

Some publishers deduct the credit card processing charge incurred for each transaction (1.5%–2.9% average). This is acceptable because it's an actual cost incurred by the publisher in selling your book.

The "net sales price" approach can become muddied when publishers inflate the actual cost to print a book and then calculate a royalty based on this figure. For example, if the publisher is able to include the printing markups as part of the cost of printing, which is deducted from any net royalty amount calculation, they are double-dipping, but not disclosing it.

Take a 200-page paperback that costs $3.90 to print ($.015 per page and $.90 per cover) and sells for $15 from your publisher's website. Assume a 50% royalty. If the publisher is using the actual print cost in determining the royalty amount, the breakdown looks like this:

$15.00   retail price
– $3.90   actual printing cost
_____

$11.10   profit to be split
x .50   author royalty percentage
_____

$5.55   author royalty

The publisher also makes a $5.55 royalty.

If the publisher tells you the printing cost is $6.00, watch what happens:

$15.00   retail price
– $6.00   inflated printing cost
_____

$9.00   profit to be split

x .50   author royalty percentage

$4.50   author royalty

The publisher makes a $4.50 royalty, plus the printing markup of $2.10, bringing its total profit to $6.60.

That's double-dipping. The publisher is making money on both ends of each sale. See how important it is to find out what the publisher includes in printing costs?

Publishers who pay based on a net price defined as something other than taking the retail price of the book and backing out the cost of production and credit card processing fees can be problematic. These companies often define "net price" however it best suits them. For example, some publishers give themselves a trade discount (similar to that given to third-party retailers that sell your book). This is very shady. Don't worry, I'll tell you about the ones that do that. A trade discount is usually 40% to 55% off the retail price. When the publisher builds the inflated printing charge into the equation and then subtracts an additional 40% for the trade discount it gives itself, the math looks like this:

$15.00   retail price
– $6.00   40% trade discount publisher gives itself for selling your book
– $6.00   inflated print cost

$3.00   profit to be split
x .50   author royalty percentage

$1.50   author royalty

The publisher makes a total of $12.60 from this sale (royalty + printing markup + trade discount).

Finally, stay away from any publisher that arrives at the "net sales price" by deducting vague items such as "administrative costs" and "marketing costs." That is a black hole that will suck up most, if not all, of your profits.

ROYALTIES PAID BY THE PUBLISHER FOR SALES BY THIRD-PARTY RETAILERS

Most self-publishing companies state that your book has distribution through Ingram and is available through all major online retailers and 25,000 other retailers. This is half-true. What this statement means is that your book is available on Amazon.com, BarnesandNoble.com, etc., and through a bookstore if someone were to walk in and specifically ask the store to order a copy.

When publisher XYZ lists your book for sale on Amazon.com, BarnesandNoble.com, or any other third-party retailer, the money the retailer makes comes from the trade discount, which is typically 40% for brick-and-mortar retailers (i.e., bookstores) and 50%–55% for online retailers (like Amazon, etc.). Unless you have actual bookstore distribution, you only need to be concerned with the online retailers' trade discount. Whether your publisher pays you based on the retail price or on the net sales amount, when calculating the royalties for sales made by third-party retailers, the trade discount will almost always be taken off the top first (many publishers, who base their royalties on the retail price rather than net, will simply give the author a lower royalty percentage on sales via third-party retailers in lieu of the discount).

In order to compensate for the steep trade discount and for printing markups, self-publishing companies usually inflate the retail price of an author's book in order to create a situation where the author can see some kind of a royalty from sales on Amazon (or similar sites). The result is a book that should be retailing for $13–$15 ends up selling for $20–$22. Why would a consumer pay that much for a paperback copy of your book, when a book by an author they know is sold for a retail price the market supports? This is a huge problem in self-publishing and the reason why it is imperative that you find a publisher that pays the author the higher royalty percentage and doesn't mark up the printing costs ridiculously or set the retail price artificially high.

Assume you choose a self-publishing company that marks up the printing costs 40% (which is quite standard), gives a 50% trade discount to online retailers, and pays the author a 50% royalty based on the net sales price. For the 200-page, paperback example I've used throughout the book, here's how the math works:

$15.00	retail price
− $7.50	50% trade discount to third-party online retailer
− $6.00	inflated print cost

$1.50	profit to be split
x .50	author royalty percentage

$.75	author royalty

The publisher makes a total of $2.85 on this sale (royalty + printing markup).

This should anger you. You pay a company a lot of money to publish your book, then every time someone purchases your book from Amazon (so the company is doing nothing to facilitate this sale), the company makes 2.5 times what you do.

Unfortunately, this scenario is the rule; the exception is the company that doesn't inflate the printing costs. In that scenario, the numbers look like this:

$15.00	retail price
− $7.50	50% trade discount to third-party online retailer
− $3.90	actual printing cost

$3.60	profit to be split
x .50	author royalty percentage

$1.80	author royalty

The publisher makes a $1.80 royalty.

At least in this scenario, the publisher isn't making more than the author. However, I don't believe a publisher should make any royalties unless it is helping an author sell the book in some way, either by spending its own money on advertising or by marketing the book. Very few publishers covered in this book agree with me.

THE ROYALTY CALCULATION CHECKLIST

For each publisher covered in this book, I provide calculations similar to those above so that you can see if the author's royalty percentage is as good as the publisher wants you to believe. Some of the royalties are just as good as the publishers represent them to be, but some border on blatant misrepresentation. One goal of this book is to make it harder for unscrupulous publishers to fool writers.

To determine whether a proposed royalty is acceptable, evaluate:

- The publisher's method of royalty calculation: Is the royalty based on the retail price of the book or the net sales amount? If it's based on the net sales amount, the calculation should rely on hard numbers, such as production costs and credit card processing fees, and not on vague items such as administrative costs.
- Whether the publisher backs out the actual production cost of the book (production costs should fall between $.013 and $.015 per page and $.90 to $1.00 per cover) or some random, inflated printing cost.
- How much royalty is paid to the author: If an author receives less than 50% of the royalty amount, he should consider that a sign to pick another publisher.

Low Printing Costs and High Production Value

A publisher can pay the highest royalty percentage in the world, but if that publisher artificially inflates the printing costs of a book, then the retail price must also be set artificially high. Why expect casual readers to pay $19.95 for your paperback thriller when they can pay $7.95 for a Grisham thriller? Make sure the publisher prices your book in the "retail comfort zone" of the average reader who's willing to take a chance on an unknown author.

A nonfiction reference type book (like this one) can be priced higher than a novel of the same page count. Consumers are willing to pay more for certain types of nonfiction. That said, $13–$15 for a 250- to 300-page paperback is about as good as it gets in the self-publishing world, where production costs are generally much higher than books printed in runs of several thousand or more. If your book is only available through online retailers, copies won't be printed until they are ordered. This is much more expensive than offset printing (which makes sense once you start printing more than 750 books at a time).

Most self-publishing companies use Lightning Source to print and ship books. If you haven't already received your money's worth from this book, the payoff is here. As I have mentioned many times already, publishers typically pay about $.013 to $.015 per page and $.90 per cover for each book ordered. A 200-page paperback costs the publisher approximately $3.90 You've read this next line a dozen different ways in this book, but it's important, so read it again: Any publisher that tells you the per book production costs are higher is gouging you and making a tidy profit on printing.

In most distribution through self-publishing companies, if your book is sold through an online retailer like Amazon, the order goes directly to Lightning Source, who prints and ships the book. When Amazon pays Lightning Source (or any other distributor for that matter), it takes its trade discount off and then sends the remainder. Lightning Source keeps its $3.90 (in the case of our 200-page example) and sends the rest to the publisher, who then pays the author the agreed upon royalty. As of April 15, 2008, Amazon.com has been forcing some publishers that previously used Lightning Source for on-demand printing to use Amazon's own printer. If publishers do have to use Amazon's printer, the process of having no books in inventory but available on Amazon will be similar to what it is now with Lightning Source. It is still not clear if every publisher covered in this book will be affected, because so far Amazon seems to only be going after the biggest ones. With Lightning Source, authors and publishers were able to offer Amazon a trade discount as low as 20% of the retail price. It appears now that Amazon's minimum trade discount will increase.. Such an increase would affect several companies discussed in this book that give Amazon (and others) a lower trade discount than the standard 40%-55%.

If you want to make any money from books that you resell yourself, don't sign with any publisher unless and until you know what the printing markup is and the publisher has justified it in some way. However, you'll read some of the "justifications" I received while researching this new edition. Most are doublespeak made to confuse the author. None of the publishers will adjust their printing markups to get you as a customer (at least none of the big ones will). But feel free to really press them. Let them know that you know what's really going on. Anything more than a 15% markup on printing is simply not acceptable, unless you know what it is for and don't mind paying more than you should. With all of this talk about production costs, don't forget about production value. The book must look nice. The cover must be clear, not blurry or cheap looking. The book must withstand multiple reads. The best way to determine the publisher's production value is to order one of its books before signing the contract.

Favorable Contract Terms

Before you sign any publishing contract, you need to make sure the contract contains the following provisions:

- A way for you to terminate the contract within 30–90 days without any penalty
- A clause that states that you own all the rights to your work and any derivatives of your work, such as movie rights
- A clause that requires the publisher, upon termination of the contract, to provide you with all original production files that contain the cover art, formatted version of your book, and any other material you paid to have created

A very detailed discussion of specific contract terms can be found in Chapter 4.

Fair Policy Regarding the Return of Your Book's Original Production Files

You pay a lot of money to have a publisher create your book. A portion of that money goes into the creation of a cover design (assuming a custom cover not a template-based one) and the formatting of the interior of your book. I believe you should own those original production (or source) files. Unless you have Adobe InDesign and Photoshop (the software most designers use to create the cover and interior files) you wouldn't be able to do much with the files. That isn't the point. The reason you want these files is because, should you terminate your contract and decide to publish the book on your own or with another self-publishing company (perhaps one that offers better royalties and smaller printing markups), you will have to pay for typesetting and a cover again. Now, if you have the source files, rather than redesigning the book, you can simply swap out the old copyright page, bar code, and publisher's ISBN, etc., which will cost much less money.

If all you can get are the press-ready PDF files, you may still be able to get a designer to tweak the parts of the book that need it (copyright page, bar code and publisher logo). Cutting out the copyright page from the book and inserting a new one in a press-ready PDF is easy, but depending on the complexity of the cover design, covering up the bar code and replacing the publisher's logo, etc., could be trickier.

Many publishers will give you (or sell you) the press-ready PDFs of your cover and interior, but relatively few publishers will give you the original production files, even though they are useless to the company if you leave. The only reason they make you pay for the production files is to squeeze a few extra dollars out of you while you're walking out the door. It's wrong and you should demand that a clause be inserted into any contract you sign that gives you these files for free upon termination.

The most egregious violator is iUniverse: it makes you pay $750 for a press-ready PDF interior and $750 for the press-ready PDF cover should you terminate your contract within 18 months. All of the good strides this company has made to be author-friendly have been erased by this one greedy maneuver.

Fairly Priced Add-on Services

When considering add-on services, keep in mind that you're entering a gouging zone. The four main areas where rip-offs occur are cover design, editing services, copyright registration services and printing of promotional material.

Cover Design

A custom cover is essential, so figure its cost into your calculations. Some publishers include a custom cover design in their publishing packages. Avoid any cover template, which I define as any pre-designed cover into which you add a picture, photo, text or graphic. Your book will look cheap and self-published (or at least what people think a self-published book looks like).

Prices for a custom cover range from $200 to $2,000. It is so subjective, that I can't say that a $2,000 cover is always a rip-off or that a $200 cover is always a great deal. You need to examine sample covers created by the publisher's artists before you decide to purchase one (some companies now include a custom designed cover in their packages).

EDITING SERVICES

There are several levels of editing services:

- Copyediting: involves correcting basic errors in spelling, grammar, punctuation, and syntax. For a copyedit, don't pay more than $.01 per word. If you do, you'll only be padding the publisher's pockets.
- Line Editing: is copyediting on steroids—a detailed line-by-line process to correct errors in spelling, grammar, and punctuation. The editor will also make suggestions to improve syntax and word choice. A reasonable line edit costs between $.015 and $.02 per word.
- Content Editing: ensures the general accuracy and consistency of content and focuses on more extensive restructuring of sentences and theme and character development. A fair price for a content edit is between $.034 and $.044 per word.

Some publishers offer a sample edit, but most do not. Some publishers guarantee that, if you do not like the edits (after reviewing an edited chapter), they will reassign your book to another editor at no additional charge. Both of these are a good way for you to make sure the editor assigned to your book is right for it. Also, make sure your editor has actually edited books; some publishers use college students and interns as editors. Your book needs editing. You can't do it yourself, and your friend, the English major or teacher, can't provide the same level of editing as a professional editor. Editing is not something you can skip if you want to put out a professional product. Again, you must have your book edited.

COPYRIGHT REGISTRATION

Copyright registration is important, especially if you think you have a book that may really sell well, thus becoming a target for those who may want to misappropriate your work. By registering with the U.S. Copyright Office, you are eligible for statutory damages and attorney fees in the event that someone steals or otherwise uses your work without your express permission. Many publishers include copyright registration as part of their packages. You should never pay more than $150 for this service (which should include the Copyright Office filing fee of $45). For more details on the benefits of copyright registration go to http://www.clickandcopyright.com/what_copyright_protection_do_I_get.asp

Standard Inclusion of ISBN, UPC Bar Code, and LCCN as Part of Any Basic Publishing Package

An ISBN number, UPC bar code, and LCCN (Library of Congress Control Number) are explained below. The publisher should provide these three numbers as part of its basic publishing package. If you're required to obtain these items on your own, you might as well publish the book on your own.

Some self-publishing companies provide these services à la carte, but be wary of the charges.

THE INTERNATIONAL STANDARD BOOK NUMBER (ISBN)

The International Standard Book Number (ISBN) is a 10- or 13-digit number that uniquely identifies books and book-like products. Eventually, the 10-digit ISBNs will be phased out, so when you get one for your book, you'll be assigned two (for now).

The ISBN allows libraries and bookstores to find information about the author, the author's book, the book's price, ordering information, and other related information.

You'll need an ISBN to sell your book through any online or offline bookseller. Each edition of a book, whether in paperback, hardcover, e-book, audio, or other such form, requires a separate ISBN.

Almost all of the publishers in this book purchase ISBNs in blocks (the smallest is a block of 10). The publisher then assigns an ISBN to an author for each edition of the book the author has licensed it to publish. The ISBN attached to the book lists the publisher as the party to contact for information.

If a publisher assesses part of its fee toward the ISBN, make sure it isn't higher than $30 because even if the publisher is buying ISBNs in the smallest block possible ($275 for 10, including processing fees), the one for your book should only be around $30. Some publishers allow authors to provide their own ISBNs, but it's more hassle than it's worth. Keep in mind that if you purchase your own ISBN, most self-publishing companies won't allow you to use it for the version of the book they publish. However, you will be able to then publish your own version of your book either during or after the term of your contract with the publisher (assuming you have a contract that allows for that). Yes, if you terminate your contract you'd have your ISBN already and wouldn't have to swap it out in your interior, but it makes it more difficult for the publisher to handle orders and royalty payments to you. If you purchase your own ISBN, you can purchase a small block of 10 for $275 (which includes processing fees). You can assign them to any versions of any books you write (e.g., if you write three books and each has an e-book, paperback, and hardcover edition, you'd use nine of the 10 ISBNs purchased). You can complete the entire process online at http://www.isbn.org/standards/home/isbn/us/secureapp.asp. A non-priority application takes about 10 days to process.

Once the ISBN has been assigned to a book, it should be reported to R.R. Bowker, the database of record for the ISBN agency. Your book can be listed for free in R.R. Bowker's Books In Print as long as you submit the information about your title at http://www.bowkerlink.com.

If a publisher wants to charge you for submitting your book's information to Books In Print, make sure the charge is reasonable, because there is no fee to register at Books In Print.

UPC BAR CODES

All books use the Bookland EAN bar code because it allows for the encoding of ISBNs. Almost all book retailers and wholesalers require the Bookland EAN bar code somewhere on the back cover of a book because this is what the retailer scans at the point of sale to identify the price and information from the bookseller's database. Like any other bar code, the computer then automatically reports the price to the cash register.

If you're interested in learning the meaning of the numbers in a bar code, go to http://www.barcode-graphics.com/info_center/bookinfocoontent.htm.

For mass market books, which are sold in drug stores, department stores and other non-bookstore retailers, a UPC bar code will likely be required since these non-bookstore retailers are not properly equipped to scan the Bookland EAN symbols (this isn't something you need to worry about if you're published by a self-publishing company that doesn't sell your book in such venues).

Bar codes can either be on a film master (a negative or positive piece of film), an EPS file (an electronic file that can be provided to printers and graphic designers so that they can include the bar code within the cover design), or on preprinted labels utilized when an item or packaging has already been printed or requires unique identification.

The publisher should take care of the bar code without requiring you to pay any fees. If you are using a self-publishing company that provides bar code services as an à la carte service, never pay more than $25.

Prices vary by supplier. Accugraphix (http://www.bar-code.com), one of the larger companies that provide this service, sells a film master bar code for $24 (plus tax and shipping) and an EPS file for $29 (total).

Bar Code Graphics (http://www.barcode-graphics.com), another large provider of bar code services, charges $15 for either a film master or EPS bar code symbol. It also offers the option of creating your own bar codes (EPS only) online for $10 at http://www.createbarcodes.com.

Although you don't need to purchase a bar code from a vendor in your home state, a state-by-state list of Bookland EAN bar code suppliers can be found at http://www.isbn.org/standards/home/isbn/us/barcode.asp.

LIBRARY OF CONGRESS CONTROL NUMBER (LCCN)

The Library of Congress Control Number (LCCN) is a unique identification number that the Library of Congress assigns to titles most likely to be acquired by the Library of Congress. This is not the same as a copyright registration with the Library of Congress.

Librarians use the LCCN to access the associated bibliographic record in the Library of Congress's database or to obtain information on various book titles on other databases.

The publisher prints the LCCN on the back of the title page in the following manner: "Library of Congress Control Number: 2001012345."

Only U.S. book publishers are eligible to obtain an LCCN. To receive an LCCN, publishers must list a U.S. place of publication on the title page or copyright page and maintain an editorial office in the country capable of answering substantive bibliographic questions.

There is no charge for registering, but the publisher must send a copy of the "best edition" of the book for which the LCCN was pre-assigned (you apply for the LCCN prior to publication) immediately upon publication to: Library of Congress, Cataloging in Publication Division, 101 Independence Ave., S.E., Washington, DC, 20540-4320. The "best edition" of a book is the retail paperback or hardcover version of the book.

Books published in electronic form are ineligible for an LCCN.

Should you wish to obtain an LCCN on your own, the first step is to complete the Application to Participate and obtain an account number and password, which takes one to two weeks. The application is online at http://pcn.loc.gov/pcn/pcn007.html. Complete information about the LCCN process can be found at http://pcn.loc.gov/pcn/pcn006.html.

A publisher may try to tell you that there is a fee for an LCCN or that it has to charge you a fee because it needs to obtain one for each edition of your book. Don't believe the publisher. Unlike an ISBN, the LCCN is assigned to the work itself and doesn't change with each new edition or version. Certainly, it takes time and effort to submit the application, and it is fair for a publisher to build this into its fee. It's not fair for a publisher to pretend that the Library of Congress charges a fee for the LCCN.

Ability to Register the Author's Book with R.R. Bowker's Books In Print, Make It Available through a Book Distributor like Baker & Taylor or Ingram, and List It on Amazon.com, BarnesandNoble.com and Other Large-Scale Sellers

Most self-publishing companies have a relationship with one of the major book wholesalers: Baker & Taylor or Ingram. If you want to make your book available in brick-and-mortar bookstores, it must be available through one of these wholesalers. This doesn't necessarily mean that your book will be carried in any bookstore. It means that your Aunt Mabel can walk into her local Barnes & Noble and special-order a copy of your book.

In order to increase your sales opportunities, make sure your publisher lists your book on Amazon.com or BarnesandNoble.com (most do). Everyone knows Amazon.com, and should someone hear about your book, chances are that person isn't going to know or remember the URL of the publisher's online store. The first instinct of many consumers when looking for a book online is to go to Amazon.com or Barnesand-Noble.com. Having your book available through Amazon.com makes it appear more legitimate in the eyes of many consumers. Anyone can put a book on Amazon.com, but to the general public seeing a book there is a big deal. Another important reason to list your book on Amazon.com is that, if you ever start to really sell books, a traditional publisher may consider Amazon.com's sales rankings to be more accurate than sales figures from your publisher's website. The downside of selling only on Amazon.com is that because of the trade discount that Amazon.com takes you will make considerably less in royalties per book than you would from sales through your publisher's website or your own.

There are about 4,000,000 products on Amazon, so the "Amazon Sales Rank" number you see on a book's sales page means that out of the 4,000,000 products on Amazon.com that book is number X. A sales rank of 100,000 or less is fantastic. So, if your book has a sales rank of 50,000 that means that it is the 50,000th best-selling item on Amazon on that day.

Other online retailers such as Borders.com, Powells.com, and BooksA-Million.com, are also worthwhile venues for selling your book, but first make sure it's available on Amazon.com or BarnesandNoble.com.

Alexa.com ranks websites in terms of traffic. It isn't always the most accurate, but it's a good gauge of online retailers and can help determine where you should list your book. Like Amazon.com, the lower the number, the better. As of February 2008, Alexa.com ranked Amazon.com as the 29th most visited website in the world. BarnesandNoble.com was at 1,585, BooksAMillion.com was at 37,532, and Borders.com was at 376,475.

Any self-publishing company claiming to provide a complete publishing service will have your book listed with either Ingram or Baker & Taylor, and will make it available for sale on Amazon.com or BarnesandNoble.com.

CHAPTER 4

THE FINE PRINT OF PUBLISHING CONTRACTS

Lawyers have often been accused of creating a language that only they can understand. This legalese forces the layperson to hire a lawyer who can decipher a document written in this funky little language. It took me three years of law school and many years of practice, which involved drafting hundreds of contracts, to approach these documents with ease.

The contract terms discussed in this chapter are common in most self-publishing contracts. Publishers all use slightly different verbiage in their contracts, so one termination clause may differ slightly from another, even though they mean essentially the same thing. The idea here is to help you recognize and understand the various terms when you read through the contract of any publisher whose services you're considering.

I discuss the specific provisions and problems of each publisher's contract in their respective overviews, and I also suggest ways to make the clauses more advantageous either by persuading the publisher to omit or modify certain language, or by finding another publisher.

Surprises are fun, but not in publishing contracts. My number one goal is to help you understand what you sign.

Read this carefully right now and then read it again: If a publisher refuses to let you see a copy of a publishing contract before you provide them with a copy of your book, run away as fast as you can. If a publisher doesn't want you to see what it will ultimately ask you to sign, take that as the big, fat, clue that it is!

Now that we have that out of the way, here are some general provisions found in most self-publishing contracts:

Parties to the Contract

This will always be you (the author) and the publisher. This introductory language identifies names that appear throughout the contract.

The author will often be referred to as the "Author," and not by his or her name.

The publisher will often be referred to as the "Publisher" or "Company," and not by its name.

Your manuscript will usually be referred to as the "Work," and not by its title.

License of Rights

This is one of the most important provisions in any publishing agreement because it states the precise rights the author licenses to the publisher during the term of the contract.

In most self-publishing contracts, the author grants either an exclusive or a nonexclusive license during the contract term. An exclusive license prevents anyone who is not the license holder, including the author, from publishing the author's book in the format for which the right is being licensed. A nonexclusive license allows others, such as the author or other publishers, to sell, distribute, and publish the book during the contract term.

If you're having your book published as an e-book, you will grant the publisher either an exclusive or nonexclusive right to print, publish and sell your book in an electronic format, which typically includes a downloadable e-book, a CD-ROM, or another file type that can be read on an e-book reader like Amazon Kindle or other similar device.

If you're publishing your book as a paperback or hardcover, you will grant those specific rights. Granting paperback rights does not automatically include hardcover. Contract language that describes "all print rights" includes print and hardcover rights.

Some publisher contracts are for "worldwide" rights. During the term of the agreement, the publisher can sell your book anywhere in the world in the format(s) you've agreed upon.

Some publishers only ask for rights to sell the book in the United States, Canada, and the United Kingdom. For example, if a publisher only has print rights in the United Kingdom, the author would still have the right to sell, distribute and publish the book in print anywhere else in the world.

Print and electronic rights are the only rights that should ever be at issue in a contract you sign with any of the publishers covered in this book. Stay away from a contract that grants the publisher "all rights whatsoever," which would include subsidiary rights, such as movie, television, radio or stage play rights.

There are companies listed in this book that take a percentage of any fees derived from an author's sale of subsidiary rights (e.g., the movie rights). Still other companies build in a contractual right to sell the subsidiary rights and then keep a percentage of the sale. It won't be hard to find them—they're all in the Publishers to Avoid chapter.

Stay away from any publisher that demands an option or right of first refusal on any other books you may write. It's one thing if you sign a three-book deal with a major publisher and receive payment up front, but it's an entirely different matter in the self-publishing world.

Many self-publishing contracts specifically state that the publisher is not claiming an interest in any other rights other than those directly related to the publication of your book (and then only those that allow them to print and distribute the book on your behalf). It's not required or necessary language to have in a contract, but it does make your rights indisputable. I prefer such language myself, and I include it in the contracts that I draft for publishing companies.

Term and Termination

The term and termination provisions are just as important as the license of rights. The term defines how long the contract will last. The termination provision describes what either party must do to cancel the contract and when they must do so.

The term and termination sections are often written together as one provision. It is important to read the license of rights and the term and termination provisions together to determine whether a contract is author-friendly. I always discuss these three provisions together when analyzing a particular publisher's contract.

LOOK FOR CONTRACTS THAT HAVE TERMS THAT DO NOT LOCK THE AUTHOR INTO A CONTRACT FOR A LONG PERIOD OF TIME

The most author-friendly contracts will have one of these terms:

- Exclusive, but only for one year
- Exclusive for X years, but the author can terminate at any time by giving X days written notice
- Nonexclusive for X years, and the author can cancel at any time

There are, of course, a few exceptions to the general rules. The goal is to always have the least number of restrictions on your rights, freeing you to search for a better publishing deal with a traditional publisher or other self-publishing company.

If a publishing contract you're considering doesn't have a term like one of these three terms, then you should think long and hard before signing (and probably not sign at all). If you attempt to terminate a contract that doesn't have a term like one of these three, you're going to wish you'd followed my advice.

AVOID CONTRACTS THAT PERMIT A PUBLISHER TO RETAIN NONEXCLUSIVE RIGHTS AFTER TERMINATION

Avoid any contract that grants the publisher a nonexclusive right to publish and sell your book after contract termination. I'm not talking about contracts that permit the publisher to sell its remaining inventory of your book after termination. There are few cases I can imagine where a self-publishing company would even have more than a few copies of your book in stock. Here are two unacceptable situations:

A. The publisher receives an exclusive term for one year, which the author can cancel at any time during that year. But if the author cancels the contract before the term is up, the publisher retains a nonexclusive right to sell the book through the original one-year term.

B. The publisher receives a two-year, nonexclusive right, which allows the publisher to publish, distribute and sell your book during that time period regardless of what you do.

The problem with both situations is that the author isn't in full control of his or her rights.

The ability to sell your book while someone else continues to sell it is not the same as having full control of your rights. Suppose a big-time publisher, such as Random House, wanted to purchase rights to your book. Before approaching Random House, you had signed a contract under scenario A or B. Although you'd have the right to sell Random House the right to publish your book, your old publisher's nonexclusive rights would remain effective. Once Random House learned about this publisher's rights, it might lose interest. At best, Random House would first have to purchase your publisher's nonexclusive rights before it would purchase any licensing rights from you.

From your ex-publisher's perspective, the nonexclusive right is worthless unless a traditional publisher decides to publish your book. It's unlikely that your publisher will actively market or sell your book. When Random House enters the picture, your ex-publisher's rights to your book become valuable. Your ex-publisher may try to sell its nonexclusive rights to you or Random House, or it will publish as many books as it can sell. What you want to avoid is a situation where your current publisher is suddenly a factor in your negotiations with a traditional publisher.

You must address these nonexclusive contract provisions, which are present in many self-publishing contracts, in one of these ways:

- Remove the language that gives the publisher nonexclusive rights after termination.
- Modify the language to permit the publisher to sell any remaining inventory it has as of the termination date, but prohibit the publisher from printing and selling additional copies after the termination date.
- Modify the language to give the author the right to purchase the publisher's nonexclusive rights upon termination for an amount equal to the publisher's net profit from sales it would have made during the nonexclusive period. The net profit should be based on the net profit during the previous X months (equal to the remaining term of the nonexclusive period after termination). For example, if the publisher had a nonexclusive right to sell the book for a year after termination, then the buy-out price should be based on the net profit dur-

ing the year that proceeded the termination date. Define the net profit as the retail price of the book less production costs, author royalties, and trade discounts.

If I terminated the agreement to sign with a bigger publisher, I'd nonchalantly try to buy out my current publisher's nonexclusive right before signing the new contract with the bigger publisher.

AVOID CONTRACTS WHOSE TERMS EXTEND FOR THE LENGTH OF THE COPYRIGHT

If you learn only one lesson from this book, remember this: never, ever, under any circumstances, enter into a contract containing a term that equals the length of the copyright.

A copyright term lasts for the life of the author plus another 70 years. This allows your heirs to receive your copyright's benefit after you're gone. Once you sign a contract that has a term that extends for the life of your book's copyright, you've lost control over your work forever.

Watch out for publishers that try to back-door such a provision into a contract. Only one publisher covered in this book actually had the gall to include a clause that gave it the rights for the term of the copyright. Guess which section of this book that publisher is in?

PAY SPECIAL ATTENTION TO TERMS THAT RENEW AUTOMATICALLY

Some publishing contracts have an initial term of X years that automatically renews on a year-to-year basis until terminated. Oftentimes, termination requires the author to give notice at least X days before the expiration of the initial or renewal term. In theory, there's nothing wrong with this requirement.

In practice, it may prove tricky. Let's say you signed a one-year agreement on January 1, 2008, which renews automatically on a yearly basis unless terminated 90 days before the expiration of the initial or renewal term.

If you want to terminate the agreement after the first year you must give notice at least 90 days before December 31, 2008, or by September 29, 2008. If you gave notice on November 15, 2008, the publisher could require you to honor the automatic renewal term through the end of 2009.

Automatic renewal clauses exist for your convenience as much as for the publisher's. Without the clause, the publisher must stop selling your book and remove it from its website at the end of the initial or renewal term. To resume sales and earn more royalties, you would have to notify them of your desire to extend the contract.

Most self-publishing companies include renewal clauses. The best way to avoid a problem is to schedule a reminder on Outlook or other calendar system before the deadline passes.

Author Warranties and Publisher Indemnification

WARRANTIES

Author warranties are promises the author makes about the submitted work. These warranties are usually the most intimidating provisions of any self-publishing contract because of their lawyerly sounding language.

Author warranties can be summed up like this: don't break the law or violate anyone else's rights with your book and you'll be OK.

Below are eight author warranties commonly found in self-publishing contracts. Not all publishing contracts contain all eight warranties, nor will the language match exactly, but the information below should give you the gist of what each means:

1. *"Author is the sole author and proprietor of the work."*
If another writer has any interest in the book, other than a writer that you paid to provide certain services such as ghostwriting, you cannot make this representation unless you have a written agreement with the other writer in which he or she has agreed that you are the sole author and owner of the work. Examples of individuals who may have an interest in your book are coauthors and illustrators, unless you have work-for-hire or other similar agreements with them.

2. *"Author owns all rights in the work free of any liens and encumbrances and has full authority to enter this agreement."*
This clause expands on the first and confirms that no one else has, will, or can make a claim to any of the rights. For example, if someone sued you for copyright infringement and the case was ongoing

at the time you signed the publishing contract, the lawsuit would be an encumbrance because you would not have the ability to sell your work in its present condition until the lawsuit was favorably resolved.

3. *"The Work is original and has not been previously published."*
This one is self-explanatory. The work is your own and not created by another person, and the work hasn't been published anywhere else. If you have published the work previously, make sure you inform the publisher so that this clause can be amended.

4. *For work not in the public domain legally effective written licenses have been secured."*
This section means that for any work not in the public domain (something you can use because the copyright protection has expired) you are warranting that you've obtained legal permission to use it.

5. *"No part of the work, including the title, contains any matter which is defamatory, unlawful, or which in any way infringes, invades, or violates any right, including privacy, copyright, trademark, or trade secret of any person."*
It's easier to break this one down by giving examples:

- If your book claims that your neighbor, John Smith, is a child molester, then that would be defamation, unless the claim is true. Truth is always a defense to defamation.
- If your book instructs people how to blow up government buildings, most publishers consider this instruction to be unlawful, regardless of your First Amendment Rights.
- If you put your girlfriend's private diary in your book without her permission, you are violating her right to privacy and infringing on her copyright in her diary. If you take a portion of this book and use it in your book without obtaining my permission, you've infringed on my copyright.
- If your book has Harry Potter as a character, you've infringed on J.K. Rowling's copyright and trademarks. However, stating that a character drank Coke or appeared on CNN isn't considered infringement.
- If you print Coke's secret recipe in your book, you've infringed on Coke's trade secret (its recipe).

6. "The publication doesn't breach any oral or written agreement the author has made with anyone else."

You are confirming that you don't have any other agreement with any publisher or third party that would preclude you from publishing your book with the publisher whose contract you're about to sign.

7. "The representations and warranties are in full force and effect on the date of publication."

You are promising that all representations and warranties you made will be true on the publication date as they are on the day you signed the contract.

8. "The warranties survive the term of the Agreement."

This means that if you defamed someone in your book who then sues the publisher several years after the publishing agreement expired, you will still be liable for the representations and warranties you made.

INDEMNIFICATION

When you indemnify a publisher you are saying that if any warranties you made turn out to be false, you will cover all of the publisher's legal expenses if it gets sued.

Here are three typical indemnity clauses you may see in publisher contracts:

1. "The author indemnifies and holds the publisher harmless from any losses, expenses, or damages arising out of or for the purpose of resolving or avoiding any suit, demand, etc., as a result of the author's breach of the representations and warranties."

If you used someone else's copyrighted material in your book, all legal expenses incurred by the publisher in defending a copyright infringement lawsuit, any damage awarded by a court, and any settlement amount the publisher makes to avoid a lawsuit or settle one, will ultimately be paid by you.

It's simple. Make sure your representations and warranties are true, or prepare for a legal mess should a third party sue.

2. "The Publisher can extend the benefit of the Author's representations and warranties and indemnities to any party affected by the Author's breach."

If the publisher sells your book through Amazon.com and the person defamed in your book sues Amazon.com, the representations, warranties, and indemnifications you made to your publisher will also cover Amazon.com. You'll be responsible for Amazon.com's costs, attorney's fees, losses, damages and more.

3. *"Author has to pay legal fees, costs, etc., to defend any suit brought against the publisher as a result of the Author's breach of any representation or warranty."*

This language is usually included in the first indemnification clause mentioned earlier. The publisher may choose to set it apart so that it's crystal clear that the author is responsible for the publisher's legal fees and expenses if the author breaches representations and warranties.

Permission and Releases

"Provided there is a legal review of the final, complete manuscript of the work, the Author, at the Author's own expense, agrees to obtain from any person or entity from whom, in the publisher's opinion, permissions, releases, or licenses shall be required in order to exercise the rights granted hereunder...."

If your characters work at XYZ Cafe, and XYZ Cafe happens to be a real restaurant in the city in which the story takes place, the publisher may require you to secure written permission to use the cafe's name from the establishment's owner. However, this is sort of a gray area because unless there is something happening in your book at XYZ Café that puts the real XYZ Café in a bad (and false) light, you may not need to obtain permission. If you have questions, I suggest contacting an intellectual property lawyer.

USE OF AUTHOR'S NAME AND LIKENESS

Language for this type of clause may read like this:

"The Author grants the publisher and its licensees the right to use the Author's name and likeness in the sale, promotion, and advertising of the work...."

Granting a publisher the right to publish your book doesn't automatically give it the right to use your picture or name on its website or a third-party's website (like submitting it to Amazon.com), or in retail stores where your book is for sale. This clause gives the publisher permission to use your name and picture in the marketing and promotion of the book.

Publisher Bankruptcy

"If the publisher commences bankruptcy proceedings, all rights to the work shall immediately revert to the author."

This clause protects the author. All assets of a publisher who files for bankruptcy become the property of the bankruptcy trustee. Without this clause, the license you gave to the publisher under the publishing agreement also becomes the bankruptcy trustee's property. This creates problems for the author because the author must then deal with the court-appointed person handling the publisher's affairs.

In some bankruptcy situations, the publisher "reorganizes" and continues to run the company. Bankruptcy clauses in the publishing contracts, however, don't differentiate between the various types of bankruptcy.

In theory, the second the publisher files for bankruptcy protection, all of the author's rights immediately revert to the author. In reality, the clause may not be enforceable. The automatic stay provision of the bankruptcy section of the U.S. Code (11 U.S.C. §362[3]) controls what would happen in a situation like this. The provision states that upon filing for bankruptcy, a stay applies to any act to obtain possession of property of the estate or of property from the estate or to exercise control over property of the estate. Of course, a creditor can always apply for relief from the stay, but for an unsecured creditor like an author, good luck. When a publisher files for bankruptcy, most bankruptcy trustees return the rights to authors in exchange for the authors' agreement to drop any claims for all unpaid royalties or other monies due.

Notices

Notice provisions explain how the author and publisher must provide notice of events or situations requiring notice, such as termination of the contract.

Some termination clauses permit notice by fax, e-mail, or regular mail. Others require notice by certified mail only.

If a contract requires delivery of notice in a specific manner, you must follow that manner for the notice to be effective. For example, if a contract requires notice to be sent using certified mail and you fax the notice, your notice is not legally effective.

Governing Law; Venue; Attorneys' Fees

These individual clauses are sometimes combined under one clause. If your contract lacks a separate clause, look for relevant language in the "General Provisions" or "Miscellaneous" contract clauses.

In the example below, I use Minnesota and Hennepin County (Minneapolis) as the venue. The counties and states will be different depending on the location of the publisher. The clause may read like this:

"This Agreement will be construed and controlled by the laws of the State of Minnesota, and each party consents to the exclusive jurisdiction and venue by the state or federal courts sitting in the State of Minnesota, County of Hennepin. If either the publisher or author employs an attorney to enforce any rights arising out of or relating to this Agreement, the prevailing party will be entitled to recover reasonable attorneys' fees and costs."

Let's break it up to review each point.

Governing Law

"This Agreement will be construed and controlled by the laws of the State of Minnesota...."

Should a legal dispute arise, the court will use Minnesota's case law and statutes to interpret the provisions of the contract.

Usually the laws of the state where the publisher or its lawyers are located will be used to interpret contract terms. Why? Because the publisher's lawyers are familiar with the laws of the state in which they already practice. The publisher won't be billed extra fees while its lawyers learn the nuances of another state's laws.

There are times when a publisher may choose to have the contract governed by the laws of another state because a particular state may have a statute or law more favorable to the publisher.

Note that the publishing contract clauses discussed in this book cover basic contract law principles and are not particular to any state.

VENUE

"…and each party consents to the exclusive jurisdiction and venue by the state or federal courts sitting in the State of Minnesota, County of Hennepin…"

This provision specifies that if one party sues the other party for a contractual breach, the lawsuit will be brought in the state or federal court located in the state identified in the agreement—in this case, a state court in Minnesota or federal court in Hennepin County, Minnesota.

Without the author's consent to a specific venue in the state of the publisher's choosing, the publisher could have a difficult time suing the author in that state. By agreeing to sue and be sued in the state of the publisher's choosing, the author cannot sue the publisher in the author's own state (unless it's the same state) because once the publisher's lawyers move to dismiss the author's action and present the contract to the court, the author's case will be dismissed assuming the contract is valid and enforceable (e.g., not signed under duress, fraud, etc.)

ATTORNEYS' FEES

"If either the publisher or the author employs attorneys to enforce any rights arising out of or relating to this Agreement, the prevailing party will be entitled to recover reasonable attorneys' fees and costs."

I call this provision the "keep-it-honest" clause because it makes a party think twice before filing a lawsuit. If you bring a weak case and lose, you will likely pay 100% of the publisher's attorneys' fees. The reverse is also true. These "prevailing party" clauses are fair.

Some publishers try to sneak in language that says: (1) the author pays the publisher's attorneys' fees regardless of the case's outcome, or (2) the publisher recovers its attorneys' fees if it prevails in a lawsuit but the author cannot. Many publishers get away with this tactic because people don't bother to read these clauses before signing the agreement. The party who drafted the contract banks on the other party overlooking it.

While I've yet to encounter an unfavorable attorneys' fees clause, I've seen these exact clauses in other commercial contracts. Request elimination of the unfavorable attorneys' fees clause or a modification to a "prevailing parties" clause, and some publishers will agree rather than risk losing you as an author. If the publisher refuses, then it's time to find another publisher. Reluctance to change this clause indicates the company will use it as a way to prevent even legitimate author claims from being brought. If you have to pay the publisher's legal fees regardless of the outcome, you lose either way. An inequitable attorneys' fees clause makes it financially difficult, if not impossible, for you to pursue legitimate claims against a publisher. To me, that is unacceptable.

Entire Agreement

"This Agreement constitutes the entire agreement between the Publisher and the Author with respect to the subject matter hereof and supercedes all prior written or oral agreements made by the parties. This agreement may not be modified or amended except in writing and signed by both parties."

Virtually every commercial contract I've seen includes this standard clause, and I've never drafted a contract without including it.

Look for this clause as a separate section entitled "Entire Agreement" or as part of the "General Provisions" clause.

The only terms included in the contract count. Nothing said or written prior to the execution of the contract is valid or enforceable. If you received an e-mail from the publisher telling you that the royalty is 50% of the retail price of your book, and the contract you later sign states a royalty of 30% of the net, the prior written communication by the publisher is meaningless.

If you could show that 50% was an inducement to get you to sign the contract and that it was fraudulent, you might be able to get out of the contract. Maybe. But, how far are you willing to go and how much money are you willing to spend to compensate for not reading and understanding the contract?

Read the bold language in the paragraph below continually until it is branded in your brain: Carefully read the contract and make sure it is complete. It must include every promise and representation by the publisher, whether oral or written, based on your review of the publisher's website and any other relevant information.

If you believe the written contract is incomplete or different than what you understood it to be, DO NOT SIGN the contract until you are absolutely satisfied with the written terms!

General Provisions/Miscellaneous

Often, the governing law, venue, attorneys' fees, and entire agreement clauses may all be part of the "General Provisions" or "Miscellaneous" provisions. Here are three additional clauses typically found in these contract provisions:

1. "Author may not assign this Agreement or any rights or obligations hereunder, by operation of law or any other manner, without Publisher's prior written consent, such consent which will not be unreasonably withheld."

This language prevents you from transferring your rights under the contract without the publisher's permission. However, the publisher can't unreasonably refuse permission if you request to assign your rights. For example, if you're assigning your rights to the new corporation you formed or to your wife, the publisher should agree to your request. If you assign your rights to another publisher, you'll probably encounter resistance.

2. "If any term or provision of this Agreement is illegal or unenforceable, this Agreement shall remain in full force and effect and such term or provision shall be deemed deleted or curtailed only to such extent as is necessary to make it legal or enforceable."

If a court finds a portion of the contract illegal and unenforceable, the rest of the contract remains valid. The problematic term will need to be deleted or rewritten to make it comply with the law.

3. "No modification, amendment, or waiver shall be valid or binding unless made in writing and signed by all parties hereto."

I've already covered this, but it bears repeating. If you and the publisher orally agree to change your royalty percentage, the agreement will carry no weight and remain meaningless until it is put in writing and made an addendum (addition) to the original publishing contract. Both you and the publisher must sign the new agreement.

A few final thoughts on these publishing contracts: Don't expect much flexibility from publishers when it comes to changing minor provisions of the contract. If there are one or two major points you want revised, suggest it. If your issues are mostly semantic, skip it. Even the best publishers aren't going to rewrite a contract just to accommodate you. Having a lawyer review the contract before you sign it is always a good idea. Having that same attorney start negotiating with the publisher is not. In many cases, the lawyer is nitpicking unimportant language just to justify his or her legal fees. Authors who get bogged down in meaningless contract semantics are people publishers want to avoid. If you get a lawyer involved and the process becomes adversarial before you even start, you'll get off on the wrong foot with your publisher. So remember, for major issues (like subsidiary rights), it may be worth making suggestions if you really like everything else about a publisher. For minor issues, if the contract terms bother you, find another publisher.

CHAPTER 5

ANALYZING THE FINE PRINT OF EACH PUBLISHER'S CONTRACT AND SERVICE

In an earlier version of this book, all publishers were given an author-friendly rating between 0 and 10. That system differentiated between a 9.4 and 9.7, at which point the differences became minute and subjective, and some publishers started using their rankings to advertise themselves as the highest-rated company in my book. As a result, excellent publishers ranked at 9.5 were overlooked by writers, who focused on publishers ranked at 9.8.

I now have an author-friendly ranking that groups publishers by category. The four categories are:

- Outstanding
- Pretty Good
- Just OK
- Avoid

The factors used to determine a publisher's ranking have evolved. For this edition, my editor and I posed as ordinary authors and contacted each publisher to inquire about the publisher's services. The difference between us and you is that we asked the questions you may not know to ask until after you've read this book. What we found was shocking, especially when we started asking the tough questions about excessive printing markups and demanding justification for the publishers' policies regarding the production files for the author's book.

Some publishers treated us with respect, provided thoughtful answers, and offered professional customer service. Other publishers lied to us about the costs of printing, chastised us for asking the questions we did, and instructed us that we should find another publisher if we wanted the original production files returned to us. Some publishers took weeks to respond to initial inquiries. As you read through the reviews of each publisher, you'll read about our experiences with the publisher as a prospective author.

All of the publishers were asked the same basic questions in the categories below. Obviously, based on the answers we veered off onto different lines of questioning.

The retail price of the book. The average reader who peruses Amazon.com, and finds a novel by an unfamiliar author will probably not spend $22 for it. People who argue otherwise live in a fantasy world. Who is going to spend $22 on your book (other than your friends or family) when Patricia Cornwall's latest thriller costs only $7.99? The reason so many books published by self-publishing companies have retail prices that are out of line with the market is because those prices include steep printing markups and fat publisher royalties. It's my goal to uncover these ploys.

The price the author pays for the author's books. Another biggie. Aggressive marketing of your book is essential to its overall success. You will need sales avenues besides any provided by your publisher. In order to actually make money selling your own book you need to be able to purchase it at a reasonable price. Companies that allow you to purchase books at no more than a 15% markup of the actual print cost score high in this book. Some publishers double and triple the printing costs, and that's one reason so many authors fail to make any money self-publishing. Few things irk me more than a publisher who charges a ton of money up front and then gouges the author when she purchases copies of her book. Since almost all publishers pay about the same amount of money to print books digitally, you will be amazed at how some charge so much more than others for copies.

Allow bookstore returns. I believe authors can successfully sell books through personal appearances, their websites, and Amazon.com and other online retailers. Most self-publishing companies critiqued in this book don't have distribution that will ever result in a bookstore actually ordering books, except in situations where the author arranges for it or where someone asks the store to order them a copy. However, you have even less of a chance of getting into bookstores if your publisher won't accept bookstore returns. You must find a publisher who accepts returns from bookstores. Some publishers include bookstore returns as part of their packages, and others charge approximately $400 for returnability.

Customer support for authors. You're a customer of the publisher. You pay them money for a service—to publish your work—and as a customer, you should be able to call them with questions. Your book is a personal and important achievement. You're entitled to talk to the people you've entrusted it to and not someone in Karachi, Pakistan, who knows little about your book.

Author-friendly contract terms. Author-friendly publishing agreements contain most or all of these provisions:

- Authors grant only print and electronic rights on a nonexclusive basis that is terminable at any time or for an exclusive term that is terminable at any time or extends for less than one year.
- The publisher doesn't retain a right of first refusal or other such option on any future books, and the publisher doesn't require payment from the author in the event the author signs with a bigger publisher or sells television or movie rights.
- Authors can terminate the contract easily and with no further obligation.
- Upon termination by the author, the publisher only maintains a limited nonexclusive right to sell any of the author's remaining books the publisher has already printed.
- Upon termination, the author receives original production files containing the book's cover art, layout, design and more—all products the author has paid for.
- Calculation of royalty amounts is based on a percentage of the retail price of the author's book, or if based on a percentage of the net price, the calculation is clear and not subject to padding.
- Competitive pricing of the author's book in the marketplace
- Author is allowed to purchase his or her books for no more than 15% more than the actual printing costs.
- No requirement that the author pay the publisher's attorneys' fees in the event of a dispute, except for defamation or the author's misrepresentation as to ownership of rights. Clauses that require the non-prevailing party in a lawsuit to pay the prevailing party's legal fees are equitable.

Based on these factors and a few intangibles, such as how fast the publishers responded to my requests, their sales techniques (some are pure shakedown artists), and the truthfulness of their website and sales materials, I grouped the publishers into one of four categories. For easy reference, I've listed publishers alphabetically within each category. The order is not a ranking within that particular section.

One important thing to note while reading through the publisher descriptions in chapters 6–9 is that the publishing packages and services change periodically and, depending on when you are reading this book, may not be exactly as described here. The contract terms, price authors pay for books and royalty amounts often remain the same despite changes in services and pricing. These three things are more important than any price increase or alteration of publishing packages and services.

Note on URLs found in the book: Some of them are hyphenated at line breaks in the text for formatting reasons. If you attempt to type any of them into a search engine (assuming you aren't viewing the clickable links in the ebook version), make sure you remove any hyphens that appear at a line break.

CHAPTER 6

OUTSTANDING SELF-PUBLISHING COMPANIES

The publishers in this category are simply the best in the business. These companies are the most dedicated to providing the author with a great publishing experience. Not every publisher here meets every ideal quality, some mark up printing costs more than I think is reasonable, but then they provide a lower publishing package. Overall, you can't go wrong with any publisher listed in this category. My ranking of these companies does not guarantee that your experience with them will be wonderful, as every publisher has authors who are disgruntled for one reason or another. But, my ranking does guarantee that you will get a fair deal at a fair price, that you will retain all of your rights, and that you won't sign a contract that contains questionable clauses.

Understand that not every publisher in this section is right for every writer, but there is a publisher here for just about everyone. Both the most expensive and one of the least expensive self-publishing companies made this list. All these companies share a proven commitment to author-friendly policies. Five of the "Outstanding" publishers, after speaking with me, modified their contracts to make them more author-friendly. They all get it. It's about understanding writers, who treat their books like they treat their children. Their books are dreams fulfilled and often represent a lifetime of work. These publishers work with you to achieve the results you want.

AVENTINE PRESS

http://www.aventinepress.com

FORMAT OF BOOKS: paperback and hardcover

GENRES ACCEPTED: all

PUBLISHING FEES: The $399 paperback package (http://www.aventinepress.com/services.html) includes:

- Choice of covers:
- For an extra $175: A template-based cover, for which author supplies the art or images
- For an extra $295: A custom cover, which includes consultation with the designer, choice of two designs, and a reasonable number of modifications (more than about five and the designer starts charging a $50 hourly rate)
- No extra charge: Author supplies a press-ready cover
- Choice of interior style templates
- ISBN
- Author's bio, photo, and cover photos or graphics supplied by author included in the book and on the cover
- Indexing, up to 25 words
- Electronic galley proof: Includes only minor changes that do not affect the layout; substantive changes are billed at $50 an hour
- UPC bar code
- Two copies of the book
- Listing with online booksellers: Amazon.com, Barnesand-Noble.com, and more
- Book and cover art production files on a CD

OTHER SERVICES OF INTEREST: All optional services, which can be viewed at http://www.aventinepress.com/services.html, include:

Copyediting for $.015 per word: Includes spelling, grammar, syntax, and punctuation.

Aventine Press Marketing Program: This service, which costs $995 and is detailed at http://www.aventinepress.com/market. html, includes:

- Website: Six pages, non-template design, domain name, and a year of hosting (after which, hosting is $50 and any updates are $75 per hour). See a sample at http://www. midriffatmidlife.com.
- Ingram Advance Catalog listing
- Professionally drafted press release
- Library of Congress Control Number (LCCN)
- U.S. Copyright Office registration

RETURN OF DIGITAL COVER AND INTERIOR FILES: Authors are given a copy of the digital cover and interior production files as part of their package.

RETAIL PRICE OF AUTHOR'S BOOK:

Number of pages	Retail price
108–200	$10.95 to $12.95
201–300	$13.95 to $16.95
301–400	$17.95 to $20.95
404–500	$21.95 to $23.95

PRICE AUTHOR PAYS FOR BOOKS: The author's price is based on the cost to produce the book ($.015 per page plus $.90 for cover of paperback or $7.55 for cover of hardcover) plus 10%. So a 200-page book would cost:

$.015	per page production cost
x 200	number of pages
+ $.90	cover fee
+ $.39	10% Aventine markup
$4.29	author price per book

ROYALTIES PAID TO AUTHOR: All of Aventine's books are sold through a third-party source, such as Amazon.com. The publisher pays authors 80% of the "net amount"—the retail price of the book less the trade discount and actual cost to print a single copy—received from each book sale. So a sale on a 200-page book will look like this:

$12.95	retail price
– $7.12	55% Amazon.com discount
– $3.90	printing cost

$1.93	net profit
x .80	author royalty percentage

$1.54	author royalty

Although this isn't much of a royalty, Aventine isn't getting rich taking what's leftover—$.39. A royalty ratio that favors the author is highly unusual in self-publishing.

NOTABLE PROVISIONS OF THE PUBLISHING AGREEMENT: The contract, which is straightforward, is available at http://www.aventinepress.com/pub_agree.html.

The "Warranties" section is standard and reasonable.

"The Rights to Your Work" makes it clear that the publisher claims no right to the author's work. The author also acknowledges that the publisher has no responsibility to correct or review the work prior to publication.

"Indemnities" says that, if warranties made by the author are false, the author is financially liable for any losses sustained by the publisher as a result of a lawsuit, including legal fees. This is fair. If an author lies about ownership of the work or even assumes she can use some material without checking to see if it's copyrighted and the publisher is sued by the actual owner because of it, the author should have to pay the publisher's legal fees.

"Terms and Exclusivity" is as author-friendly as it gets: it's nonexclusive so the author can enter into other publishing agreements. This section also describes the publishing fee portion, which will be refunded to the author depending on specific circumstances.

"Complete Agreement" voids any and all promises made prior to the signing of the contract that fail to appear in the contract.

"Law & Venue" requires arbitration for all monetary disputes. This requirement doesn't preclude equitable relief, such as a court order prohibiting the publisher from distributing the book after termination of the contract. Court action must be brought in California, but the contract doesn't necessarily require arbitration hearings to be held in California. This evens the playing field when a dispute arises, since an author won't have to travel to California to arbitrate. When a contract doesn't state where arbitration must occur, it can be done either by phone or somewhere convenient to both parties.

AUTHOR-FRIENDLY RATING: Aventine is one of the few self-publishing companies that don't gouge authors on printing fees and royalties. The only downside to Aventine is that it doesn't have a way for authors to sell books directly (either through Aventine or their own websites). So, while the 80% royalty is great, by the time the trade discount and printing costs come out there isn't much left. However, this deficiency isn't enough to keep Aventine from being a great company. If you choose Aventine, make sure you have a way to sell books directly.

The $995 marketing package is good, but it's not really a marketing program. A six-page website isn't robust enough to ever get a lot of traffic on its own. But, the sites the company creates are nice—not worth $1,000, but nice. A press release without anywhere to send it isn't worth much. Overall, the marketing package won't even get you close to where you need to be marketing-wise, but you'll get a nice site out of it.

Aventine is doing things the right way and is worth your consideration.

BOOKLOCKER
http://publishing.booklocker.com

FORMAT OF BOOKS: e-books, paperback and hardcover

GENRES ACCEPTED: BookLocker accepts all genres of nonfiction and fiction. The publisher claims to take only 30% of all submissions because the bulk of its money comes from selling books.

PUBLISHING FEES: BookLocker offers two publishing packages, one for black-and-white and another for color. The latter will not be discussed here, but can be found at: http://publishing.booklocker.com/booklocker-color-pod-program/.

Black & White Interior: This package is priced at $299. Authors must provide their own cover or purchase cover art from Book-Locker, either custom-designed or template-based. BookLocker graphic artists work with authors to come up with cover ideas. Authors may provide images but are not required to do so. Minor changes are included in the price (i.e., font, color, copy), but if an author requires a full redesign of the cover, he or she will have to repay the cover fee. For a paperback book, a template-based cover is $125, and a custom cover is $175. For a hardcover book, a template-based cover is $189, and a custom cover is $239. This package also includes:

- Interior formatting, including graphics, charts, and photos
- Choice of trim size:
      5.5" x 8.5"
      6" x 9"
      8.25" x 11"
- Distribution through Ingram
- Listing with online booksellers: Amazon.com, BarnesandNoble.com and others
- Free e-book version
- Printed galley proof: Includes 1 set of free changes. The next set is $99.50. Changes made after you approve the final PDF are $199.
- ISBN
- Bar code
- Option to print in hardcover for an additional $239 with a custom cover or $174 with a template-based cover
- Option to list in the Ingram catalog, a one-time group print ad, for a $60 fee
- Author blog (for example see http://travel.booklocker.com)

RETURN OF DIGITAL COVER AND INTERIOR FILES:
BookLocker says on its website that departing authors will be given copies of their digital interior and cover production files at no charge—a rarity in the self-publishing business. However, that is only half true. The book is provided in a formatted MS Word document, but the cover is in a flat PDF file, which is printable but not editable, so you would not be able to add an ISBN number to it, for example. When I asked why, the publisher's representative replied:

We can't distribute layered files of covers because that involves distributing individual images of artwork. If those were obtained from an image company, distributing just the image to another party (not as part of the cover) would be a violation of their user agreement.

I doubt that would be the case, since you pay a fee to use these images for a specific purpose. Transferring within the original file created and for the exact same purpose would not be a violation. However, without knowing the specifics of BookLocker's relationship with any third-party stock photo site, I can't comment on it specifically.

RETAIL PRICE OF AUTHOR'S BOOK: Authors have the option to set the retail price of their books, provided they are at or above BookLocker's minimum price, based on the length of the book:

Number of pages	Retail price
Up to 108	$11.95
109–150	$12.95
151–200	$13.95
201–250	$14.95

PRICE AUTHOR PAYS FOR BOOKS: BookLocker's author discount is 35% for purchases of up to 24 books; larger quantities garner higher discounts, determined by the size of the book. For a 200-page, paperback book, the price will go down to $8.57 for 50 books, $7.27 for 100 books, and $6.82 for 500 books, and so on. You can find a complete author discount chart here: https://secure.booklocker.com/booklocker/book/authordiscounts060107.pdf.

For a 200-page paperback at the minimum list price, the numbers would run like this:

$13.95   retail price
– $4.88   35% author discount
————————————————
$9.07   author price per book

We know the book costs $3.90 to print, so it follows that Book-Locker makes $5.98 for every book you buy.

ROYALTIES PAID TO AUTHOR: BookLocker's royalties are paid on the book's retail price. For e-books, royalties are 70% for those that retail for $8.95 or higher and 50% for those that retail for less than $8.95. For paperback or hardcover, royalties are 35% for those sold through BookLocker's online bookstore and 15% for those sold through Amazon.com or another third party.

If a 200-page, paperback book retails for $13.95, your royalties on a book sold through Amazon.com (which receives a 30% trade discount from BookLocker) would look like this:

$13.95   retail price
x .15   author royalty percentage
————————————————
$2.09   author royalty

On that same sale, BookLocker takes:

$13.95   retail price
– $4.19   30% Amazon.com discount
– $3.90   printing cost
– $2.09   author royalty
————————————————
$3.77   BookLocker profit

For sales on BookLocker's website for that same book, the breakdown is as follows:

$13.95   retail price
x .35   author royalty percentage
————————————————
$4.88   author royalty

BookLocker makes $5.17 in profit on each sale of this book through its site.

NOTABLE PROVISIONS OF THE PUBLISHING AGREEMENT: BookLocker's author agreement can be found at http://publishing.booklocker.com/contract.txt.

Section I makes it clear that the contract is nonexclusive.

Section II states that the author can terminate his or her relationship with BookLocker at any time, for any reason, effective immediately via e-mail. It also requires the author to terminate the contract with BookLocker prior to entering into another contract (7th paragraph from the end).

Section IV states that the publisher will review book sales annually, and if the author's book is not selling at a rate of at least five copies per month, the company reserves the right to remove the work and terminate the contract.

Section VI sets forth publishing fee information. Paragraph 6 states that only the author has final approval of the work. If publisher mistakes are discovered after the author has approved the work, the author will be charged a $199 change fee. If the author is at fault for the mistakes, the publisher will charge a new setup fee for corrections. So, either way you are going to get charged, so make sure you review the proof carefully before approving it.

Section VII provides pricing guide information for hardcover and paperback books. The last paragraph in section VII confirms that the author is free to sell the book on his own. However, as long as you are under contract with BookLocker you agree to not sell the e-book for less than the price BookLocker sells it.

Section VIII discusses royalty payments and states that the author can monitor sales and royalties via the Internet. If the author thinks the fulfillment system might not be recording sales accurately, he or she can order an audit, but it is at the author's expense.

Section XI discusses promotional activity of the authors, stating that authors who use spam messages—defined primarily as an unsolicited e-mail sent en masse—to promote their books will no longer be eligible to sell books through BookLocker and will lose their contracts.

In section XVII, in the third to last paragraph, any lawsuit against BookLocker must be brought in Bangor, Maine, and the forum will be binding arbitration. This clause is standard in all commercial contracts in which one party drafts the document.

AUTHOR-FRIENDLY RATING: BookLocker will let you know whether or not they want to publish your book within five days of submission. Its authors receive their print galley within four to six weeks of completing the final manuscript. Although the initial package fee is low, I don't believe that one can get truly custom designed covers and layout for the price BookLocker offers. However, I've never heard complaints from BookLocker authors. Perhaps the higher printing markups help offset the price of layout and design.

The e-book royalties are high, but so what? Unless an e-book is a nonfiction, reference type, they don't sell well enough to matter. The Amazon.com (and other retailer) royalty is decent, but the 35% royalty for sales through BookLocker is only average. However, because the initial publishing package is low, there is a trade-off here.

The publishing agreement is easily terminated at any time, and you can take the bulk of your production files with you, without charge.

I know that this publisher is selective, but I'm not sure that matters so much these days, unless the publisher has wider distribution or is spending its own money to promote books, neither of which Book-Locker has or does. It's nice for authors to feel that their books were accepted on grounds more selective than their checks clearing, but at the same time, don't let the exclusiveness lull you into thinking you'll have a leg up. You won't. The book-buying public has no idea who BookLocker is or that it publishes selectively.

If BookLocker was actively promoting its authors' books and spending some of those printing markups on advertising, it would be on to something. However, BookLocker remains a solid choice especially for the author who wants to dip his or her toe into the publishing pond. You'll get fair treatment, and the prices are reasonable. They have a policy of only communicating with authors through e-mail, so you lose some of the personal touch you may desire, but the e-mail only policy ensures a quicker response time according to Angela Hoy, one of the owners. The e-mail only policy is the one downside for me, but if it works for you, then great. If you book starts selling well, you may want to seek out other publishing alternatives that offer better royalties and smaller printing markups.

BOOKPROS

http://www.bookpros.com

FORMAT OF BOOKS: paperback and hardcover

GENRES ACCEPTED: BookPros states that it only accepts a certain percentage of submitted manuscripts, although it receives hundreds of inquiries a month. The low acceptance percentage, BookPros says, is due to the nature of their publishing program, the cornerstone of which is traditional book PR campaigns and traditional distribution. Most submissions aren't accepted because the book's PR hook isn't strong enough. The company accepts all genres of books, with the exception of poetry and romance. In order to help determine a book's PR potential, BookPros conducts a free analysis of each title submitted for consideration (http://www.bookpros.com/free_book_analysis).

PUBLISHING FEES: BookPros has three publishing imprints: Bridgeway Books, Synergy Books, and Ovation Books. The fees range from around $13,000 to publish under the Bridgeway Books imprint to as much as $40,000 for the top-tier Ovation Books imprint. BookPros does not offer set package prices; instead, the previously mentioned "media analysis" is conducted to determine what level of services an author's book would require based on its media and distribution potential. These individual services are charged by line item and presented to the author as a custom package. Services are not available on an à la carte basis.

Bridgeway Books: The base price for this package (http://www .bookpros.com/bridgeway_books) is $5,950; total price ranges from $13,000–$25,000, plus the cost of printing a minimum of 1,250 books. This package includes, but is not limited to, the following services:

- Editing: A professional edit is required and includes grammar, syntax, spelling, and content (plot, character, flow, consistency, etc.). This service is priced on a sliding scale from $.049 to $.028 based on the total number of words (longer is less per word).

- Layout: Includes manual formatting of the book, with up to 1 chapter and 3 sections per every 10 pages, as well as title page, dedications, table of contents, drop caps, etc.
- Cover Design: Pricing includes custom design of the book's front, rear, and spine; two reviews of the design; and one optional stock photo. Author must provide an author photo and 100–200 words of back cover content. Approximate cost attributed to cover design is $3,000.
- U.S. Copyright Office registration in the author's name
- ISBN
- Bookland EAN bar code
- Library of Congress Control Number (LCCN)
- R.R. Bowker's Books In Print registration
- National direct wholesale distribution through Ingram Book Group and Baker & Taylor, including listing in catalogs
- Listing in BookPros's catalog, which is distributed at BookExpo America and mailed to bookstores around the U.S.
- Listing and monitoring of your book with online booksellers: Amazon.com and BarnesandNoble.com
- Book submission to Amazon Search Inside and Google Book Search programs
- BookPros's management of stock and inventory of book, which includes management of the author's book at a third-party warehouse and transfers to author, company, and distributor (author pays fees associated with shipping and handling)
- Monthly sales and activity reporting via e-mailed reports to authors
- Guidelines for successful book signings and a list of the best bookstores for events
- Tip sheet: A basic fact sheet serving as a sales tool for a distributor's buyer
- Sell sheet: An illustrative sheet designed to sell an author's book, for use by the author in scheduling book events (for Synergy Books and Ovation Books titles, the sell sheets will also be used by the distributor's sales force when pitching the book to buyers)
- Print method: Offset—Bridgeway Books requires authors

to print a minimum of 1,250 books, which will be stocked in a third-party warehouse.

· Professional book publicity campaign: BookPros uses Phenix & Phenix Literary Publicists (http://www.phenixpublicity. com), its corporate partner. Services vary depending on book and campaign length, but basically include strategic planning; a media campaign including television, daily newspapers, radio, and print; galley submissions; media training; press materials creation; and detailed reporting. Bridgeway Books requires a minimum campaign of two months, and fees range from $3,000–$4,000 per month (plus any associated postage, galley book fees, etc.)

Synergy Books: The base price for this package (http://www. bookpros.com/synergy_books) is $7,950; the total price ranges from $23,000–$28,000, plus the cost of printing a minimum of 2,500 books. This package includes everything in the Bridgeway Books package, plus:

· Cataloging-in-Publication (CIP) registration
· Direct distribution in the U.S. and Canada through Midpoint Trade Books
· Publicity and marketing updates to distributor
· Print method: Offset—requires minimum run of 2,500
· Publicity campaign: Minimum of three months—fees range from $3,000–$4,000 per month (plus any associated postage, galley book fees, etc.)

Ovation Books: The base price for this package (http://www. bookpros.com/ovation_books) is $9,950; the total price ranges from $29,000–$37,000, plus the cost of printing 5,000 books. According to the literature, BookPros only offers this imprint to five to ten titles per year and is selective in determining the titles that qualify for it. The package includes everything in the Synergy Books imprint but with a different distribution program, plus:

· National distribution through National Book Network, Inc: NBN is the largest independent book distributor in North America, having represented mid-size to large publishers in the industry for more than 20 years. BookPros is the only fully author-funded publishing company to have a distribution relationship with NBN.

- International distribution to Canada, Australia, and New Zealand through National Book Network, Inc.
- Print method: Offset—requires minimum run of 5,000
- Publicity campaign: Minimum of five months—fees range from $3,000–$4,000 per month (plus any associated postage, galley book fees, etc.)

RETURN OF DIGITAL COVER AND INTERIOR FILES: Per BookPros's contract, departing authors take all of the book's artwork and production files with them, should they determine to leave BookPros, without further fee.

RETAIL PRICE OF AUTHOR'S BOOK: BookPros works with authors to set a retail price. For example, a visit to the Bridgeway Books website found books between 215 and 228 pages ranging from $13.95 to $16.95.

PRICE AUTHOR PAYS FOR BOOK: BookPros manages the printing process for each author. Although book printing prices are not listed on the website, BookPros requires printing larger runs of books, from 1,250 books to 5,000. BookPros does not print the books themselves; instead, they act as a "print broker" and take competitive bids from a wide range of printers both in the U.S. and abroad.

Note: Since you are paying all of the setup fees and printing costs, BookPros does not require you to work with one of its printers; however, if you choose your own printer, the publisher will require you to present it with three samples of the printer's work and reserves the right to reject the printer's services. If they approve your printer, you will have to manage the printing process yourself, from start to finish, including shipping and customs clearance if your printer is outside the U.S. Whether you are printing in small or large runs through BookPros, the printing markup is approximately 15%–20%. Much of BookPros printing is done domestically, although some books are printed overseas. All costs associated with shipping the books are built into the price.

ROYALTIES PAID TO AUTHOR: BookPros does not take a royalty. Authors receive 100% of the amount paid by the distributor. Unless the author is selling the book through their own website or directly to the consumer, author payments from the distributor are as follows: a Bridgeway Books author will make 45% of the retail price, a Synergy Books author will make 36% of the retail price, and an Ovation Books author will make roughly 32% of the retail price, depending on the wholesale discount offered by the distributor. It's harder with this company to figure out exactly how much the author's profit will be on each book because there is no way to know exactly what the author paid for printing. The book printing cost of $.015 per page and $.90 per cover, which is often quoted in this book, mainly applies to digital printing, which is not available through BookPros. Offset printing requires larger print runs and more expense up front but is cheaper per book than digital.

Let's say you publish under Bridgeway Books, and your publishing package total is $17,000 (this is the cost to edit, design, publish, and publicize your book). Assume also that the book will retail for $15.95, and the cost to offset print 2,500 copies of your book turns out to be $3.00 per book. So your total cost for printing is $7,500.

Your royalty per book is 45% of the retail price, which is $7.18.

If you were to sell all 2,500 books through retailers, you would receive:

2,500	number of books
x $7.18	author royalty per book

$17,950	author royalty
− $7,500	printing cost

$10,450	author net profit

You invest $24,500 between the package and printing. If you sell all 2,500 books, you recoup $10,450, but still have another $14,050 to go before you've paid for this investment. Obviously, this is not the best way to make your money back. So let's look at a different scenario that includes direct selling, as well as retail sales. BookPros encourages authors to make direct selling part of their overall marketing and sales plan, since it helps increase your visibility with readers and you recoup money much faster. When you sell the book direct (i.e., "back of the room" sales at an event or direct from your website), you make the full margin between what you sell it for and what it costs to print, because there is no retailer or distributor to take a cut. So, in this case:

$15.95   retail price
− $3.00   printing cost
_____

$12.95   author royalty

Let's say you plan to sell 40% of your inventory through retail and 60% direct. Of your 2,500 books, that's:

1,000   for retail
1,500   for direct

So for the retail sales, you would make:

1,000   number of books
x $7.18   author royalty per book
_____

$7,180   total author royalty for retail sales

For direct sales, you would make:

1,500   number of books
x $12.95   author royalty per book
_____

$19,425   total author royalty for direct sales

Your total gross sales would be:

$7,180   royalty for retail sales
+ $19,425   royalty for direct sales
_____

$26,605   total royalty
− $7,500   printing cost
_____

$19,105 author net royalty

It gets you closer to recouping your initial $24,500 investment, but you are still $5,395 in the hole, and keep in mind that these scenarios are not taking into account miscellaneous shipping or storage fees. Also, you can't just assume you will sell 2,500 books. It could take you months or even years to sell your entire inventory—or you may never sell it. On the other hand, if your book takes off through publicity and marketing, you may sell your entire inventory within a matter of weeks.

NOTABLE TERMS OF THE CONTRACT: The contract isn't available online; you'll only receive one if your book is accepted. I do not like that you cannot see a contract prior to submitting your book. However, because I have worked with the publisher in the past, it sent a contract to me.

The first five sections spell out the services BookPros provides and the prices of each service. If you are unclear about any of the services or prices, you should request clarification.

Subsection 5.11.4 states that the author is responsible for all shipping and postage fees incurred during the publicity campaign, up to a cap of $500, after which the publisher must seek permission from you before spending more. The author will be invoiced for fees and has 15 days from the invoice date to pay the invoice.

Section 6.1 states the minimum number of books the author must print. Subsections of 6.1 state that the author is not required to use the publisher's printer, but any other printer they use must provide three sample books and is subject to the publisher's approval. Further, the publisher will not manage the printer found by the author, so you'll be on your own dealing with the printer.

Printer payments are also outlined in subsection 6.1.1., which states that the author will receive a price quote including printing costs and shipping and handling fees, which the author must pay 50% of within 15 days of receipt. The rest of the payment is due 10 days from the author's notification that the book is ready to print.

Sections 6.2 and 6.3 cover off-site storage (not to exceed $100 per month/every 2,500 books) and annual service fees ($250).

Section 7 addresses expenses associated with additional services requested by the author that are not outlined in the contract—such as last-minute additions of images or indexing—stating that the publisher must inform client of expenses associated with these services.

Section 8 deals with accounting and payments to the author. Since each imprint has a different distribution arrangement, the amount that you make for retail sales varies, but the Bridgeway Books contract we looked at offered 45% of the retail price of the book.

Subsection 8.1.1 also states that the author will be subject to various fees charged by the distributor, which are here undefined, and the author may ask the publisher to provide definition and documentation of the fees. Payments come from the distributors, and the method of payment is very different from other self-publishing companies. Typically, the distributor pays BookPros about 120 days after the reporting period. Then BookPros pays the authors about 15 days after that. So, for sales made in January 2008, an author would be paid on or about May 15, 2008.

Section 8.2 deals with accounting and payments.

Subsection 8.2.1 says that returns will be charged against the author's royalty payments and clarifies the payment schedule. Payments of net amounts (meaning sales less any of those undefined fees) will be paid:

> 50%—120 days after the close of each accounting month, with a 30-day grace period

> 50%—150 days after the close of each accounting month, with a 30-day grace period

Subsection 8.2.2 says that if the author doesn't make enough money to cover distributor fees, the publisher will carry the negative balance forward, but also has the right to demand payment of the author (due within 30 days of receipt).

Subsection 8.2.3 says that all returns are charged against the author's royalties, and the distributor will withhold 15% of royalties as reserve payment for returns. If no returns are made, or the reserve is unspent, the money will be returned to the author a year from the date it was pulled for the reserve.

Subsection 8.2.4 says that the distributor can set a higher reserve payment if it thinks the author's book is more likely than others to be returned.

Subsection 8.2.8 indicates that the author will be paid monthly, once his or her royalties equal $50 or more; otherwise, payments rollover until the next period.

Section 11 clarifies that not only do you own the book's content, but also you own the layout, the design, the cover art, etc., which is important. BookPros allows you to take all the production files with you, so you won't have to recreate the cover art or reformat the interior of the book should you determine to print the book on your own or with another publisher.

Section 12 is a bit confusing, but it basically says that the publisher will provide the author proofs to review changes made in preliminary revisions of the book. The publisher will also provide one opportunity to review the finished layout and edits. After these proofs, there will be a final proof; any changes the author makes after the final proof may be subject to undefined fees. Authors will have five days to review the proof, which is reasonable if you want to keep production of the book moving.

Section 13 says that the author indemnifies the publisher against any claims should the book, allegedly or otherwise, violate someone else's copyright or intellectual property, which is reasonable. You plagiarize, you pay.

Section 15 says that either party can cancel with 60 days written notice. If BookPros cancels, they will refund all of the monies you paid that have not been spent in the production of the book. If you cancel, you will be refunded up to 15% of the monies you have paid at the time of cancellation. BookPros says this is because when you sign its contract, the publisher makes "commitments to different vendors and provides a lot of information and expertise to the author that can't really be quantified." Nevertheless, 85% of a $25,000 contract is quantifiable: you'll lose at least $21,250 if you cancel your contract after paying the full fees associated with your project. BookPros says it will consider special cases for terminating the agreement (death, illness, etc.), but this is not included in the agreement, so if you sign up with them be prepared to follow through or pay anyway.

Section 17 states that any arbitration over the agreement is subject to the laws of and must occur in Travis County, Texas. Such a clause is standard.

Section 19 says neither the publisher nor the author is responsible for acts of nature that may hinder the publishing of the author's book—such as a flood, fires, strikes, etc. Basically, if the printer's offices collapse in an earthquake, the publisher is not responsible for the fact that your book cannot be printed on schedule.

Section 20 states that the entire agreement is contained in the contract and that any amendments must be made in writing and signed by all parties.

AUTHOR FRIENDLY RATING: BookPros is one of the publishers that does not provide a contract or fee schedule to querying authors until it has accepted their book, which is generally a bad sign—in fact, at the beginning of the book, I say that this will often land a publisher in the "Publisher to Avoid" section of *The Fine Print*. However, because I have worked with BookPros in the past and they were willing to send me a contract to review, I have more information about the company than I would if I were simply an author querying the publisher for information.

BookPros provides a high-quality service with a dedicated staff of people who know the publishing business. Is the BookPros model worth the money? That is something you'll have to decide yourself. As with any business venture (or investment of any kind, really), if you can't afford to lose the investment, then don't make it. That's true whether you're paying a few thousand dollars or $13,000–$40,000 with BookPros.

You have to get out there and sell a lot of books to make your money back under the BookPros model. Unless you already have a following of some kind, are on the speaking circuit, or have other ways to sell large quantities of books, you have to be prepared to personally get out there and work hard at selling your books. That's not to say you won't have sales through BookPros's distributors, but book sales are not automatic. No matter how good BookPros is, if you're an unknown author, you still have an uphill battle.

I always say that the success of a particular book comes down to the participation of the author. So, you need to be sure that the BookPros model will work for you. If, after you sign the contract and pay, you have second thoughts, it may be too late. BookPros makes it clear that once you pay and they start working, you are not getting your money back for services they've provided—and that isn't just the stuff you see, like editing and design. Publishing a book requires a lot of background work with distributors and registrations, too. So keep that in mind, and don't sign up with them unless you're serious about seeing the project through to completion.

The BookPros model relies on book distribution and traditional book publicity to make a book sell. Can a $3,000-a-month publicist make your book sell? Every book is different, and even the greatest publicist can't guarantee results. While BookPros's corporate partner, Phenix and Phenix, is a highly respected publicity firm—the company handles publicity for some major publishing houses—whether that experience will pay off for your book is not something you'll be able to measure until you've completed a publicity campaign.

Will BookPros provide a service that is $20,000 better than anyone else in this book? If your book takes off, then yes. However, if your book isn't very successful, you may not think so.

I know the people at BookPros well. They are a professional, dedicated group of individuals, and the company will provide a publishing experience similar to what you might encounter at a traditional publishing house, with large distribution opportunities and experienced publicists. It comes down to this: there is no question that it's a class operation, but before you agree to tens of thousands of dollars to publish your book, make sure it is something you can afford. If you can afford to make the investment, and if you have realistic expectations, you will have a fantastic publishing experience.

COLD TREE PRESS

http://www.coldtreepress.com

FORMAT OF BOOKS: hardcover and paperback

GENRES ACCEPTED: all

PUBLISHING FEES: Cold Tree offers five packages:

The Paperback Package: This package (http://www.coldtreepress.com/publish/choice1.html) is priced at $1,400 and includes:

- Custom designed 4-color cover
- Author photo supplied by author included in book and on cover
- ISBN
- Bookland EAN bar code
- Library of Congress Control Number (LCCN)
- Up to 15 interior images

- All books are returnable by retailers at no charge
- Electronic PDF proof
- Author review copy of the completed book prior to release
- Five finished author copies of the book
- E-book formatting and online e-book sales
- R.R. Bowker's Books In Print registration
- Author sell sheet (printable PDF document)
- Free marketing design assistance
- Online sales placement in Cold Tree's catalog section for electronic distribution, which includes ability for authors to monitor sales through an Internet-based reporting system
- Listing with online booksellers: Amazon.com, BarnesandNoble.com and BooksAMillion.com; includes a quarterly report of sales with royalty
- Ability for the book to be ordered through bookstores
- Choice of trim size:
    5" x 8"
    5.5" x 8.5"
    6" x 9"
    7.5" x 9.25"
    7" x 10"
    8.25" x 11"

The Hardcover Package: Priced at $1,600, this package (http://www.coldtreepress.com/publish/choice2.html) includes:

- All features of the Paperback Package
- U.S. Copyright registration
- Cover type/graphic treatment on interior title and chapter pages
- Up to 30 interior images
- Up to five interior tables
- Ten finished hardcover author copies of the book
- Choice of trim size:
    5.5" x 8.5"
    6" x 9"
    6.14" x 9.21"
    7" x 10"

The Combination Package: Priced at $2,100, this package (http://www.coldtreepress.com/publish/choice3.html) includes:

- All features of the Paperback and Hardcover Packages
- Ten finished hardcover copies and five paperback copies of the book
- Choice of trim size:
  - Hardcover:
    5.5" x 8.5"
    6" x 9"
    6.14" x 9.21"
    7" x 10"
  - Paperback:
    5" x 8"
    5.5" x 8.5"
    6" x 9"
    6.14" x 9.21"
    7.5" x 9.25"
    7" x 10"
    7.44" x 9.69"
    8.25" x 11"

The Pinnacle Package: Authors must apply for this option, which costs $9,800 and includes everything in the combination package, plus a full line-by-line edit, distribution through Ingram Book Group, and a full public relations campaign. The PR campaign is tailored to the book and managed by a PR agency, either local to the author or Cold Tree's agency, Steven Style Group, which will provide a press release, media kits, and review copies. The press kits will be distributed to 2,500 to 5,000 media outlets in radio, television, and print. Editorial Service: For $3,500, Cold Tree offers an editing package that includes character development, continuity and flow, as well as a line-by-line edit for spelling, punctuation and grammar.

RETURN OF DIGITAL COVER AND INTERIOR FILES: Cold Tree authors own the original digital cover and interior files of their books, which is important if an author decides to print her book with another self-publishing house or a traditional publisher. Cold Tree will return digital art and files either in press-ready PDF or production files to the author without charge. Honsberger admits, however, that in one recent case, in which an author flipped a book to Penguin, the new publisher did not want to use many of the production files.

RETAIL PRICE OF AUTHOR'S BOOK: Cold Tree does not publish its retail book prices, however a peak at the online bookstore suggests that a 200-page, paperback book would retail for $12.95, which is a reasonable price.

PRICE AUTHOR PAYS FOR BOOKS: Cold Tree offers authors a 40% discount off the retail price of their books, paperback or hardcover. Here's what that looks like for a 200-page book (5.5" x 8.5", perfect-bound):

$12.95	retail price
– $5.18	40% author discount
$7.77	author price per book

Another way of looking at it:

$7.77	retail price
– $3.90	printing cost
$3.87	Cold Tree profit

I asked Cold Tree where the $3.87 per book was going, and here is the response we got from the company's founder and CEO, Peter Honsberger:

To answer simply, [that]…is our return on a book sale. We do make more money on a short paperback. On the longer ones we make less. On hard covers [sic], we just about break even (usually, between $.50 and $1.00 per book). We usually suggest a retail price to the author which is the minimum we can sell it for and not lose money. On the shorter paperbacks…we also want to keep it in a fair market value range. Too low and its perceived value is not there and too high people won't purchase it. So most of those price around the $10.95 area. All *our books are priced within fair market value. The issue with the formula is that it slightly favors us in the smaller books. If someone out there has a better formula that is manageable, I'm always open to suggestions.*

But what are you, the author, getting for that $3.87? Honsberger says superior service. Unlike many self-publishing houses, every Cold Tree book is marked returnable; authors have access to Honsberger ("I have close to 30 years of experience in graphic design, advertising, and marketing, with national and international awards to my credit, prior to starting Cold Tree," he says. "So there is a pretty good well to draw from. We never charge for this."); a close working relationship with the book designers, who actually read the books; and Cold Tree often stocks copies of higher demand books at its own expense so that orders are filled more quickly. And, he says, the company works hard to accommodate its authors, which in the past has meant everything from covering the cost of a rush print job to getting a great book into hardcover even if the author can't afford the upgrade.

ROYALTIES PAID TO AUTHOR: The royalty is 30% of the retail list price for sales made directly by Cold Tree and 15% of retail list price for sales made through third-party retailers. Using the same 200-page book, the royalty on a book purchased from Cold Tree would be:

$$\begin{array}{ll} \$12.95 & \text{retail price} \\ \times .30 & \text{author royalty percentage} \\ \hline \$3.89 & \text{author royalty} \end{array}$$

Cold Tree makes $5.16 on that same sale (retail – printing costs – author royalty).

The royalty on a book purchased from Amazon.com would be:

$$\begin{array}{ll} \$12.95 & \text{retail price} \\ \times .15 & \text{author royalty percentage} \\ \hline \$1.94 & \text{author royalty} \end{array}$$

On that sale, Cold Tree makes:

$12.95   retail price
– $5.18   40% Amazon.com discount
– $3.90   printing cost
– $1.94   author royalty

———————————

$1.93   Cold Tree profit

Any retailer buying a book from Cold Tree is entitled to a 40% discount on paperback books and a 30% discount on hardcover, which is standard industry practice. However, unlike some self-publishing houses, Cold Tree does not extend itself a trade discount for the books sold on its website. "No, that would mean that we would take the 30 or 40% and pocket it," Honsberger wrote. "And we don't do that."

NOTABLE PROVISIONS OF THE PUBLISHING AGREEMENT: The publishing agreement can be found at http://www.coldtreepress.com/contract/index.html.

Sections 4 and 8 grant nonexclusive rights to the publisher for one year, but either party can terminate at any time with 30 days written notice. After an author's cancellation, the publisher has 90 days from the end of the month in which the cancellation occurred to sell all remaining copies of the work.

Section 6 representations, warranties, and indemnifications are standard and reasonable.

Section 7 clarifies that the publisher only provides printing and book sale services.

Section 12 requires any lawsuit arising from a dispute between the parties to be brought in Davidson County, Tennessee.

AUTHOR-FRIENDLY RATING: The contract contains author-friendly terms: short, nonexclusive, terminable by the author at any time, and decent royalty percentages.

Peter Honsberger is also an award-winning graphic designer. His work has received recognition from various organizations and publications, including the New York Art Directors Club, *Communication Arts magazine, Print magazine*, the National Advertising Federation, and the International Poster exhibition. Honsberger shows his dedication to authors and their work by putting out well-written and aesthetically pleasing books. That, combined with the fact that everything Cold Tree publishes is marked returnable, will not only alleviate some of the stigma attached to self-published books but will also help authors get their work onto bookstore shelves and into readers' hands.

In return for more up-front costs, you receive hands-on cover design work, which includes three separate original designs, and careful formatting of your book. The books are reasonably priced, and the authors' royalties are within range. With its author-friendly philosophy, Cold Tree's model continues to evolve. In fact, Cold Tree has formed a traditional publishing imprint, Hooded Friar Press, which will not be a self-publishing company. If the new press is successful, it can only lend more authority to what is already a credible publisher. On the service side, the publisher will also add a marketing guide to all of its programs, a self-directed guide to marketing books, which is meant to function in tandem with guidance from the publisher.

Cold Tree is one company that is doing it right. Yes, it's making money on every end of the transaction (printing markup and paying low royalties), but authors do get hands-on service. In an industry where it can be hard to get someone on the phone once your check clears, Cold Tree is a company worth considering for your book.

DOG EAR PUBLISHING

http://www.dogearpublishing.net

FORMAT OF BOOKS: paperback or hardcover

GENRES ACCEPTED: all

PUBLISHING FEES: Dog Ear offers four publishing packages.

Basic Package: Priced at $1,099, this package (http://dogear-publishing.net/pricingbasic.aspx) includes:

- Custom interior and cover design with up to 30 images
- Up to 10 free paperback books or five hardcover (dependent upon format and page count)
- Book and author webpage in the Dog Ear website that links to a sales page at Amazon.com or author's website

- Registration with all major online booksellers and national distributors
- R.R. Bowker's Books In Print registration
- ISBN
- Library of Congress Control Number (LCCN)
- Submission to Google Books

Professional Package: Priced at $1,499, this package (http://dogearpublishing.net/pricingpro.aspx) includes everything in the Basic Package, with the following upgrades and additions:

- Up to 30 interior graphics and 10 tables (supplied by the author)
- Up to 20 free paperback books or 10 hardcover books (dependent upon format and page count)
- Marketing and promotional support including:
  - Personalized domain name
  - Custom website (Dog Ear will manage the site for one year; renewal is $75 each year following.)
  - E-mail marketing campaign to your database of up to 500 addresses
  - Press release writing and distribution to 100 targeted media outlets
  - 5 posters, 100 postcards and 100 bookmarks

The website can be of value. However, understand that at best this is a "starter" website that on its own won't get you a lot of traffic. You do get your own domain name, and for an additional $175, the publisher will add a shopping cart, so you can sell books and avoid the huge discount fee to Amazon.com. Yes, you will still have to pay credit card fees, which average around 1.9% plus $.90 a transaction. Dog Ear will provide fulfillment services for a $2 handling fee per order.

The e-mail marketing campaign portion isn't worth much because you still must compile the list. However, Dog Ear uses some of the same tools that top public relations people use to customize its press release campaign for you, which adds a lot of value.

Masterpiece Package: Priced at $3,499, this package (http://dogearpublishing.net/pricingprem.aspx) includes everything in the Professional Package, with the following upgrades and additions:

- Total design customization, including up to 100 interior graphics and 20 tables (supplied by the author)
- Up to 75 free paperback books or 30 free hardcover books (dependent upon format and page count)
- Professional editing and proofreading before the book is formatted for printing (includes up to $800 in editing or 53,000 words)
- An aggressive marketing campaign that includes:
  - A press release to 500 targeted media outlets
  - 250 bookmarks, 100 postcards and 10 posters with a picture of the author and the book and ordering information
  - A custom website that features all the important aspects of the book and includes a shopping cart to process payments directly to the author's bank account. If you can get people to your website and make sales through it, then your profitability will increase.
  - A search marketing campaign, including up to 250 search terms and 5 ad categories that promote the book to search engine visitors and directs them to the author's store front or a specific page on the author's website.

Yes, this is a lot of money, but editing is something you need—you cannot self-edit your book. It doesn't work. Dog Ear assured me that all editors are professionals who edit books for a living. Out of the $3,499, that's worth $800. Authors also receive 75 books. At $5.20 per book (for a 200-page standard book), that's worth $390. But, remember, the actual price to print that book is actually $3.90 per book, not $5.20, so the 75 books are actually worth $292.50.

OTHER SERVICES OF INTEREST: Since the last edition of the book, Dog Ear has added two new services.

Expedited service: For $500, this service, under the Basic or Professional publishing packages, guarantees your books are delivered to press in 30 business days or less, color books in 60 days or less, from delivery of all materials. The package only includes one proof, so find a good editor, and make sure your manuscript is clean, clean, clean.

Bookstore Returns Service: For $499, this program marks the author's book "Returnable" in the Ingram Title Database. This is important because it reduces the risk brick-and-mortar bookstores take by stocking your book and makes them more likely to do so.

The administrative fee for this service must be paid annually, and Dog Ear will deduct the returns from your outstanding author net profit balance.

Editing Services: As is now true of many self-publishing companies, Dog Ear offers a soup-to-nuts array of reasonably priced editing services, from a simple proofread to a ghostwriter taking your project from notes to novel.

- Literary Critique: A senior editor gives your manuscript a thorough read and provides constructive criticism and an outline looking at various aspects of your writing style, all with an eye towards getting your book ready to be published. The $175 flat fee is very reasonable for this kind of feedback, which you will never get from your best friend or Aunt Joe.
- Literary Editor: For $.022 per word, an editor will give your book 2–3 deep reads and provide feedback on character, plot, development, and structure.
- Ghostwriter: For a flat fee, determined on a case-by-case basis, a writer will take your rough draft or notes and craft it, with your input, into a manuscript. The fee for an initial writing sample is $199.
- Indexer: An index will make your nonfiction work that much more useful to the reader and is priced at $.015 per word.
- Book cover copywriting: A Dog Ear marketing person will write your cover and author biography for a $99 flat fee.
- Proofreader: For $.009 per word, a post-production read through will be done to look for style issues, such as bad breaks, font changes, widows, etc.

RETURN OF DIGITAL COVER AND INTERIOR FILES: If you terminate your book contract with Dog Ear, the publisher will return your digital cover and interior files without fee.

RETAIL PRICE OF AUTHOR'S BOOK: Dog Ear allows authors to set the retail prices for their books but recommends that they set the price at least 2.5 times higher than the single-copy print price to allow for bookseller discounts and a reasonable royalty.

As explained in detail in the next section, a 200-page, paperback book costs the author $5.28. Per Dog Ear's suggestion, you should set the retail price at $13.20 at least. I would say you could go a bit higher, to $13.95.

PRICE AUTHOR PAYS FOR BOOKS: Dog Ear marks up its printing costs but does so at less than almost every other company. For a standard, paperback with a full-color cover and black-and-white text interior, Dog Ear charges $.02 per page plus $1.28 per cover for each book it prints, while the actual costs are $.015 per page plus $.90 per cover.

For the 200-page paperback referred to throughout this book, an author pays this publisher $5.28 for each book the author purchases, while the actual printing cost is $3.90. Thus, the markup is 26% per book. Because this publisher doesn't take any royalties, the 26% is a bit easier to stomach.

ROYALTIES PAID TO AUTHOR: As noted in the previous section, you make 100% of the retail price of the book less publishing fees and bookstore discount. If you sell the book on your website, you pay Dog Ear $5.28, which means that if you sell it for $13.95, you make $8.67. If you want Dog Ear to handle all book fulfillment, credit card processing, etc., a $2 per order fee is added, but you still come out ahead.

NOTABLE PROVISIONS OF THE PUBLISHING AGREE-MENT: Unlike many publishers, Dog Ear's publishing agreement is easily located on its website at http://www.dogearpublishing.net/resourcesauthoragree.aspx.

The contract is written in simple, straightforward English so a lay person can understand it the first read through. The beauty of that can also be a curse of sorts because important details are not addressed. If an issue not covered in the contract becomes a problem, it makes resolving that issue a lot trickier. For example, in some of the packages, you get a website and domain name. If you terminate the contract, who owns them? Dog Ear says you do, but that's not stated in the contract or on the website.

That said, when I pointed out to Dog Ear that it had neglected to include in the contract language specifically stating that it will give departing authors the digital production files for the interior and cover of their books, the publisher agreed to add the necessary clause. And that's what makes Dog Ear an outstanding publisher.

AUTHOR-FRIENDLY RATING: Dog Ear continues to be one of the best self-publishing companies around. Even though I'm not a fan of marking up printing at all, Dog Ear's markup of 26% is still far less than most everyone else. Taking no royalties puts them in a league with only a few other companies. I wish they would stop selling junk that doesn't matter (like bookmarks and posters) and add more services like their press release campaign. Dog Ear uses services such as Cision and Gebbie Press to handpick the media outlets most likely to find your book interesting, and sends out professionally produced releases. These are the same tools and services public relations professionals would offer.

The Masterpiece Package offers the best value for many reasons, not the least of which is that you get your own website and domain, which are essential if you plan on selling books yourself. The only downside is that while Amazon orders ship within 24–48 hours, it takes 7 to 10 business days for author book orders to ship from Dog Ear.

The company's three owners are all book industry veterans. Together, they have a true understanding of the book business and have created a company with an affinity for writers—the website is easy to navigate and almost too informative, and when we e-mailed the company we received a personal reply within two business days, without having to fill out a request form or send in a manuscript.

Dog Ear has a solid business model, one that benefits both the company and the author. Dog Ear should be on your list of companies to consider.

INFINITY PUBLISHING
http://www.infinitypublishing.com

FORMAT OF BOOKS: paperback

GENRES ACCEPTED: all

PUBLISHING FEES: The $499 publishing package (http://www.infinitypublishing.com/book-publishing-services/book-publishing-services.html) includes:

- ISBN
- Bar code
- Custom cover and template-based interior, including royalty-free or author-provided artwork and placement of all interior graphs, photos, and illustration. The graphic artist will design only one cover, and the author may ask for up to 40 corrections. After that, the author must pay $50 per set of 40 corrections.
- R.R Bowker's Books In Print registration
- Listing with online booksellers such as Amazon.com and BarnesandNoble.com
- Book and author webpage on http://www.buybooksontheweb.com, Infinity's online bookstore
- Three galley proofs—one for the author, one for corrections, and one for the U.S. Copyright Office for copyrighting; includes up to 30 corrections, and subsequent errors can be corrected for a fee of $50 an hour (this pertains to all typos, including those of the publisher)
- Choice of trim size:
    5.5" x 8.5"
    8.5" x 11"
    8" x 8"
- Optional title submission to the Ingram database for a $149 fee

OTHER SERVICES OF INTEREST: Infinity offers fewer additional services than some publishers:

Photo scanning: $7 a scan

Copyediting: Includes syntax, grammar, and spelling at $.013 per word

Advanced reading copy: Includes 24 copies of the book with mailers and labels, and announcement cards. If you bought the books with your initial 50% discount, they'd cost you $167, so that means you are paying $4.50 a book for the mailing supplies and a note card. Is it worth the extra $109?

Four marketing packages: $125 to $470 (http://www.infinity-publishing.com/bookmarketing.htm).

On the plus side, all packages include copies of two excellent books: *The Complete Guide to Book Publicity by Jodee Blanco* ($19.95) and *1001 Ways to Market Your Book by John Kremer* ($27.95). Each package also includes copies of your book (2–25), bookmarks (25–250), business cards (100–1000), and—with the exception of the $125 package—posters (5–50).

This publisher also owns a commercial-printing operation, and the pricing on the printed materials seems reasonable, but do you need them? Bookmarks and business cards for your book are fun extras, but I'd spend my money on marketing tools designed to have readers actually find my book. You can buy copies of John Kremer's and Jodee Blanco's books for a few dollars each on eBay.

RETURN OF DIGITAL COVER AND INTERIOR FILES: Although this fact is published in neither the contract nor the website, one Infinity representative assured me that the publisher will give departing authors their digital cover and interior production files without a fee. Another informed me that it would cost $125 to have the files delivered in either a press ready PDF or a MS Word document. The company, he said, does not provide production files because: "The production files we use here are not suitable for use through other printers or publishing companies."

I'd insist that language regarding the production files be put in the contract despite any oral assurances, since the contract (like every other book contract) contains a clause stating that only the written terms of the contract are binding upon the parties. Further, it is unlikely that Infinity uses something other than Quark or InDesign, the design software used by every publishing company, to create these production files. Without the original production files, you are back to square one if you want to reprint your book with another publisher or on your own.

RETAIL PRICE OF AUTHOR'S BOOK: Infinity allows authors to set the retail price for their nonfiction books as long as it meets or exceeds the publisher's minimum retail price, based on the size of the book. I couldn't find a book minimum retail pricing chart on the website, but according to the Infinity representative, the minimum price for a 200-page, 8.5" x 5.5" paperback book is $13.95.

Authors may choose any "value-added" price for their nonfiction book, and any amount over the minimum retail price will receive an additional royalty of 75%. Fiction books may not be value-added. For details on how that royalty works, see the section below.

PRICE AUTHOR PAYS FOR BOOKS: Infinity bases the author's discount on the book's minimum retail price and offers authors a 50% discount on their initial order and 40% discount on every order thereafter. So the math looks like this:

$13.95   minimum retail price
x .50   author discount percentage
_____

$6.98   author price per book

While that is certainly a hefty discount, as we know the book costs only $3.90 to print, so Infinity is still making at least $3.07 off the sale—perhaps more, since Infinity does all of its printing in-house and is surely paying less than $.015 per page and $.90 per cover to print books. It's OK for a publisher to markup printing. Yes, its one factor that makes it hard for self-published authors to actually make money, but it's an accepted business practice. You have to decide if you can live with a 50%–75% markup. I couldn't.

ROYALTIES PAID TO AUTHOR: Royalties are based both on the minimum retail and the value-added price, which is initially a bit confusing. Here's how it works:

Direct Sales: Infinity pays a 30% royalty on retail sales through its online bookstore, http://www.buybooksontheweb.com. So, let's say we have a 200-page book selling for $13.95. The royalty would look like this:

$13.95   minimum retail price
x .30   author royalty percentage
_____

$4.19   author royalty without a value-added markup

From this sale, Infinity makes:

$13.95   minimum retail price
– $4.19   author royalty
– $3.90   printing cost
_____

$5.86   Infinity profit

Now, let's say we mark up our 200-page book to $16.95. Infinity pays an additional royalty of 75% on the $3 value-added markup:

$3.00   value-added markup
x .75   author royalty percentage
_____

$2.25   author royalty on value-added markup
+ $4.19   author royalty on minimum retail price
_____

$6.44   total author royalty

That's 37% of the value-added price of your book, but Infinity makes:

$16.95   value-added retail price
– $6.44   total author royalty
– $3.90   printing cost
_____

$6.61   total Infinity profit on a value-added book

Indirect Sales: Infinity offers a 15% royalty on wholesale sales (less the 40% discount), plus 45% of the value-added markup. So on the same book, the royalty would look like this:

$13.95   minimum retail price
− $5.58   40% wholesale discount
x .15   author royalty percentage
_____

$1.26   author royalty without a value-added markup

On that same sale, Infinity makes:

$13.95   minimum retail price of book
− $5.58   40% wholesale discount
− $1.26   author royalty
− $3.90   printing cost
_____

$3.21   Infinity profit

Again, if we mark up the book to $16.95, the author gets an additional 45%:

$3.00   value-added markup
x .45   author royalty percentage
_____

$1.35   author royalty on value-added markup
+ $1.25   author royalty on minimum retail price
_____

$2.60   total author royalty

Meanwhile, Infinity makes:

$16.95   marked-up retail price of book
− $6.78   40% wholesale discount
− $2.60   total author royalty
− $3.90   printing cost
_____

$3.67   Infinity profit on value-added sale

For a complete explanation of the royalty, see: http://www.infinity-publishing.com/royalties.htm.

NOTABLE PROVISIONS OF THE PUBLISHING AGREEMENT: The contract can be found at http://www.infinitypublishing.com/publishing-contract-agreements/book-publishing-agreement.html.

Paragraphs 6–7a, under "Infinity Publishing," state that the publisher agrees to pay the royalty percentages as I've explained in the royalty section above. Section 7a of the contract is rather confusing, but basically states that the publisher will base its wholesale royalties on the discounted price (retail price less a 40% discount) of the book.

Paragraph 3, under "The Author," requires the author to register the copyright with the U.S. Copyright Office and provide a copy of the stamped form to the publisher.

Paragraph 6, under "The Author," clearly states that the publisher has no ownership in the work and that "the author is free to pursue any and all publishing ventures…." You can publish and sell your book anywhere else during the term of the agreement.

Paragraph 10, under "The Author," allows the author to terminate the agreement at any time.

The General Provisions paragraph states that the agreement is governed by the Commonwealth of Pennsylvania, USA, which is common. Oddly, the publisher does not state that all arbitration must take place in Pennsylvania, which is uncommon but works in favor of the author. Also, there is this language: "This written Agreement contains all and is the only Agreement, and supersedes any other agreement, oral, written, or otherwise construed as a prior agreement between the author and IP. This Agreement cannot be appended, changed, modified, word or words added or deleted except by the mutual written agreement of the author and IP; and further, is binding upon the heirs, executors, administrators, and assigns of the author and IP." It's standard in almost any business contract. When it comes to getting the original production files back, this clause becomes important. What this means is that even if the Infinity representative told you that you could get your original digital files back upon termination, if that promise is not in the contract it doesn't count, and Infinity is under no obligation to give them to you.

AUTHOR-FRIENDLY RATING: Despite the fact that Infinity marks up the book printing costs by 50%—perhaps even 75%—and offers low royalties, it still remains one of the "Outstanding" publishers. While both of these deficiencies are enough to cause most publishers in this book to drop in rank, Infinity stays at the top because its publishing package is one of the lowest at $499 (even though, if you want the standard distribution that every other self-publishing company offers, you'll have to pay an additional $149), yet still comprehensive. Also, Infinity is not an author mill, and its staff (once you get them on the phone) is attentive and helpful.

As with every publisher in the book, my editor and I contacted Infinity just as any other author would. Our initial e-mail query was answered, but it went to the spam filter. So, after nine days, my editor thought she had been blown off and called and spoke to a representative, who was quite helpful. We appreciated that the representative was willing to admit that she didn't know the answer to some of my questions and placed my editor on hold while she found someone who did. Oddly enough, when my editor found the missing e-mail, one of the answers was slightly different than what she got from the person on the phone. That fact aside, it's important to note that her e-mail was answered, thoroughly and promptly within 24 hours.

The website could be easier to navigate and less cluttered. Writers should not have to hunt for information, such as how much their book will cost. The royalty section in particular is very confusing.

Infinity's pricing structure and royalty model is best suited for writers who don't expect to sell a lot of books, at least initially. The low package price allows you to get into the publishing game with little risk. But, if you know that you will sell more than a few hundred books, Infinity's royalty structure will be a detriment. Because of the high printing mark-ups and low royalty, Infinity comes out much further ahead than the author does if the author sells a lot of books. There's the argument that "If you were with a traditional publisher, you'd never make royalties this generous." True, but the author takes 100% of the risk and should get much more than a paltry 15%–30% of the royalties. If you start selling a lot of books, you'll want to find a better publishing situation—one with lower printing costs and higher royalties.

The contract is very author-friendly, and you can get out whenever you want. If you do choose Infinity, make sure an addendum is added to your contract about getting any original production files upon termination.

Several years ago I toured Infinity's physical operations and was impressed by its commitment to quality and its hands-on approach with authors. You won't be just a number here. Infinity is a solid choice, but not one that makes a lot of sense once you become successful.

RJ COMMUNICATIONS

http://www.rjcom.com or http://www.selfpublishing.com or
http://www.booksjustbooks.com

FORMAT OF BOOKS: RJ Communications offers both digital
and offset printing and can provide paperback and hardcover formats.

GENRES ACCEPTED: all

PUBLISHING FEE: RJ Communications offers à la carte publishing services rather than set packages. Services range from simple
copyediting to website development, marketing and full-scale professional press release campaigns. Here is just a sampling of the services:

Editorial Services: (http://editorial.selfpublishing.com)

- Analysis: For $149, an analysis establishes the level of edit-
ing necessary to get your book ready for publishing. This
service is free with purchase of $398 or more of editing
services.
- Trade book editing: Priced from $.01 to $.035 per word,
this includes several levels of editing, ranging from a basic
edit for spelling, grammar and syntax to a thorough edit
that includes content, plot, development, and fact checking.

Design Services: (http://design.selfpublishing.com/index.php5)

- Custom interior design: This includes title page, copyright
page, table of contents, 256 pages of content with heads
and folios, final PDF proof with one round of up to 32
corrections. The service is priced at $350 plus $50 for each
additional 32 pages and $5 per graph or text box.
- Cover and dust jacket design: For $350 plus $25 for a bar
code, this service includes consultation with designers,
access to stock photos, scans, basic image manipulation, up
to two cover comps, and final PDF proof with two rounds
of corrections.

Distribution: (http://www.justbookz.com/thor)

- **The Thor distribution program** through Lightning Source utilizes a database of 26,000 stores, including Baker & Taylor, Ingram, Amazon.com, and BarnesandNoble.com. The only requirement is that you must purchase at least 100 copies for your own personal inventory. This service is priced at $49.95 plus $19.95 per year.
- Distribution through RJ's online bookstore: For a $24 storage fee, this service includes an author webpage with book info, author bio, shopping cart and customer reviews.
- ISBN: You will need an ISBN to sell your book. RJ doesn't provide an ISBN, but you can purchase your own directly from R.R. Bowker's U.S. ISBN Agency for $300 for a block of 10 ISBNs plus $25 per bar code.

RETURN OF DIGITAL COVER AND INTERIOR FILES: Although it is not stated on the website or in the contract, authors who pay RJ to create the interior or cover for their book will walk away with the production files for a modest $25 fee, which covers copying the files onto a disk. Since RJ authors also own their own ISBNs, this means they are free to print the book anywhere they please.

RETAIL PRICE OF AUTHOR'S BOOK: If you distribute through Thor, RJ allows the author to set the retail price for the book.

PRICE AUTHOR PAYS FOR BOOKS: You can find a pricing calculator on the RJ website at: http://www.booksjustbooks.com.

Here's how it works: A $100 administrative setup fee is added to all printing orders. Orders of 100 to 400 copies are printed digitally and orders of 500+ are printed on an offset printing press. The price for 100 copies of a 200-page, 5.5" x 8.5" book would be $5.41 per book, $5.23 per book for 500+ copies, and $3.01 per book for 1000+ copies. In other words:

$5.41	author price per book
– $3.50	book printing cost (.90 cover + .013 per page)

$1.91	RJ profit per book

The $1.91 profit is a reasonable markup on printing in this situation because, assuming your files arrive at RJ ready to print, there is no up-front fee.

PROFITS PAID TO AUTHOR: If you participate in the Thor distribution program, RJ distributes profits rather than royalties. Profits equal the retail price of the book less the wholesale discount and the cost to produce the book. The retail price of the book is determined by the author. For example, suppose you sold your 200-page, 5.5" x 8.5" book for $13.95:

$13.95	retail price
− $6.98	50% wholesale discount
− $3.50	book printing cost

$3.47	author profit

Now, if you retailed your book for $16, the profit would be $5.52 per book.

NOTABLE PROVISIONS OF THE PUBLISHING AGREEMENT: This isn't a contract as much as it is a purchase order. RJ takes no rights; there is no term clause or any of the other contract provisions you'd normally expect after reading this book. Instead, you execute a purchase order and include the submission checklist found at http://booksjustbooks.com/bookrequest/trade_submission.pdf. If you don't submit the files in a press-ready condition, RJ will fix them and charge you for no more than one hour's worth of time, billed at $65. The purchase order and the submission checklist are subject to terms and conditions found at http://booksjustbooks.com/bookrequest/termsandconditions.asp, which are standard and reasonable.

AUTHOR-FRIENDLY RATING: Ron Pramschufer, owner of RJ, is one of the good guys in self-publishing. He stands by the idea that anything an author pays to have done remains the property of the author (such as book covers and layout designs). Pramschufer is all about the author, and it shows in the pricing.

RJ is similar to Lulu in that it's an à la carte offering, but the quality and service are much better.

For a first-time author, RJ's à la carte offerings may make the initial publishing process more complex because the author essentially oversees every step of the process, and between RJ's multiple websites and its wide service offering, figuring out which services you need can be overwhelming.

If you have RJ provide all the services self-publishing does, you will spend about the same amount you would pay to let a company handle everything for you. However, the printing markups won't be as much, and you will make all of the revenues from your book sales.

If you aren't a first-time author and/or have press ready files of your book, you need to check out RJ's plethora of services.

Pramschufer hosts a radio show on self-publishing and often takes on the giants of the POD industry, asking the questions that need to be asked and demanding answers. RJ Communications is one of the few companies that are 100% in the author's corner.

XULON PRESS
http://www.xulonpress.com

FORMAT OF BOOK: paperback and hardcover

GENRES ACCEPTED: Xulon only accepts books that support its core Christian beliefs and values, but it publishes in many categories, including Christian living, theology, church growth, discipleship, Bible study, fiction, poetry and biography.

PUBLISHING FEES: Xulon has three publishing packages, the details of which you can find at http://www.xulonpress.com/prices_programs.htm.

The Basic Package: Priced at $999, this package includes:

- Custom book cover: Author can choose from Xulon's gallery or provide up to three of her own photos. Includes only one design with minimal changes.
- Professionally formatted text: Xulon interiors are template-based, and only Times New Roman 12 pt. font is used.
- Choice of trim size:
  - 5" x 8"
  - 5.5" x 8.5"
  - 6" x 9"
  - 8.25" x 11"

· PDF review copy of the book: Includes 10 minor changes, after which changes are $50 plus $2.50/change.
· ISBN
· Five free copies
· Personal template-based webpage via Xulon's online bookstore
· No distribution or royalty

Without any distribution or royalty, you are just paying to have your book printed. If you want to go with Xulon, this package makes no sense.

The Premium Package: At $1499, this package includes everything in the Basic Package, plus:

· Ten free copies
· R.R. Bowker's Books In Print registration
· Order/Pak & Ship Service offered 24 hours a day, seven days a week (toll-free order service takes phone orders and ships books to customers). Books are delivered 7-10 days from order. This service applies to sales that might come, for example, from your personal website. Xulon will handle fulfillment on individual sales if you don't want to deal with shipping, etc. It is part of the package, so there is no extra charge.
· Distribution through Ingram and Spring Arbor (Christian-book distributor), including a quarterly report of how many books sold and where they sold
· Author's book can be ordered in 25,000 bookstores, including 2,500 Christian bookstores
· Listing on Internet promotion on Amazon.com, Target.com, Borders.com, and BarnesandNoble.com
· Marketing to thousands of Christian bookstores and 1,000 leading churches in the publisher's catalog, *Christian Book Browser*
· Access to additional fee-based services: International distribution for $49 , Returns service for $59

The Best-Seller Package: At $2499, this package includes everything in the Premium Package, plus:

- Professionally written press release, which will be posted on Newswire and distributed to 3,000 Christian broadcasters and journalists through Xulon's Christian Media Alert publication
- Submission to Google Books
- International distribution, which means that your book can be ordered on Amazon.com, etc., outside of the U.S.
- Advertising in Advance and Christian Advance, which reach 25,000 bookstores monthly and 10,000 bookstores bi-monthly, respectively
- Promotion at the International Christian Retail Show twice a year with catalogs and multimedia presentations

OTHER SERVICES OF INTEREST: Xulon offers fewer à la carte services than many publishers, but those it offers are reasonably priced.

45-day copyedit: Includes grammar, syntax and spelling at $.015 per word. You can find good editing for $.01 per word, so shopping around for your own editor might be worth it.

10-day expedited copyedit: Includes grammar, syntax and spelling at $.030 per word.

International Distribution: This does not put your books on European bookshelves, but rather makes them available to order online, at sites such as Amazon.com and at bookstores. This service is $49.

Bookstore Returns Program: Marks books returnable. All returned books are deducted from author's royalty. This service is $59.

Rush service: Your book can be produced in 45 days rather than 90 for $299.

RETURN OF DIGITAL COVER AND INTERIOR FILES: Xulon recently resolved to destroy its authors' working files after six months because it costs the publisher too much file space and money to store every book. Similarly, any original artwork or photography will be destroyed after six months. Xulon will give departing authors press-ready PDF files of their digital cover and interior files for a $100 fee. You won't be able to do anything with these other than print copies of your book that still include the Xulon ISBN and logo.

RETAIL PRICE OF AUTHOR'S BOOK: A book's retail price is determined by page count (see the chart at http://www.xulonpress. com/orders_copies):

Number of pages	Retail price
48–104	$9.99
105–124	$10.99
125–199	$13.99
200–249	$14.99
250–299	$15.99
300–349	$17.99
350–399	$19.99
400–449	$21.99

PRICE AUTHOR PAYS FOR BOOKS: Xulon authors receive a substantial discount on books, depending on how many they buy, with the scale ranging from 40% off the retail price for 1–25 books to 70% off for 1,000 or more books. As an example, a 200-page book would look something like this:

$14.99	retail price
– $6.00	40% author discount
$8.99	author price per book
– $3.90	actual printing cost
$5.09	Xulon profit

When asked, the Xulon representative declined to say how much it costs to print a book, stating that the price fluctuates with the seasons and the variable cost of paper. The costs don't vary that much. The reason the representative didn't give a truthful answer is because Xulon marks up the book printing by at least 63%. The books are expensive, but Xulon will give you 75% to 100% of the royalties, which helps make up for the printing markup.

ROYALTIES PAID TO AUTHOR: Take the 200-page, paperback book as an example. Xulon retails it for $14.99. At a 63% markup on $3.90, the actual cost to print the book, Xulon is taking a printing fee of $6.36.

Xulon gives its authors 100% of net receipts (retail book price less the bookseller discount and the cost to print) from all sales to bookstores, libraries, and distributors. For books sold individually through Xulon, the author receives 75% of net receipts (full retail price less the cost to print the book). Here's what that will look like on our 200-page book for books sold through retailers:

$14.99	retail price
– $6.00	40% wholesale discount
– $6.36	Xulon printing cost
$2.63	author royalty

In that transaction, Xulon made $2.46 ($6.36–$3.90). So, authors don't really make 100% of the profits. They make 100% of the profits, not including the printing markup. For books sold through Xulon:

$14.99	retail price
– $6.36	Xulon printing cost
$8.63	net profit
x .75	author royalty percentage
$6.47	author royalty

In this transaction, Xulon makes $4.62 (25% royalty + $2.46 printing markup). The net profit of $8.63 is a higher royalty than many publishers will provide; however, authors don't make 75% of the actual profits, but 75% of the profits after backing out Xulon's printing markups.

NOTABLE PROVISIONS OF THE PUBLISHING AGREEMENT: The publishing agreement is not easy to find without a little digging, but it's listed on the site map as a sample agreement at http://www.xulonpress.com/sample_agreement.htm (go to "Step 4: Agreement").

"Author Right to Ownership" and "Author Right to Copyright" establish that the author holds complete control of the work at all times and can sell it to a third party at any time.

"Term and Termination" specifies that the author determines the term of the agreement.

"Cover Design" says that the author receives an original cover using stock photos or images and that designers will consider artwork submitted by the author but are not obliged to use it. It also states that Xulon controls what the cover looks like; the author has no option to decline, unless they want to pay a substantial fee for a new cover. Similarly, all interior text will be formatted, according to the publisher's template, in Times New Roman font.

"Miscellaneous Fees" imposes charges on the author for work that requires editing. The author may receive 10 minor edit changes for free. After 10 changes, the publisher charges $50 plus $2.50 for each minor change.

AUTHOR-FRIENDLY RATING: The publisher offers a nonexclusive contract and competitive pricing at the retail level. Although the author has less flexibility in book design and pays a bit more for books than with some other publishers, the trade-off is fantastic royalties.

Xulon should be more forthright about what it's really making per book or should adjust the royalty percentages to make them accurate. That being said, Xulon still pays a better royalty than almost anyone in the business.

The marketing services included in the upper-end package justify the publisher's additional fees. The publisher is a member of Christian Booksellers Association and Evangelical Christian Publishers Association, both of which may provide additional information and references.

Xulon's website is well organized and pretty much all of the fees and services are explained up front. If you do have a question, you'll need to call, as the company does not provide a contact e-mail. However, the Xulon operators were extremely responsive to questions without attempting to pressure me into placing a book with their service.

I feel that authors who select Christian publishers are under a belief that such a company would never provide inaccurate information. That is why Xulon and other religion-focused publishers need to be held to a higher standard in the way they present information about their services. Authors inherently believe them. But, if you're targeting a Christian audience, Xulon does provide a solid package and promotional opportunities. Hands down, Xulon is the best exclusively Christian self-publishing company out there.

CHAPTER 7

SOME PRETTY GOOD SELF-PUBLISHING COMPANIES

How do you separate an "Outstanding" publisher from a "Pretty Good" one? By examining factors such as the publisher's pricing, royalties and contract. Publishers that earned a "Pretty Good" rating typically exhibited one aspect that was unfavorable to authors, such as low royalties, extremely high printing markups, or a clause in their contract that wasn't author-friendly and that the publisher would not change.

The publishers in this section are good companies and provide a solid service. In fact, many of these publishers are one mere tweak away from the "Outstanding" category. Read their reviews, and if the deficiencies don't bother you, then publish your work with one of these "Pretty Good" publishers.

BLITZPRINT

http://www.blitzprint.com

FORMAT OF BOOKS: paperback and hardcover

GENRES: Blitzprint is as much a printing service as a publishing services provider and will print just about anything providing it is not libelous, stolen, or hateful.

PUBLISHING FEES: Blitzprint is more of a publishing services company than a publisher, and as such offers primarily à la carte services, although its design services include much of what one might find in a publishing package. An overview of available services can be found here: http://www.blitzprint.com/get_started.htm. Here is a broad synopsis:

> **Editing:** For $.012 per word, this service includes spelling, grammar, punctuation, syntax and word usage.

> **Marketing:** Blitzprint has partnered with Ink Tree, a professional book marketing and PR company. At the low end, the $249 Starter Kit is a self-led course on how to do your own book publicity and, at the high end, the $1,197 Powerhouse Kit is also self-led, but includes 60 days of unlimited consultation, access to media lists and other contacts, and template-based tools for putting together your publicity.

> **Design:** Blitzprint will allow authors to submit their own design files, provided they are to spec, and even provides some tools to help with the process. But, if you want more of a "package," the template ($449) or custom designs ($649) are similar to the publishing packages offered by other self-publishing companies.

> **Template-based Cover:** This cover choice includes:
>   · Choice of interior templates in a variety of trim sizes
>   · Choice of cover templates in a variety of trim sizes (including hardcover)
>   · Scanning and placement of interior images for an additional $5 each
>   · Scanning and placement of 4-color cover images
>   · ISBN
>   · Bar code
>   · Compete hard copy proof prior to any printing
>   · E-book ready PDF file
>   · Distribution and fulfillment (see description below)

> **Custom-designed Cover:** This cover choice includes everything in the template-based package, plus:

- Author works directly with the designer to come up with the cover concept, which includes the author's choice of two concepts. Author has the option to supply design layout suggestions, images or samples.
- Custom interior, which includes the author's choice of up to three layout concepts

Distribution and Fulfillment: Blitzprint distribution, called Bookstream, is priced at $99 and includes:

- Listing on the Blitzprint.com bookstore: http://www.bookstream.biz
- Distribution through Baker & Taylor
- Listing with online booksellers, including Amazon.com
- ISBN
- Library of Congress Control Number (LCCN)

Blitzprint fulfillment is optional and requires the author to buy 100 or more books. The bulk of the order is shipped to the author, the rest are held in stock.

To get what would be a basic publishing and distribution package, you would spend approximately $748.

RETURN OF DIGITAL COVER AND INTERIOR FILES: According to the Blitzprint representative I contacted, authors own all of their book files, regardless of who designed the cover. However, this fact is not included in the contract. I would recommend getting that guaranteed in writing.

RETAIL PRICE OF AUTHOR'S BOOK: The author determines the price of their book, whether they are selling via Blitzprint or some other venue. In general, a 200-page paperback retails for $13.95. Remember, though, that the author buys every book that sells through Blitzprint's fulfillment, and $13.95 will not yield much profit when it comes to Amazon.com sales, as you'll see below.

PRICE AUTHOR PAYS FOR BOOKS: Blitzprint is both a publisher and a printer and, therefore, charges à la carte pricing for each service. That said, when I asked the company what it would cost to print a 200-page, 6" x 9", perfect-bound, paperback book, the representative quoted me the following per book prices and offered to waive the setup fee and throw in a free ISBN and bar code.

Number of books	Author price per book
Up to 100	$6.31
200	$5.14
500	4.34

Although these prices are neither higher nor lower than average, the author should consider that Blitzprint makes somewhere in the vicinity of $2.41 in markups on each book but likely makes more than that since they do the printing themselves.

ROYALTIES PAID TO AUTHOR: Royalties only apply if the author uses Blitzprint for fulfillment. In that case, the author (who is the publisher) pays either Blitzprint a 20% or Amazon. com a 50% fee for any books sold on their respective websites. Remember, under the Blitzprint fulfillment plan, the author buys the books, which are held in stock.

So, if the author sells her 200-page, paperback book on the Blitzprint website, she makes:

$13.95	retail price
– $2.79	20% Blitzprint fee
– $6.31	author price per book
$4.85	author profit

That's a fine profit, relative to what you might make elsewhere, but consider that Blitzprint makes:

$2.79	fulfillment fee
+ $2.41	printing markup
$5.20	Blitzprint profit

If the author sells that same book on Amazon.com, she makes:

$13.95	retail price
– $6.97	50% Amazon.com discount

− $6.31   author price per book

$.67   author profit

Blitzprint, on the other hand, is making at least $2.41 on each Amazon.com sale. If you want to make more of a profit on Amazon.com sales, you will need to raise the price of the book. In order to earn a $2.00 profit, you would need to charge $16.60.

NOTABLE PROVISIONS OF THE PUBLISHING AGREEMENT: Although Blitzprint forwarded me this agreement, the printer's representative said that it does not require authors to sign an agreement unless Blitzprint is providing fulfillment services. However, as stated before, if the agreement is well written and fair, it can provide clarity if something goes wrong between you and the publisher, or in this case the printer—in this contract, the term "publisher" refers to the author.

In section 1, "Intellectual Property," the publisher (author) grants Blitzprint the nonexclusive license to manufacture his or her book in any language, in any country, and in any form or media. This section also states the work—including copyrights, trademarks, and intellectual and proprietary rights—belongs to the publisher (author) but is subject to the license granted to Blitzprint, which means that while Blitzprint has a nonexclusive right to print and/or distribute the book, it does not own the rights to it.

Under subsection 1.3, the publisher (author) is required to print a copyright notice on the book. That's less interesting than the fact that Blitzprint, which is not the publisher (remember, YOU are!), will put its trademark on the book—basically, that means that your book will be marked as a self-published book.

Section 2 deals with print and delivery. Of note, it states that Blitzprint will provide one free proof and one round of corrections; after that, if the publisher (author) has changes, he must pay an unspecified hourly rate for changes—unless Blitzprint made the errors, in which case there will not be a fee for corrections. This section also states that neither party will be held responsible if an act of God or nature prevents delivery of services, materials, or books. This is standard and fair language.

In section 4, "Publisher's Warranty," the author agrees that he owns all of the content in the book and that the book is original—i.e., nothing in the books is stolen. The author also agrees that the book does not contain anything obscene, libelous, hateful or otherwise scandalous. Section 4 also states that Blitzprint can refuse to print the book for any of these reasons.

In section 8, "Indemnification," the publisher (author) agrees to accept all legal responsibility for the content of the book, which means that Blitzprint and its employees will not be held responsible if you have plagiarized the book.

In section 9, "Confidentiality," both parties agree to keep any trade secrets, technology, know-how, or otherwise valuable information that is exposed in the course of this contract confidential, even after the life of the contract. This clause does not apply if either party can document that they had the confidential information prior to the contract, that it actually came from a third-party, or that they must surrender the information because of a court order.

Section 10, "Termination," states that the agreement is valid for one year and may be terminated "for the conditions expressly set forth herein" with 10 days written notice. However, if the contract is terminated, the publisher (author) "shall remain liable to Blitzprint for all sums due and owing to Blitzprint pursuant to the terms of this Agreement and Blitzprint is liable for performance as of the date of such termination, and the payment or retention of these sums shall not constitute a penalty or forfeiture." This means that if you terminate, you're still obligated to complete any unfinished business with the company and vice-versa.

Section 16, "Choice of Law and Forum," states that the agreement is subject to the laws of Alberta, Canada, and that any disputes must be argued in the courts of Alberta. This clause is fair, but it obviously does not favor anyone who happens to live outside of Alberta, let alone Canada.

AUTHOR-FRIENDLY RATING: This is, overall, an unexceptional publisher. Unless you find something terribly wrong in the contract, I see little to recommend or fault in Blitzprint. Its prices are fairly average, and its services are well defined, but it doesn't seem to go out of its way to provide a stand-out service for authors.

Blitzprint's website is clean, professional looking, and easy to find your way around, and the quote service is personal and very responsive. However, the Blitzprint bookstore, Bookstream.com, is hokey and screams self-publishing. The company has designed a beautiful site to sell itself but provides only a very basic site to sell its authors' books. Since the author will make a lot more on the books he or she sells through the publisher's online bookstore, Blitzprint owes it to its authors to improve Bookstream.com.

Blitzprint has one of the more honest offerings. Sure, they mark up the books, but there aren't any hidden costs and the author can easily figure out what they will pay and make per book and decide if the service is for them. There is something to be said for that kind of transparency.

FOREMOST PRESS
http://www.foremostpress.com

FORMAT OF BOOK: e-book and paperback

GENRES ACCEPTED: Foremost Press prefers books of not less than 104 pages or 60,000–100,000 words, but will consider longer books. Go to http://www.foremostpress.com/authors for complete guideline information.

PUBLISHING FEES: The two publishing programs are:

Plan A: Priced at $347, this plan includes:
- Light edit: On the Foremost website this is defined as the publisher's editors "examining" the manuscript to make sure it meets their standards and correcting any mistakes they find along the way. This is not a true edit, so authors should definitely pay a copyeditor to give their manuscript a thorough edit.
- 6" x 9" trim size
- ISBN
- Ten copies of the book
- PDF version of book for e-book sales
- Four-page website with a sales page on publisher's website.

An example can be found at http://www.foremostpress.
com/readers/chacko_d/shadow.html. While this is deeper
than many provided by self-publishers, it would be more
effective if the domain name was tied to the book itself
instead of to Foremost.

- Listing with online booksellers: Amazon.com and Barne-
  sandNoble.com
- Distribution through Baker & Taylor
- Customized typesetting: This is a little misleading, as the
  publisher says it uses "a classic format that has proved uni-
  versally popular," which implies that a single template is
  used. However, that is not unusual.
- Cover provided by author or purchased separately from
  Foremost's designer, Charles King. Apparently, King generally likes to design both the cover and the interior, and
  so the publisher is careful to say "he may be willing" to
  design just the cover, making no guarantees. The price for
  the cover design is about $150.

Plan B: Priced at $197, this plan includes everything in Plan A
except typesetting. Authors must pay Charles King or a third-
party designer to create a cover and typeset the book. If the
author chooses King, the cover costs around $150 and typeset-
ting ranges from $200 to $400.

RETURN OF DIGITAL COVER AND INTERIOR FILES:
Foremost supplies departing authors with their production files at no
extra charge. However, this is not written on Foremost's website or in the
contract. I would advise you to have it added as an addendum to the contract; otherwise the company is not legally bound to provide the files.

RETAIL PRICE OF AUTHOR'S BOOK: For paperback books,
Foremost bases it retail book prices on the book's page count.

Number of pages	Retail price
104–120	$10.97
124–160	$11.97
164–196	$12.97

200–236	$13.97
240–280	$14.97
284–320	$15.97
324–360	$16.97
364–400	$17.97
404–440	$18.97
444–480	$19.97
484–500	$20.97

For e-books, the author sets the sales price, although the publisher suggests a maximum of $4.97, because, it says, "electronic fiction has such a bad rap that only low prices lead to sales."

PRICE AUTHOR PAYS FOR BOOKS: Authors pay 50% of the retail book price (plus shipping) for orders of 10 books or more. So, for a 200-page book the author will pay:

| $13.97 | retail price |
| x .50 | author discount percentage |

| $6.99 | author price per book |

Foremost uses Lightning Source to print its books and publishes what it pays to print each book as $.013 per page + $.90 for the cover:

$13.97	retail price
– $6.99	50% author discount
– $3.50	printing cost

| $3.48 | Foremost profit |

ROYALTIES PAID TO AUTHOR: For paperback books, the author receives 20% of the gross sales price for sales on the publisher's website. For a 200-page book:

| $13.97 | retail price |
| x .20 | author royalty percentage |

| $2.79 | author royalty |

Meanwhile, on that same sale, Foremost makes:

| $13.97 | retail price |

$$
\begin{array}{ll}
-\ \$2.79 & \text{20\% author royalty} \\
-\ \$3.90 & \text{printing cost} \\
\hline
\$7.28 & \text{Foremost profit}
\end{array}
$$

For wholesale and third-party retail sales, the publisher and author split the net profit of the sale 50-50. The publisher defines "net" as the retail price less the wholesale discount (40%) and cost to print. So, for a 200-page book:

$$
\begin{array}{ll}
\$13.97 & \text{retail price} \\
-\ \$5.58 & \text{40\% wholesale discount} \\
-\ \$3.50 & \text{printing cost} \\
\text{x .50} & \text{author and publisher royalty percentage} \\
\hline
\$2.45 & \text{author and publisher royalty}
\end{array}
$$

For e-books, the publisher deducts a $.97 transaction fee from the retail price of the e-book and then splits what is left with the author 50-50:

$$
\begin{array}{ll}
\$4.97 & \text{maximum e-book retail price} \\
-\ \$.97 & \text{processing fee} \\
\hline
\$4.00 & \text{net profit} \\
\text{x .50} & \text{author royalty percentage} \\
\hline
\$2.00 & \text{author royalty}
\end{array}
$$

NOTABLE PROVISIONS OF THE PUBLISHING AGREEMENT: The contract is at http://foremostpress.com/authors/agreement.html. Foremost Press has the shortest publishing contract I've ever seen; it condenses the content of standard 10-page publishing contracts into one page. It sets forth royalty rights (as already discussed) and allows either party to cancel at any time by giving 120 days e-mail notice. The author confirms rights to the book with a denial of libel or copyright infringement.

Sometimes a contract can be too short. It doesn't address important elements like how long the process will take, if the author receives a proof copy, etc. If everything goes smoothly then it's not an issue, but if you run into problems with this publisher, you will be in a tough position, as the contract provides very little clarity.

AUTHOR-FRIENDLY RATING: You can't get a bookstore quality book produced for the fees this publisher charges. The publisher makes it clear, if you read between the lines a bit, that there is one standard layout and one trim size. If a 6" x 9" trim size and template-based layout are acceptable to you, neither package is a bad deal. Either way, the author needs to provide the cover design. If you are considering Foremost, go out and pay to have a great cover designed. Whether Charles King (the man touted on the website as an amazing cover designer) is the right person to design your cover, is something you'll need to figure out for yourself. Don't consider the light "look over" in the $397 package to be an edit. It's not. I'm not sure what it is, other than glancing at the book to see if glaring mistakes pop to the surface.

The printing markups are incredibly high. On the 200-page, paperback book, which costs Foremost $3.50 to print, the markup is 100%—the author pays $6.99.

The royalties are also sore spot. Foremost makes much, much more than the author and offers very limited services beyond printing the book and making it available for sale. On a 200-page book, Foremost makes a 55% profit (based on the retail price of $13.97) on each book sold from its website, while the author makes about a 20% profit.

The low-cost packages are attractive and, on the surface, seem to be a great deal. But, once you peel back the skin and look at the real numbers, you will see that the low entry point only benefits authors who don't sell many books. If your book is successful (or you're planning on its success), it's always smarter to pay more up front and avoid getting saddled with low royalties and enormous printing markups. If you don't plan on selling many books, but simply want a published book, pay as little as you can up front and don't worry about royalties.

The publisher responded within two hours to queries I sent via e-mail, and provided the most thorough, honest answers I've received from almost any other publisher covered in this book. The chances are good that a frank and responsive publisher won't ignore its authors once the check clears. That alone puts this publisher in the "Pretty Good" category.

Yet, Foremost is ranked "Pretty Good" with a disclaimer: Now that you know how much it marks up printing costs and how much more it makes than its authors in royalties, proceed with caution. I believe this publisher will deliver a fine product, but the cost is too high for me.

LULU

http://www.lulu.com

FORMAT OF BOOKS: e-books, paperback and hardcover

GENRES ACCEPTED: all

PUBLISHING FEES: Lulu is an unusual self-publisher in that it doesn't admit to being one, calling itself instead a technology company, but its service is actually closer to "self" publishing than many out there. Rather than offering set publishing packages that take you from manuscript to bookselling, Lulu simply provides the software and a place to post, sell, and buy digital content, be it books, music or photographs. Basically, it's free to set your content up using Lulu's software and publish it in the Lulu Marketplace; the company makes its money by taking a transaction fee if you actually sell something. However, if you want to take the relationship a step further, the company also offers printing and distribution services and access to third-party vendors that provide à la carte services, such as editing, layout, and marketing. There are two distribution services.

Published by Lulu: This service (http://www.lulu.com/help/index.php?fSymbol=isbn_faq#FAQLink8) is priced at $99.95 and includes:

- Book sales through Lulu.com
- A Lulu-owned ISBN
- Bookland EAN bar code
- R.R. Bowker's Books In Print registration
- Listing with online booksellers
- Conversion of your retail price into five currencies (U.S. dollars, British pounds, Australian dollars, Euros, and Canadian dollars) to facilitate global availability and purchasing

- Listing with online retailers such as Amazon.com and BarnesandNoble.com
- My Account: Lulu's Internet-based reporting system, which allows authors to monitor book sales and royalties, as well communications with the Lulu community

Published by You: This service (http://www.lulu.com/help/ index.php?fSymbol=isbn_faq#FAQLink9) is priced at $149 and includes everything in the Published by Lulu package, with the exception that you are the publisher and own the ISBN:

- You register to become a publisher
- You purchase ISBN (Note: ISBNs are sold at http://www. isbn.com as a set of 10 for $275. When considering this package, you should factor in this cost and, of course, whether or not you may have a use for the other nine ISBNs in the future.)
- Bookland EAN bar code placed on the back cover (not applicable to one-piece covers)
- Bibliographic data on your book fed to major international bibliographic databases and available to booksellers (At the booksellers' discretion, your book may be made available for sale online or in bookstores.)
- Conversion of retail price into five currencies (U.S. dollars, British pounds, Australian dollars, Euros, and Canadian dollars) to facilitate global availability and purchasing
- Listing with online booksellers: Amazon.com and BarnesandNoble.com

If you want to build your own full-service package, Lulu provides a list of vendors and links on its website at http://www.lulu.com/services. Each service is rated, similar to eBay, with one to six stars and comments from presumably happy customers. So, for the sake of comparing apples to apples, you could combine Published by Lulu with a vendor and pay $400–$500 ($600–$750 if you decide to go with Published by You and purchase ISBNs) for a complete package comparable to other publishers:

Dixie Press Custom Combo Package: This service (http:// www.lulu.com/content/141766) is priced at $300–$475 and includes:

· Custom cover design
· Custom book formatting
· Three revisions of the cover and interior
· A $2 illustration upload charge for use of your own draw-
  ings and photographs

Note: Lulu also offers free images for your use in creating your
book cover.

RETAIL PRICE OF AUTHOR'S BOOK: Authors set the price
for their books, thus determining their own royalties as well. See
the royalty section for more detailed information.

PRICE AUTHOR PAYS FOR BOOKS: Authors purchase
copies of their books for $4.53 per book plus $.02 per page.
A pricing calculator can be found at http://www.lulu.com/help/
index.php?fSymbol=ordering_faq#FAQLink4. A 200-page, 6" x
9", perfect-bound book will cost:

$4.53	fixed fee for cover, binding and setup
+ $4.00	(200 pages x $.02 per page)

$8.53	author price per book

Another way to look at that is:

$8.53	author price per book
– $3.90	printing cost

$4.63	Lulu profit

If you order fewer than 26 books, you pay $8.53 per book. After
that, quantity discounts kick in, and the price drops a small percentage
with every book you purchase:

Number of books	Discount	Author price per book
26	1%	$8.45
36	8%	$7.33

46	11%	$7.56
56	14%	$7.35
100	19%	$6.93
200	25%	$6.37
500	31%	$5.88
1000	33%	$5.69

Lulu's books are not cheap, but you can set the book up for free, and the publisher only takes a 20% royalty.

ROYALTIES PAID TO AUTHOR: Royalties are determined by the author, who sets the price of the book, and by the distribution method. If you visit http://www.lulu.com/help/index.php?fSymbol=royalty_faq you can see how the royalty is determined and calculated. For example, if an author chooses to sell her book only through the Lulu Marketplace, the publisher's online bookstore, and sets the price at $13.95 for a 200-page, 6" x 9" book, sales will look like this:

$13.95	retail price
– $4.53	fixed fee for cover, binding and setup
– $4.00	printing cost ($.02 per page)

$5.42	net profit
– $1.08	20% Lulu commission

$4.34	author royalty

If an author chooses either Published by You or Published by Lulu, the retail price will have to go up somewhat to accommodate a royalty because of the wholesale discounts to Amazon.com and other third parties. For example, you would need to set the price for the same book at $18 to make a $2 royalty:

$18.00	retail price
– $1.56	fixed fee for cover, binding, and setup
– $4.00	printing cost ($.02 per page)
– $9.90	55% Amazon.com discount

$2.54	net profit
– $.51	20% Lulu commission

$2.03	author royalty

So, the question is, will someone pay $18 for your 200-page, paper-back book?

NOTABLE PROVISIONS OF THE PUBLISHING AGREE-MENT: Lulu publishes two agreements. One is the general publisher agreement that all authors and users must use, and the other applies to those who sign on to one of Lulu's two distribution programs.

The Publisher's Member Agreement: This agreement can be found at http://www.lulu.com/about/member_agreement.php. Although it is used by authors and website users, only the portions relevant to writers are discussed here.

Section 3 states that Lulu makes no claim to the copyright in your work but has permission to post and sell the author's work. This section lists all author representations and warranties, which are reasonable.

Section 6 discusses payment terms and agrees to pay you the "creator revenue" or royalty amount you chose, while charging a service fee of 20% of the gross margin. The gross margin is the net amount actually received for your content after freight and manufacturing costs are subtracted. It also tells you how to access information about how many of your books have sold and how to choose how you will be paid your creator revenue.

Section 7 explains that Lulu is not responsible for the content, and therefore will not accept returns unless there is physical damage (i.e., a torn page) to the book.

Section 9 is significant because it explains how an author removes his or her work for sale from the publisher's website. It's a simple process that can be done at any time.

Section 12 allows Lulu to shut down its website at any time. It simply means that if Lulu goes out of business, you don't have any recourse.

Section 13 confirms that services to the author are provided on an "as is" basis. If there's a glitch in the system, such as a technical error that prevents your book from being ordered from its website for 10 days, there's nothing the author can do about it. This is a standard clause and not unreasonable.

Section 14 disallows an author's claim for damages resulting from circumstances described in sections 11 and 12 beyond the amount the author paid Lulu in connection with the transaction giving rise to the claim. For example, if Lulu issues an ISBN that's already issued to another author, you could only sue them for the amount you originally paid for the ISBN number. Again, this type of language is reasonable.

Section 15 confirms that Lulu owns everything on its website that isn't submitted by a member.

Section 16, paragraph 1 requires changes to the contract to be in writing and signed by both parties. Paragraph 2 says that either party who could have made a claim under the contract but didn't does not give up the right to do so later. Paragraph 3 means that if a section of the contract is deemed invalid, the rest of the contract remains valid. Paragraph 4 points to the laws of North Carolina as the governing authority. Any dispute will be handled by a single arbitrator and arbitrated in Raleigh, North Carolina. The arbitrator's ruling is final and enforceable in court.

Section 17 states that the agreement continues until either party terminates, but that certain provisions such as warranties survive termination.

Section 18 says that the publisher may change the terms of the agreement from time to time and that you agree to monitor the agreement for changes. If a change occurs that you don't like, you can stop using the website and remove your work.

The Published By Lulu agreement: This agreement is written in clear language and presented in a simple list form at http://www.lulu.com/help/index.php?fSymbol=pbl_agreement.

Item 1 says that you grant Lulu the right to act as a publisher on your behalf with retailers and wholesalers globally.

Item 4 asserts your right to remove your work from Lulu at any time, with the caveat that it may take six to eight weeks for the work to be removed completely.

Item 8 states your agreement to buy a review copy prior to approving the first copy of your book.

Item 10 says that you agree to set the Lulu Marketplace price (Lulu's online bookstore) of your book equal to or greater than the retail price of your book.

Item 11 says that you agree not to sell a duplicate of your book at a lower price while the original Lulu print is still in circulation. This is

a terrible clause. It prevents you from selling your book in the "new &
used" section on Amazon.com or technically through any other venue,
like an author appearance, at a price less than the inflated ones on Lulu.

Item 12 clarifies that your royalty will initially be set at $4 a book,
but you have the option to change that at anytime prior to the printing
of the book.

Item 13 states that you understand that any changes made to your
book after a final copy has been approved for distribution will result in
a $79 revision fee.

AUTHOR-FRIENDLY RATING: Lulu (and the copycats, Wordclay and CreateSpace) actually punishes authors who sell a lot of books
because of its high printing costs, which result in artificially high retail
prices. Lulu (and the others) is designed for those who want to dip a toe
in the publishing waters with little risk and those with a lot of self-publishing experience. If you are not experienced in handling every aspect
of the publishing process on your own (hiring cover designers, editors,
book formatters, etc.), essentially being your own general contractor,
then the Lulu model, in my opinion, is not the best option.

Lulu requires that you do a lot of the leg work yourself and, by the
time you pay the preferred service providers (all of whom give Lulu a
percentage of what you pay them), you will have spent close to what it
would cost to let one company handle everything. In publishing as in
life, you get what you pay for.

But, if you are a skilled designer or a basic book meets your needs or
you simply don't have enough money to publish any other way, Lulu is a
company to consider. And Lulu is well suited to the experienced author
whose book is already designed and formatted and who only needs a
simple distribution package.

That being said, Lulu's website has recently been redesigned, and it
is very easy to navigate. Less than an hour after getting on the site, I had
a book loaded and ready for sale, and that included a short chat with the
folks at Live Help when I was having trouble with my Word document.
The Lulu template software was really easy to use and flexible; unlike
Wordclay's, it allowed me to add in photos, choose from multiple book
sizes and bindings, and to look at and edit my book after it had been
published without starting from scratch. Also, the folks at Live Help

were actually able to look at my project—unlike CreateSpace—and walk me through the problem.

Live Help is great, but Lulu's user forums also provide a wealth of information. Knowledgeable Lulu Power Posters man every string, providing clear and complete answers to questions within hours, sometimes minutes, of their posting.

And, as I have already mentioned, Lulu is a good way to test things. You can shop à la carte and put together a complete publishing package for around $400–$500 ($600–$750 if buy your own ISBNs). If you're going to spend $500, you have to really decide if going the do-it-yourself route will result in a better book and if you can afford the time, too.

The agreement is as author-friendly as they come. The ability to set your price is a great feature, and the royalties can be as high or low as you want based on your projections. But, the fact that you can't sell your own books for less than the purchase price on Lulu will be restrictive.

If all you have is $500 and you want to see if you can generate some viral buzz about your book, Lulu could be an option for you. If you plan on actually selling your book at a competitive price, Lulu will never be an option. But, Lulu is the best for what it is and easily wins out over its competitors, Wordclay and CreateSpace.

MAGIC VALLEY PUBLISHING
http://www.magicvalleypub.com/index.html

FORMAT OF BOOKS: paperback

GENRES: all

PUBLISHING FEES: Magic Valley offers one, pared down package.

Publishing Package: Priced at $379, plus $45 for a proof, this package includes:

- ISBN
- Bar code
- US. Copyright Office registration

- Listing with online booksellers, including Amazon.com and BarnesandNoble.com
- Cover design, which includes a total of four hours of design time
- Typesetting
- Choice of trim size:
  - 5" x 8"
  - 5.5" x 8.5"
  - 6" x 9"
- Inclusion in catalog—free for first year, $22 for each year after that

RETURN OF DIGITAL COVER AND INTERIOR FILES: Magic Valley's author agreement says that the "Publisher will retain possession of all materials submitted by Author. Publisher will have no obligation to provide Author any submitted materials or production files at anytime or for any reason."

However, a representative for the publisher told me that the working files could be purchased. She was not able to come up with a fee offhand but said this is something that could be added to the author's contract. However, the contract language is definitive, and the fact that the representative couldn't come up with a fee means there probably isn't one.

RETAIL PRICE OF AUTHOR'S BOOK: Magic Valley allows its authors to set the price of their books but asks them to keep in mind a 40% Amazon.com discount.

PRICE AUTHOR PAYS FOR BOOKS: Magic Valley provides the following equation for wholesale or author orders: $2.00 cover charge per unit plus $.015 per page. So, your price on a 200-page, 6" x 9" paperback would be:

$2.00	cover charge
+ $3.00	(200 pages at $.015 per page)
$5.00	wholesale price

Since we already know the actual cost to print a 200-page book digitally is $3.90, the publisher makes $1.10 in this scenario, which is not a huge markup in the relative world of self-publishing.

ROYALTIES PAID TO AUTHOR: Oddly, the author agreement references a royalty, but no where on the website or the agreement does it mention how much of a royalty the author will receive. When I talked to the publisher's representative, she explained that the author earns 100% of net sales, which in this case means retail less the wholesale/author price and any discounts.

If the author sells the same 200-page book on the Magic Valley website, she makes:

$13.95	retail price
– $5.00	author price per book

$8.95	author profit

If that same book sells on Amazon.com, the author makes:

$13.95	retail price
– $5.58	40% Amazon.com discount
– $5.00	author price per book

$3.37	

NOTABLE PROVISIONS OF THE PUBLISHING AGREEMENT: The publishing agreement can be found at http://www.magicvalleypub.com/publishingagreement.pdf.

Paragraph 1 states that the author is responsible for sending the publisher the agreement, payment, and his work in a ready-to-publish format. If the author does not submit the work in an acceptable format (note that this is not defined in the contract) or requests subsequent revisions, the publisher will apply an unspecified fee.

Paragraph 2 covers the ownership of the production files: "Publisher will retain possession of all materials submitted by Author. Publisher will have no obligation to provide Author any submitted materials or production files at anytime or for any reason." It is fairly standard for a publisher to decline responsibility for the safekeeping of the author's materials, but not providing the production files is another thing. If the author decides to leave Magic Valley and cannot take his production files with him, he will have to pay another designer to create a cover and typeset the book. When I called and asked the publisher about this clause, she agreed that the author could have them for a fee but was unable to offer a number on the fly.

Paragraph 3 is a fairly standard warranty section in which the author agrees that he is the author of the book, that it does not contain libelous or hateful material, and that he has the right to publish it.

Paragraph 4 is also a standard clause, stating that Magic Valley Publishers does not own the work and assumes no responsibility for editing the work. It also says that either party can terminate the agreement at any time, without cause. The publisher is not responsible for errors introduced by its distributors, and "Publisher shall be held harmless for any damages Publisher sustains by distributing the Work." This means that if an author defames someone in her book, and that person sues Magic Valley (since it is the publisher), the author agrees that any damages assessed against Magic Valley will be the author's responsibility. This is a fair and reasonable clause.

In Paragraph 5, the publisher agrees to prepare the work for distribution, assign an ISBN, and register the book with distributors so it is available via print on demand. It also says that the "Publisher shall keep records of all book sales and distribute Author royalties quarterly."

Paragraph 6 deals with pricing and says that it will be determined per title and subject to change without notice, which means that if you publish a second book with the company you will not necessarily pay the same fees. The breakdown of the fees is as listed previously. This clause also guarantees an original book cover, which includes either stock photography or an image created by the author, and up to four hours of design production time. The clause also states that the publisher will typeset the book. Additional time with the design department is available for purchase at an hourly rate of $75.

Paragraph 7 states that the author will pay an annual catalog fee of $22 and that the first year is included in the package price.

AUTHOR-FRIENDLY RATING: There isn't a lot to this publisher, and that may be why my overall gut reaction is that it's honest. The site is a bit hokey, but the fees are low, the book printing markups are respectable, and the royalties are high.

I e-mailed my first query and received no reply. However, when I called, the publisher answered the phone and was extremely friendly and informative. She also explained that the general e-mail box is full of spam, so she has a "secret" e-mail address that she uses for her authors.

This publisher seems like a good option for an author who only has $400 to spend on publishing and just wants a book on Amazon.com. If you want anything more than that, you'll need to look elsewhere.

OUTSKIRTS PRESS
http://www.outskirtspress.com

FORMAT OF BOOKS: e-book, paperback and hardcover

GENRES ACCEPTED: all

PUBLISHING FEES: There are five publishing packages ranging from $199 to $999. A side-by-side comparison of all the packages can be found at http://www.outskirtspress.com/publishinginformation. php. It's not especially descriptive, so if you want to know more about the various services look here: http://www.outskirtspress.com/help.php. For a list of à la carte prices, look here: http://www.outskirtspress .com/outskirts_pricelist.pdf.

The Emerald Package: Priced at $199, this package includes:

- Choice of two full-color cover templates
- Digital author review: Includes 25 changes, after which every change is
- $.50. Additional galleys are $49 plus $.50 per edit.
- One free author copy
- Interior layout template with choice of fonts
- Interior graphics: First five graphics are placed for a $29 fee, additional graphics are $4 each
- Template-based author webpage
- Marketing toolkit
- Local radio contacts
- One book size: 5.5" x 8.5" and between 30–800 pages in length
- Listing on Outskirts's website
- Manuscript evaluation

- No distribution, royalty, ISBN or bar code
- File storage for an additional $18 annual fee

The Sapphire Package: For $399, this package includes everything in the Emerald Package, plus:

- Three copies of the book
- Choice of nine full-color cover templates
- Choice of trim size:
     5" x 8"
     5.5" x 8.5"
     6" x 9"
- Author website with choice of two templates
- Ability to set the royalty
- Distribution through Ingram and Baker & Taylor
- Listing with online booksellers: Amazon.com, BarnesandNoble.com, Borders.com and BooksAMillion.com
- Access to the Author Center, where authors can monitor sales of the book
- ISBN
- Bar code

The Ruby Package: At $599, this package includes everything in the Sapphire Package, plus:

- Worldwide distribution
- Choice of 16 full-color cover templates
- Six free author copies
- Author website with nine template options
- Choice of 13 book formats (see http://www.outskirtspress.com/rubypublishing.php)
- Marketing coach
- R.R. Bowker's Books In Print registration
- Access to other fee-based services, including:
- Library of Congress registration (LCCN)
- Ingram Publishing announcement
- U.S. Copyright Office registration
- Custom cover, which includes a copy polish and custom

interior, and choice of photos from the image gallery
· Retail Returns program

The Diamond Package: For $999, this package (http://www
.outskirtspress.com/diamondpublishing.php) includes every feature of the Ruby Package, plus:

- Fifteen available formats for the book
- Ten free author copies
- Twenty-five customizable cover choices, including free
  cover image gallery
- Author website with 16 template choices
- Professional interior layout, including drop caps
- Free e-book version
- Loyalty program: If author publishes a second book through
  the Outskirts Diamond program, the author will receive
  a 10% discount. A third book gets an additional 10% off,
  which becomes the publishing price moving forward.
- Audio excerpt: A three-minute recording of the author's
  voice either talking about or reading from the book
- Back page promotion: A printed page at the back of the
  book that promotes the author's previously published books
- Press Release distribution: Book release written and distributed by an Outskirts PR professional to 100,000 media
  outlets
- Qualify for EVVY nomination: The EVVY Awards are
  sponsored by the Colorado Independent Publisher's Association and recognize excellence in self-published and
  independently published books. Outskirts nominates less
  than 5% of its authors.
- OTHER SERVICES OF INTEREST: Outskirts offers a
  smattering of à la carte services. Here are a few of note:

Edit: Basic copyediting includes typos, spelling and syntax at
$.014 a word with a minimum of 15,000 words. Books of poetry are
$50 an hour with a minimum of four hours. More extensive editing
services are available and charged by the project.

Custom designed professional cover: Author works with designer to create a 100% original cover. The cost is $299. Designer will provide two options and one round of changes, after which all changes are charged in 15-minute increments at $50/hour.

Hardcover edition: Price is either $199 or $298, depending on whether the hardcover edition is the same size as the paperback edition or different.

Standard press release: For $99, Outskirts's publicity professionals create a standard book release announcement, which is then distributed to a database 100,000 media contacts. But, since it's not targeted, you're taking a $99 gamble that one or two people out of 100,000 will respond. (I didn't see anything to indicate the publisher has 100,000 media contacts interested in romance novels and 100,000 interested in self-help books, for example)

Custom press release: For $199, Outskirts's publicity professionals write a customized press release, which is then distributed to the 100,000 media contacts. Here, you're just sending a better written press release to a non-targeted list. The results won't be much different.

Returns: For a $499 annual fee, this program, which is not available on hardcover books, allows retailers to return unsold books to Ingram. However, because Outskirts strongly suggests giving only a 20% trade discount to third-party retailers (like Amazon.com and bookstores), it is unlikely that any brick-and-mortar retailer will order copies of your book. These retailers usually require at least a 40% trade discount. Thus, paying for this service, if you're only giving a 20% trade discount, is a waste of money.

Unique photo image from gallery: $99

RETURN OF DIGITAL COVER AND INTERIOR FILES: Departing authors may take their files with them in a press-ready PDF file for a fee of $99 each for the interior and cover files. If you decide to publish your book yourself, you can take a press-ready PDF to any printer and print it. However, you can't sell the book through any third-party retailer or wholesaler without an ISBN and bar code.

So, unless you have the design software to do it yourself, a new publisher would need to be able to get into these PDFs and replace the ISBN, etc. So you're paying $198 for something that has little value to you—or to Outskirts for that matter—unless you want to print the book for your personal use.

RETAIL PRICE OF AUTHOR'S BOOK: Outskirts allows authors to set the retail price of their books, within limits, and therefore their own royalty. Because the two are so inextricable, a detailed description of retail pricing is contained below in the royalty section.

PRICE AUTHOR PAYS FOR BOOKS: Author price is determined by the size of the book and the package, and though the author is able to determine royalty and retail discount amounts, the price remains the same regardless. The higher the package price, the lower the cost of the book to the author and, thus, depending on how the author prices it, the higher the profit margin on the book. So, for example a 200-page, 5.5" x 8.5", paperback book will cost the author between $6.16 and $9.16 depending on the package purchased. Since it costs no more than $3.90 to print this book, if you buy Outskirts's most expensive publishing package, Outskirts still makes $2.26 off of each book you purchase. Another way to look at it:

$6.16   author price per book
– $3.90   printing cost
_____

$2.26   Outskirts profit

That's more than a 50% markup from the actual printing costs. Add in the royalty amount Outskirts takes, and suddenly the royalty percentages touted on the website are not as wonderful as they first appear.

ROYALTIES PAID TO AUTHOR: Royalties are between 20% and 50% of the net wholesale payment that the publisher receives from sales, less shipping and handling charges, sales tax charges, and returns or refunds. Authors set the book retail prices, so royalty amounts will vary. You can calculate your royalties at http://outskirtspress.com/calculator.

php. For example, for a 200-page paperback book, the retail price and royalties published under the Diamond Package could be as follows:

Retail price	Royalty	Royalty earnings
$10.95	20%	$2.19
$12.95	30%	$3.89
$15.95	40%	$6.38
$20.95	50%	$10.48

The trade discount defaults to 20%, and according to the calculator, you'd make the royalties (even on sales through Amazon.com, etc.) as set forth in the table given. Outskirts acts as though it has some special relationship with the distributor and with Amazon.com that allows them to set a 20% trade discount. It doesn't. Most publishers don't encourage or offer such a low trade discount because it almost guarantees that no brick-and-mortar retailer will ever consider ordering your book, as they typically require a 40% trade discount. The problem with paying Amazon.com such a low trade discount is that it won't make any effort to move your books. When Amazon.com receives at least a 40% trade discount, it will often discount the price of the book online (and that reduction comes out of Amazon's cut).

If making sure the wholesale discount (for Amazon.com, etc.) is high enough to support sales is important to you, you can use the calculator to set the discount and determine the royalty and retail price automatically. Putting a 50% wholesale discount on the same 200-page book published under the Diamond Package gives the following numbers:

Retail price	Wholesale discount	Royalty	Royalty earnings
$16.95	50%	14%	$2.37

"The new decision by Amazon to force publishers to use its printer could eventually destroy Outskirts' entire business model, which is predicated on giving Amazon (and other online retailers) only a 20% trade discount. If Amazon ups the minimum trade discount it will accept to 40%-55%, Outskirts will need to change its model. An author considering Outskirts must find out what kind of deal this publisher has with Amazon before signing a contract."

Outskirts makes $2.21 on the sale while you make $2.37.

NOTABLE PROVISIONS OF THE PUBLISHING CONTRACT: There are four contracts for each of the publishing packages, but they are identical except for the specifics outlined in "Attachment A." A sample contract is available at http://www.outskirtspress.com /Contract_OutskirtsPress.pdf. The review below covers all four contracts.

Section I, "License," subsection (c) gives the publisher a worldwide, nonexclusive license to print and distribute the work as an e-book or print book.

Section III, "Publisher Services," subsection (a) limits the submission to publication timeline to 90 days, and no more than 180 days.

Section IV, "Author Warranties," and section XI, "Indemnification," are standard and reasonable.

Section X, "Termination," allows either party to cancel the contract on 30 days written notice, which is good. Subsection (e), the last subsection in XI, reiterates that the author retains all the rights to the book, front cover, back cover, spine, and the digital files developed by the publisher if either party terminates. But if this is the case, why does the publisher charge a departing author $198 for press-ready PDFs, which aren't the digital files developed by the publisher?

Section XI, subsection (c) contains a clause often found in such publishing agreements. The publisher does not warrant its services, which are provided on an "as is" basis. Damages owed to the author are limited to fees "actually paid by the author to the publisher for the one month period prior to publisher's act" that gives rise to the liability. The publisher also rejects liability for any damages that could possibly result from publisher error. This clause has little to do with any intentional acts by the publisher, such as refusal to pay royalties or refusal to cease book sales after termination. Instead, it covers situations like Outskirts failing to send you copies of your book in time for a scheduled book signing. You wouldn't be able to sue Outskirts for damages that resulted in the inability of people to purchase the book at the book signing.

Section XII, "Force Majeure," means that if the publisher cannot fulfill its obligations under the contract in a timely manner due to reasons out of its control, it is not liable. For example, if a tornado destroys the facility housing the printing press, which delays publication of the book within the time required by the contract terms, the publisher is "excused" from the time requirement. This clause is standard in most commercial contracts.

Section XIII, "Governing Law," specifies Douglas County, Colorado, as the venue for all legal proceedings.

AUTHOR-FRIENDLY RATING: Although Outskirts's package fees are in the ballpark, you'll need to add $299 for a custom-designed cover to any package you choose if you want something more than a basic cover. Paying to publish with a template cover is throwing money away, because you'll never have a "real" looking book.

Outskirts will be one of the most affected publishers should Amazon require self-publishing companies that use print-on-demand distribution to print with Amazon's own printer. Even if Amazon doesn't require such printing, but no longer allows publishers to give it a 20% trade discount, Outskirts' publishing model is severely impacted. The rest of this section must be read with the understanding that by the time you read this, Outskirts' could be paying Amazon a much higher trade discount.

While the 20% trade discount to Amazon.com seems great and is not a bad strategy if that is the place you care most about selling books, realize that your book will not receive any special attention from Amazon.com in terms of discounts to consumers, and few if any brick-and-mortar retailers will buy your book (most require at least a 40% trade discount). But, if you can direct readers to Amazon.com and they are going to buy your book anyway, the 20% trade discount will improve your bottom line. The fact that Outskirts gives authors the option of lowering the trade discount is a plus, but what Outskirts doesn't explain to authors, unless pressed, is that distribution will be limited only to online retailers. Unless all you care about is selling your book on Amazon.com, Outskirts doesn't make a lot of sense.

Outskirts allows authors who terminate their contracts with the publisher to take a press-ready PDF with them, albeit for a $198 fee. While I believe that authors pay for this right initially, Outskirts's fee for the return of these files is still one of the lower ones.

The royalties paid to authors are low; Outskirts makes more on each sale than the authors do in most cases. The author price for books isn't as high as other publishers, but it's still at least 50% of the actual printing costs. That being said, if you are comfortable with an overall bookselling strategy that only involves Amazon.com and you understand the limitations to this approach, Outskirts should be on your list of publishers to consider.

UNIVERSAL PUBLISHERS
http://www.universal-publishers.com

FORMAT OF BOOK: e-book and paperback

GENRES ACCEPTED: Universal publishes nonfiction books on scientific, how-to, technical, academic, and other specialized topics.

PUBLISHING FEES: The publishing package, which costs $495, includes:
- · ISBN
- · Bar code
- · Formatting for printing
- · Optional custom cover for an additional $100 fee. Author must provide images.
- · Conversion to PDF format ($100 discount if submitted formatted)
- · Author page on Universal's website. The page includes author biography, book synopsis, and a 25-page preview of the book.
- · R.R. Bowker's Books In Print registration
- · Listing through online booksellers: Amazon.com and BarnesandNoble.com
- · Standard trim size: 5.5" x 8.5"

RETURN OF DIGITAL COVER AND INTERIOR FILES: According to the Universal help desk, the digital cover and interior files belong to the author at the termination of the contract. However, this information is not posted on the website or in the author agreement.

RETAIL PRICE OF AUTHOR'S BOOK: All e-books are $12. Paperback pricing is based on the book's page count:

Number of pages	Retail price
Up to 200	$19.95
201–300	$25.95
301–400	$29.95

These prices are very high, even for nonfiction; however, technical and specialized how-to books can command a higher retail price. When I asked the publisher why its books are so expensive, both for readers and authors, a customer service representative replied via e-mail: "We primarily publish technical, how-to, and academic books. Our pricing, distribution, and royalty structure is optimized for this type of publication."

PRICE AUTHOR PAYS FOR BOOKS: The customer service representative's reply to my e-mail makes no sense when it comes to an author purchasing copies of his or her own book. The price authors pay the publisher for their books is 40% off the retail price. If they buy 100 or more books, the discount is 55%. For a 200-page paperback, here's what the math looks like:

$19.95	retail price
– $7.98	40% author discount
$11.97	author price per book
– $3.90	printing cost
$8.07	Universal profit

So the only party for whom the pricing is "optimized" is the publisher, not the author, since the publisher makes a 200% profit on the printing each time an author orders less than 100 books for his or her own use.

ROYALTIES PAID TO AUTHOR: Royalties are based on where the book sells. For books sold on Universal's website, the royalty is 40% of the retail price. For books sold at third-party retailers like Amazon.com, the royalty is 20% of the retail price. The kicker is that, according to the Universal publishing agreement, authors earn no royalties until the fourth book sold each quarter.

For a 200-page book sold on Amazon.com or other third parties, your royalty would be:

$19.95	retail price
x .20	author royalty percentage

$3.99   author royalty

That's a generous royalty by anyone's standards, but if we look at what Universal is making on that same sale, note that it is 20% more than the author's royalty:

$19.99	retail price
– $3.99	author royalty
– $6.99	35% Amazon.com discount
– $3.90	printing cost

$5.11   Universal profit

For books sold through the Universal site, the math works like this:

$19.95	retail price
x .40	author royalty percentage

$7.98   author royalty

And here is what Universal makes on this same transaction:

$19.95	retail price
– $7.98	author royalty
– $3.90	printing cost

$8.07   Universal profit

NOTABLE PROVISIONS OF THE PUBLISHING AGREEMENT: The agreement can be found at http://www.universal-publishers.com/agreement.php. The agreement is short: only three-fourths of a page. The third paragraph is the most important. It states that the contract is nonexclusive and can be canceled by either party with 90 days written notice. Two things to note: (1) if the publisher decides to terminate, the publishing fees paid by the author are nonrefundable, regardless of when the termination occurs, and (2) the publisher reserves the right to make the author repay all fees if author submits changes to the manuscript after it's been accepted for publication. In other words, if the book is ready to go and the author discovers an error that must be changed, the publisher could make the author pay an additional $495.

While a contract this short seems great, it can cause problems as the publisher and author may have different expectations about timing of the book release, printing, etc. A short contract isn't necessarily bad, but you need to trust your publisher if you sign a contract that is this vague.

AUTHOR-FRIENDLY RATING: Universal's contract is non-exclusive and easy to terminate, and the publisher's setup fee is reasonable. For $495, your book is set up to be printed as a paperback; you get a page on the publisher's website, where the book will be offered for sale; and your book is registered with Amazon.com and other online booksellers.

The royalty amounts are generous. The $9 price for e-books makes sense, but the $19.95 cost for a 200-page book is high considering fledgling authors have few loyal followers willing to pay the price. But nonfiction how-to and technical books can command a bit more than other types of books. For this publisher to work for you, given the high retail prices, you need to have a how-to book that is so unique that a book buyer won't mind spending whatever the price is to get a copy.

Universal's website is one of the easiest to negotiate—all of the information you need is spelled out in easy terms. I was heartened, after being ignored by so many publishers, to have the help desk get back to me within 24 hours, even though the answers were somewhat obtuse.

If you have a really specialized nonfiction how-to or technical book, this publisher might be one to consider. If you have any other kind of book, Universal's high retail prices make it a poor choice.

THIRD MILLENNIUM PUBLISHING
http://www.3mpub.com

FORMAT OF BOOKS: e-books and paperback

GENRES ACCEPTED: all

PUBLISHING FEES: For $300, the package includes the following:

- Manuscript preparation, which includes creating a press-ready PDF of the manuscript and using commercial clip art to create a cover and interior images if the author so desires. Author may also provide her own art.
- Author webpage, including summary and biography pages and a click-to-buy service with Paypal, check, or credit card options. The webpage is located on the publisher's website (for an example, see: http://3mpub.com/rominek).
- ISBN
- Bar code
- Book displayed and sold on publisher's website for two years (after two years, there is a fee of $100 per year)

RETURN OF DIGITAL COVER AND INTERIOR FILES: Third Millennium Publishing (3MPub) makes it clear in its author agreement that while the author owns the work, the publisher owns all digital files it creates to get the work online or in print. In correspondence, the publisher told me he would make the production files available to an author, for example, if needed to print at a capacity above what the 3MPub presses can manage, but nothing of this sort is in the contract.

RETAIL PRICE OF AUTHOR'S BOOK: Author determines the price, although 3MPub suggests setting the e-book price between $4 and $6 and the paperback price between $15 and $20.

PRICE AUTHOR PAYS FOR BOOKS: For books over 126 pages, the author pays a flat fee for copies regardless of page count. The price is dependent on the order size and ranges from $11 for 1–9 books to $7.50 for 100 or more books. So, let's say you purchase 100 copies of your 200-page book. The math would look like this:

$8.00   author price per book
– $3.90 printing cost
─────────────────────
$4.10   3MPub profit

A $4.10 profit is more than a 100% markup on the cost of printing your book, but considering the fact that the publisher only takes a $1 royalty, it's not as bad as it could be.

ROYALTIES PAID TO AUTHOR: Royalty equals the selling price of the book less the cost of credit card processing ($.50 + 2.6% of the selling price) and a $1 per book publisher's fee per transaction. So for an e-book, the royalty would be calculated as follows:

$5.00   retail price
– $.63   credit card processing fee ($.50 + 2.6% of $5.00)
– $1.00 3MPub fee
─────────────────────
$3.37   author royalty

In order to lower costs and increase royalties for print books, the author must invest in inventory. For example, if the author wants to sell his 200-page paperback for $13.95, he'll make more money by buying 60–99 books at the lower price, like so:

$13.95   retail price
– $8.00 author price per book for 60–99 books
– $1.86 ($.50 + 2.6% of $13.95 + $1.00) 3MPub fees
─────────────────────
$4.09   author royalty

You'll find few better deals in self-publishing.

Note: For a $25 annual fee, 3MPub will list your book on Amazon.com. Amazon will charge you 15% of the retail price + $1.00 to fulfill the order, but because the bookseller is charging you those fees, 3MPub will forgo its fees.

NOTABLE PROVISIONS OF THE PUBLISHING AGREEMENT: The "Third Millennium Publishing Electronic Work Hosting Agreement" is available upon request from the publisher. Many of the important terms are covered at http://3mpub.com/services. Section B (5) is perhaps the most important term. Any files that the publisher creates for the book are the publisher's property. After termination of the agreement, the publisher has no obligation to provide the author with the formatted production files of his or her book. When asked about this clause, the publisher responded as follows:

> *The author owns the book and the right to publish the book, but we own the files that we created to produce the book....If the author's book becomes a best seller, we will aid that author in transferring to a high volume printer when the volume exceeds our printing capacity. In such cases, we provide the necessary files reformatted for the printer. We have done so 3–4 times now, both for authors who wanted to buy a lot of commercially printed books to obtain the lower unit price, and for authors who have used other services, such as Booksurge, in addition to Third Millennium Publishing.*

We also provide files to authors who request them for archival purposes. However, to prevent misunderstandings, we include Section B(5) in our agreement.

In addition, the second half of the clause states that while the publisher owns the files, it does not have the right to reproduce the work outside of this agreement. So the author maintains control of all rights to the book and can still sell it anywhere while it's being sold on the publisher's website. However, in order to do so, the author would have to have it formatted again, unless the publisher provides the author permission to use the formatted files for outside sales. Also, the author can remove the book from the website at any time. See http://www.3mpub.com/services/faqs.htm for an FAQ section. The publisher states, "We do not own the rights to publish your book...you own those rights...."

Section C(1) states that author and publisher can withdraw from this agreement at any time, effective immediately. However, if the author withdraws, he or she loses all fees paid to the publisher. If the publisher withdraws before the author's book has been on the site for 90 days, all fees will be returned to the author; after 90 days but under two years, and the publisher will return a prorated portion of the fees.

AUTHOR-FRIENDLY RATING: Third Millennium Publishing doesn't offer bells and whistles, but it runs a solid operation. After all, owner Michael McCollum has sold 250,000 copies of his own books, which were published by Ballantine / Del Ray, over a 10-year period.

Having said that, here are the problems: For $300, it's impossible to get a book that is indistinguishable from those on the shelves of any bookstore. High quality, professional layout and cover design alone usually costs more than the $300 this publisher charges for its entire package. Yet, this publisher has many repeat authors, so they must be happy with the results.

The $300 fee is low, but the only way for the author to make the service worthwhile is to purchase 60–100 books up front because the larger volume decreases the per book cost, which in turn allows the author to set a competitive book price. This of course, increases the basic cost of the package from $480 to $800, but such an increase is worth it.

Although the publisher's royalties are practically nonexistent—with the exception of a $1.00 processing fee for orders made via the publisher's website—the cost an author pays to print copies of his book is inflated by more than 100%, which is not acceptable.

The website is outdated and a bit cumbersome to use, especially when trying to order an author's book. Plus, if an author drives potential book-buyers to the website, the sales page looks amateurish and "self-published."

The fact that the author doesn't own the working files for his or her book and/or cover is cause for concern, too. If an author chooses to terminate the contract, he or she will have to start over in terms of layout and cover design. I'd like to take McCollum at his word that he would make it easy for authors to print elsewhere; you shouldn't, get it in writing.

But, for all that, McCollum replied to my e-mail query within hours, and two days later, an autographed copy of his book and a sample contract appeared in my mailbox. That attention paid to the authors is commendable and worth noting.

This is another publisher right on the border between "Pretty Good" and "Just OK." The benefits—low entry costs, low publisher royalties, and McCollum's attention to authors—all push this publisher toward "Pretty Good." But the publisher's huge printing markups, stock cover designs, claim on production files, and outdated website pull it back to being "Just OK." If all you have to spend is $300, and you want to get in the game, this publisher is a good option.

WAHMPRENEUR BOOKS
http://www.wahmpreneurbooks.com

FORMAT OF BOOKS: paperback

GENRES: Wahmpreneur is a no-frills publisher specializing in books for the small business market, such as small business management, online and offline marketing, Internet systems and strategies, and relevant policy issues for micro-business owners.

PUBLISHING FEES: This publisher offers one package, which you can read about here: http://www.wahmpreneurbooks.com /services.html. For $400, this package includes:

- ISBN
- Bar code
- Interior formatting
- Cover formatting for print, which means the author provides a complete book cover and the publisher then adds an ISBN and bar code
- Distribution through Ingram
- R.R. Bowker's Books In Print registration
- U.S. Copyright Office registration
- Online and offline distribution selling
- Listing in Wahmpreneur Books online bookstore
- Ten copies of the book
- No returns
- Shipments directly from the printer to the author within two business days, and shipments of retail purchases within one business day, provided the title is in stock; for back orders, shipments within five business days

OTHER SERVICES OF INTEREST: Dawn Rivers-Baker, the publisher at Wahmpreneur books prides herself on being a no-frills house, so she doesn't offer a ton of services.

As I already noted, Wahmpreneur does not provide a cover, but Dawn Rivers-Baker works with a variety of cover artists who can produce covers in a range of $150 to $500. I asked for a sample of the covers, and the publisher sent me the most recent nonfiction book produced by Wahmpreneur Books, Awake Publishing's *Life Beyond Belief,* which you can see at http://www.awakepublishing. com. She also sent me her own book, *E-Commerce for the Unfunded,* which you can find on Amazon.com at: (http://www.amazon.com /E-Commerce-Unfunded-Dawn-Rivers-Baker/dp/0971327807 /ref=sr_1_2?ie=UTF8&s=books&qid=1201206748&sr=1-2)

RETURN OF DIGITAL COVER AND INTERIOR FILES: When I asked Dawn Rivers-Baker who would own the cover and interior files if I went with her cover design services, she wrote back:

> *You own the book. If you hire someone to produce original artwork for the cover, they would own the copyright but the agreement between Wahmpreneur Books and the artist would include permission to use the artwork, in perpetuity, specifically in connection with production, marketing and sales of the book.*

RETAIL PRICE OF AUTHOR'S BOOK: According to publisher Dawn Rivers-Baker, a 200-page paperback will retail anywhere from $15 to $20, give or take a few dollars, depending on the market, how many competing titles exist, and other variables. She is willing to discuss the price with the author.

PRICE AUTHOR PAYS FOR BOOKS: Author discounts are based on the page count. The formula is $.015 per page + $.90 for the cover. So, if you publish a 200-page, paperback book, your price would be:

$3.00   (200 pages x $.015 per page)
+ $.90   cover fee
_____

$3.90   author price per book

And that's basically one of the fairest deals I've heard of in the self-publishing industry.

ROYALTIES PAID TO AUTHOR: Wahmpreneur authors make 75% of net, which is described in the author agreement as sales less the author price per book for sales on Wahmpreneur.com and sales less the author price per book and any discounts for sales elsewhere. So, for a 200-page, paperback book sold on Wahmpreneur.com:

$15.00	retail price
– $3.90	printing cost

$11.10	net profit
x .75	author royalty percentage

$ 8.33	author royalty

And for a book on Amazon.com:

$15.00	retail price
– $6.75	45% Amazon.com discount
– $3.90	printing cost

$4.35	net profit
x .75	author royalty percentage

$3.26	author royalty

NOTABLE PROVISIONS OF THE PUBLISHING AGREEMENT: The publishing agreement can be found at http://www.wahmpreneurbooks.com/services.html.

In section 1, the publisher agrees that in exchange for the publishing fees, she will prepare your book for publication, including: interior and cover formatting, assignment of ISBN and procurement of bar code, and title setup with printer. In exchange, the author gives the publisher nonexclusive rights to print, publish, and sell the book.

In section 2, the author agrees that within 10 days of signing the contract she will send the publisher an electronic copy of the book's text and its cover files. If she fails to do so, the contract is considered void, and the publisher will return all fees.

In section 3, the author agrees to send the publisher a complete manuscript that is ready to be published, meaning edited and reasonably competent. If the manuscript is not ready for print, the publisher reserves the right to reject it, void the contract, and in that event, will refund any and all fees to the author.

In section 4, the publisher agrees not to make substantive changes to the work without the written approval of the author.

In section 5, the publisher agrees to have the work printed in perfect binding, trade paperback form within three months of the author delivering her files to the publisher, barring any reasonable delays, which would include natural disasters, war, strikes, etc. The publisher also promises to print the book one month after said disaster and in no case longer than six months after the manuscript is delivered. If she fails to do so, the author can void the agreement in writing, and will receive a refund of all fees.

In section 6, the publisher reserves the right to determine the format and style of the book, although she says she will consult with the author.

In section 7, the publisher agrees to pay the author 75% of the net proceeds from the sale of each book. Net, per this agreement, is defined as: "Any payments received by the Publisher, after deduction of printing charges, for any and all direct-to-consumer sales and any payments received by the Publisher, after deduction of printing charges, for any and all discounted wholesale trade sales."

The contract says that the publisher offers a wholesale discount of 55% to qualified booksellers, but in an e-mail she asserted that she gives Amazon.com a 55% discount and everyone else 45%.

In section 8, the publisher agrees to pay the author royalties on a quarterly basis and to include a report of sales with each royalty statement. If the publisher is later than 30 days after the close of the quarter, the author can demand payment to be made in 10 days. If the publisher refuses, the "Author may immediately terminate this Agreement without prejudice to any claims Author may have against publisher for amounts due and owing under the terms of this Agreement." This is a very fair and honorable clause, as it allows the author to immediately terminate while still maintaining any rights to sue for unpaid royalties.

Section 9 outlines what the publisher's statement will look like, which includes the number of copies sold, total sales to date, price of the books sold, gross amount received by the publisher, cost to print the books sold, publishers receipts, and the royalty owed to the author.

Section 10 says the publisher will give the author 10 copies of her book upon publication.

Section 11 says the author owns the book's copyright.

Section 12 is standard and basically insures that the author wrote the book and has the right to contract with the publisher and sell the book, and also that the book does not contain libelous or stolen material. Further, it says that the author will not hold the publisher legally or otherwise responsible in any lawsuits that arise out of the book.

In section 13, it says that either of the parties may terminate the agreement with 60 days written notice, sent via e-mail or post. At that point, the "Publisher shall provide Author with any and all electronic files containing the Work, including but not limited to those electronic files prepared by Publisher for printing of the Work." This is one of the few publishers who, without fee, give the author her design files!

Section 14 states that, upon termination of the agreement, the publisher may continue to sell the remaining stock of the author's book unless the author determines to buy the stock, at cost, from the publisher.

Section 15 says that this is the whole agreement and that any amendments must be made in writing.

Section 17 says that the agreement is governed by the laws of the State of New York.

AUTHOR-FRIENDLY RATING: This is one of the most pared down services out there, but it's also one of the fairest. The publisher says that she created a no-frills website so that her authors wouldn't have to pay for the bells and whistles through high fees, and she seems to actually mean it.

Wahmpreneur is good for what it is. But, if you want your book to stand out and be a centerpiece of your writing career and not just an addition to your business, there are better companies more focused on just book publishing. However, the royalties are generous, and if you're selling a book that is in conjunction with your already existing business and you want to test the viability of the project, this publisher is one to consider.

WASTELAND PRESS
http://www.wastelandpress.net

FORMAT OF BOOKS: hardcover and paperback

GENRES: Wasteland Press's submission guidelines do not address content, so one can assume they will accept any genre.

PUBLISHING FEES: This publisher offers six black-and-white packages and three color packages. For the purposes of this overview, I will only delve into the former. A comparison chart of the black-and-white packages is available at http://www.wastelandpress. net/Compare.html. Wasteland's base prices refer to books that range from 40 to 125 pages after production. If your book is longer than that, there is an additional charge of $30 to $400 per 50 page increase (it's unclear from the website how the price jump is determined, because there is so much variance). Note that I have included the price for a 200-page book in parentheses next to the base price.

Basic Plan: At $195 ($195 for a 200-page book), this package is for authors who simply want to get their book in print for personal use. It includes:

- Five paperback books, shipping included
- Four-color custom cover, designed in-house with input from the author. The designer creates one cover and then works with the author on any changes for an undefined amount of time.
- Option to print a hardcover version of the book for an additional $250
- Limited distribution, which means the book will be available through Wasteland's online bookstore only. For $50, authors have the option to purchase an ISBN and bar code and list their book on Amazon.com.
- Choice of trim size:
    5.5" x 8.5"
    6" x 9"
- Unlimited black-and-white photos throughout the book

- Silver Plan: This package is priced at $350 ($440 for a 200-page book). In terms of services, the Silver Plan is identical to the basic plan with the exception that it includes a total of 25 paperback books, shipping included. It also offers a higher royalty (see royalty section for details).
- Gold Plan: At $650 ($925 for a 200-page book), this package includes everything in the Basic and Silver plans, plus:
- A total of 75 paperback books, shipping included
- ISBN
- Bar code
- Full-service marketing, which includes a press release written and distributed by Wasteland to more than 2,000 media, alerting them to the release of your book and providing follow-up information. It only includes two review copies of your book, but since this is basically an untargeted blast, that may not be an issue.
- Full distribution, which makes your book available on major online retailers, as well as available to order via brick-and-mortar stores. It does not provide online tracking of your book sales, but that information is available via an e-mail query to the publisher.
- Five hours of copyediting, which the publisher tells me can include formatting, structuring, and spelling and grammar check, but does not include rewriting or restructuring the author's work

Platinum Plan: This package is priced at $950 ($1,400 for a 200-page book). Wasteland promotes this package to "career-minded writers." It includes everything in the Basic, Silver, and Gold plans, plus:

- A total of 150 books, shipping included
- Ten total hours of copyediting
- Five total review copies as part of the marketing plan described in the Silver Plan

Titanium Plan: This package is priced at $1,250 ($1,700 for a 200-page book) and is for authors who want their book published in hardcover and paperback versions. It includes everything in the Platinum Plan, plus:

- · A total of five hardcover copies of your book, shipping included
- · Fifteen total hours of copyediting

The Ultimate Plan: This package is priced at $2,250 ($3,000 for a 200-page book). Wasteland bills this package as its "most efficient." Naturally, it includes everything in the Titanium Plan, plus

- · A total of 500 paperback copies of your book, shipping included
- · Twenty-five total review copies as part of the marketing plan described in the Silver Plan.
- · Twenty total hours of copyediting

RETURN OF DIGITAL COVER AND INTERIOR FILES: Publisher Timothy Veeley assured me, via an e-mail conversation, that the author can keep all of her files, without extra charge: "The designed files belong to you. No fee needed. They are already yours." However, there is nothing to that effect in the author agreement, so consider getting this assurance written into the contract if you decide to publish with Wasteland.

RETAIL PRICE OF AUTHOR'S BOOK: Wasteland authors determine the price of their books within a range limit set by the publisher. For example, I queried the Wasteland help desk with a 200-page, 6" x 9", paperback book and was told that the retail price range for my book would be $8.95 to 16.95.

PRICE AUTHOR PAYS FOR BOOKS: Although the website assures potential authors that their author discounts start at 50% off the retail price and then get higher based on the quantity ordered, that's strictly only true if you set your retail price at the highest level. For example, I was quoted a retail price range of $8.95 to $16.95 for a 200-page 6" x 9" paperback book with these corresponding discounts:

Number of books	Author price per book
1–99	$8.25

100–199	$7.75
200–499	$7.25
500–999	$5.50
1000+	$4.55

Wasteland uses Lightning Source to print its books, so we know that each book costs around $3.90 to print. That means that Wasteland is marking up the books more than 100% above the actual print cost and making $4.35 on every book you buy (assuming you order less than 100).

ROYALTIES PAID TO AUTHOR: Royalties are 15% to 30%, depending on which plan the author buys, and are based on net sales, which Wasteland defines as:

Retail price – 55% of retail (Ingram's fee) x .15 to .30 = Profit x .15 to .30 = Author royalty.

Royalties for each of the packages are:

- · Basic plan: 15%
- · Silver plan: 20%
- · Gold Plan: 25%
- · Platinum, Titanium, Ultimate plans: 30%

So, on the same 200-page, paperback book, if you charged $13.95 for the book on the Gold plan, you would make:

$13.95	retail price
– $7.67	55% Ingram discount
$6.28	gross profit (without backing out printing expense)
x .25	author royalty percentage
$1.57	author royalty

Is that reasonable? Well, let's look at what Wasteland makes:

$6.28	gross profit
– $1.57	author royalty
– $3.90	printing cost
$.81	Wasteland royalty

Wasteland is one of the few self-publishing companies that make less in royalties than its authors. Because Wasteland calculates the author's royalty before deducting the printing cost, the actual royalty is much higher than 25%. In the example given, the author's royalty is actually 66% of net.

NOTABLE PROVISIONS OF THE PUBLISHING AGREE-MENT: The publishing agreement can be found at http://www. wastelandpress.net/Compare.html. Although the Wasteland website posts different agreements for each of its publishing plans, they all offer the same legal information; the only thing that is different between them is the individual plan details.

In the "Warranties" section, the author agrees that she is indeed the author of the book and that she has not engaged in plagiarism or libeled anyone in the writing of it. This is standard language.

In the "Right To Your Work" section, Wasteland states that it does not own the book and that it is not responsible for editing its content. In other words, if your book prints with a massive typo in the first paragraph, you are responsible. This is fair and standard language.

The "Book Royalties" section explains that Wasteland will pay the author a royalty, which differs depending on which publishing plan you purchase, and will be based on Wastelands "payments actually received" in each sale, less any shipping and handling, taxes, or returns. Wasteland defines payments received not as net, which would include cost to print, but as what it makes after Ingram takes its 55%. See the royalty section for further explanation.

In the "Indemnities" section, the author agrees that, in the event that a lawsuit arises from the book, for any reason, neither Wasteland Press nor its employees will be held responsible, including any attorney fees. This is a fair clause.

The "Disclosure of Royalties" section simply states that the royalty checks are sent out every quarter, if there is a royalty to send, within 30 days of the end of the quarter. Royalty reports are available via an e-mail to the publisher at webmaster@wastelandpress.net.

The "Shipping and Handling" clause basically says that Wasteland Press is not responsible if the books they are shipping on your behalf go astray. However, under the basic plan, the author can insure the arrival of her books by paying an extra $12, which would then guarantee a refund of any fees (i.e., the cost of the books ordered) if the books are lost. This fee is built into all of the other plans.

"Terms and Exclusivity" states that either party can choose to terminate this agreement at any time. Refunds are based on who terminates and when:

1. If the author terminates before the book is printed, she will receive a full refund less 30% for pre-publication services, not to exceed $999.
2. If the publisher terminates before the book is printed, and no breech of contract has occurred, the author will receive a full refund. If a breech of contract has occurred, then the author will not receive a refund.
3. If either party terminates the agreement after the book has been printed, the author does not receive a refund.

In "Worldwide Distribution", the author gives Wasteland, Lightning Source, and Ingram permission to distribute her book. This service is included in all of the publisher's plans for one year. After one year, the author must pay $25 a year in order to keep the book in circulation. It also says that if the author terminates, Wasteland has up to three months to clear the book from its database, which makes sense because the publisher needs time to fulfill any outstanding orders.

AUTHOR-FRIENDLY RATING: The retail price of Wasteland's books is too high and so is the cost at which authors can buy copies of their own books. But, those are the only drawbacks to an otherwise impressive service. The packages turn out to be a good value when you include the printing costs for the free books with each package.

The actual royalties are better than the percentages Wasteland states on its website. It's a rare moment in this industry when a publisher understates and over-delivers, but this one does on the royalty percentages.

Again, the huge downside is the cost at which an author can purchase his or her books. If you plan on buying a lot of copies of your book and reselling them, this will end up being an issue for you.

In e-mail exchanges with publisher Timothy Veeley, I learned that the bulk of the services are the same, no matter which plan you purchase; the main difference between the plans seems to be more copyediting time, more review copies, and more author copies.

The covers are pretty good—not fabulous, but better than average.

Wasteland has a live chat window, which is very politely authored. The website is very easy to use and, though it could provide a greater level of detail, relatively useful. When I overwhelmed the Live Chat window, publisher Timothy Veeley wrote a personal note within 10 minutes of my having closed the chat window; subsequent questions were also followed up promptly.

If Wasteland lowered the cost at which authors can purchase copies of their own books, it would be one of the "Outstanding" self-publishing companies. Until it does that, it's still a pretty good company.

CHAPTER 8

PUBLISHERS WHO ARE JUST OK

If none of the "Outstanding" or "Pretty Good" publishers discussed in this book fits your needs or will publish your work, then by all means comb the "Just OK" group to see if a publisher meets your requirements.

What does "Just OK" mean? It means just what you think it means—that it's something less than average, but not horrible.

There are many publishers far better than ones covered in this chapter. These "Just OK" publishers offer deficient and overpriced products and services and have issues that preclude them from inclusion in the better categories.

However, these publishers probably aren't scams or fly-by-nights, which is why they're on my "Just OK" list instead of my "Avoid" list. Like I said, consider a publisher in the "Just OK" category only if you can't get a publisher in either the "Outstanding" or "Pretty Good" groups to accept your work.

BLOOMING TWIG BOOKS

http://www.bloomingtwigbooks.com

FORMAT OF BOOKS: e-book, paperback and hardcover

GENRES: Billing itself as "The Humane Publisher," Blooming Twig Books appears to focus on self-help, spirituality, and related poetry and fiction. Submissions are accepted in a variety of forms, and if there are stringent guidelines they are not mentioned on the website: http://www.bloomingtwigbooks.com/submissions.html.

PUBLISHING FEES: This publisher offers three packages. Each package has three levels. For the sake of brevity, only the highest level of each package is discussed here. The packages are described in a chart and in a pop up window, but neither gives a concrete idea of what is actually included in the packages, i.e., how many copies of the book the author gets, whether copyediting is actually included or available for an extra fee, etc. (Note: A more detailed chart was available when I started this overview but has since been removed. The publisher is in the middle of redesigning the website and its service offering, so things at Blooming Twig were fairly confused, albeit very friendly, when I set out to write this overview.)

Standard Package: This package has three levels priced at $149, $349, and $499. The two lowest levels of this package do not include an ISBN or printing. The $499 level includes:

- Author page (see http://www.straightintogayamerica.com)
- Online sales via http://www.bloomingtwigbooks.com/shop (With this and all packages, if you want to add Amazon .com, BarnesandNoble.com, etc., you need to pay an additional $200.)
- Book printing of a limited number of books to be defined by you and the printer
- ISBN
- Bar code

Standard Plus Package: This package has three levels priced at $995, $1,995 and $2,995. Oddly, jumping up to the $995 package appears only to add copyright registration and an e-book, which many publishers throw in at no additional cost. (However, the à la carte Blooming Twig e-book costs $295, so...) The top level, at $2,995, includes everything in the Includes everything in the Standard Package, plus:

- Cover design The author and designer work together collaboratively. Although there is no limit to cover design revisions, the publisher asks that (the author keep it to two or three drafts.)
- Interior design and layout, including an unlimited number of images and graphics

- Author website (for an example see http://www.rewritethescript.com)
- Author blog (for an example see http://rewritethescript.wordpress.com)
- U.S. Copyright Office registration
- E-book version
- Copies of the book, but it's unclear how many. Here's what the publisher told me via e-mail:

It depends on the features we include, and on how many copies you need! We work with you to customize the package to your needs…It might be 300 copies, and it might include 50! It depends on the specific project and its goals…

- It would seem to me that the author needs more, not fewer copies of his book.

Professional Plus Package: This package has three levels priced at $4,000, $5,500, and $7,000. At the highest level, this package includes everything in the Basic Plus package, plus:

- Copyediting: The publisher describes this as a collaborative "passing back and forth" of the book and says that it does its best to "find all errors and awkwardness within the manuscript."
- Author podcast (for an example see http://www.cynthiagustavson.com/podcast)
- Marketing resources, including tour booking, press releases, and promotion. The publisher was vague about what this entails. In general, the answer was, "We'll do what it takes." Press releases are written in-house, and distribution can be as targeted or open as the author desires—again, the publisher didn't provide a real concrete answer.
- CD media kit: The rep told me this includes an e-book, author bio, publicity pictures, and anything else the author would like to include.
- Audio book

OTHER SERVICES OF INTEREST: Blooming Twig offers a myriad of à la carte services. Prices are listed here, but you'll need to contact the publisher to find out what is included in the fee.

Copyediting: Pricing is based on the number of pages (0–25 pages for $5.00 a page, 50–100 pages for $4.00 a page, and 200 pages for $3.00 a page).

· Cover design: $170 an hour
· Cover art: $225 an hour

RETURN OF DIGITAL COVER AND INTERIOR FILES: Although it is not specifically stated in the Blooming Twig author agreement, a representative of the company assured me that the author owns all the artwork and files used to create the book. Of course, the best way to insure that you get your digital files is to have that assurance added to your contract.

RETAIL PRICE OF AUTHOR'S BOOK: The author has the ability to set the retail price of the book, and Blooming Twig does not set a minimum price.

PRICE AUTHOR PAYS FOR BOOKS: Author discounts are based on quantity, trim size, and page count. Although the publisher's website does not provide a formula for determining a price, it does give this example of what a 6" x 9", 100-page paperback might cost:

Number of books	Retail price
25	$12.00
50	$9.50
100	$7.50
200	$6.00
500	$5.00

That's not much of a discount, considering Blooming Twig would pay Lightning Source $2.40 to print that 100-page book. Basically, if you buy 50 books, Blooming Twig makes:

$9.50	author price per book
– $2.40	printing cost

$7.10	Blooming Twig profit

This is almost a 300% markup on printing.

ROYALTIES PAID TO AUTHOR: According to the website, it would appear that Blooming Twig only offers to sell books on its website rather than on a retailer like Amazon.com. For each book it sells, Blooming Twig takes a $4.00 fee.

This fee structure, and the cost of the book, basically means that, in order to make any profit at all on a 100-page paperback, you would need to charge $15.50 a book. Here's what you will make by selling it on Blooming Twig's website:

$15.50	retail price
− $4.00	Blooming Twig royalty/fee
− $9.50	author price to print book

| $2.00 | author profit |

So, what you need to ask yourself is:

1. Is profit important to you?
2. Will someone pay $15.50 for your 100-page book?
3. Is it OK with you that Blooming Twig essentially makes $11.10 ($7.10 markup on printing + $4.00 royalty/fee) on the sale, while you make $2.00?

NOTABLE PROVISIONS OF THE PUBLISHING AGREEMENT: Blooming Twig's author agreement is not available online, but I was able to get a copy through a prospective author.

In section 1, "Term," the term is for two years, after which it automatically renews annually, unless either party terminates with written notice 60 days prior to the end of the current contract year. This is a bad clause. Even though the contract is nonexclusive, you are locked in for two years at least. The only way to terminate early, per section 9 (which is mistyped as a "B" in the contract) is if the publisher breaches a part of the contract and fails to fix the breach within 30 days after receiving written notice from the author. If I were going to choose this publisher, I'd request an addendum that allowed me to terminate the contract at anytime with 60 days written notice. If the publisher wouldn't go for that, I'd move on.

In section 2, "Grant of Rights," the author maintains all rights for the work, including copyright, and gives the publisher nonexclusive license to print and distribute the book worldwide. Further, the author allows the publisher to put its logo on the book and to advertise it.

In section 4, "Payments," the publisher agrees to pay the author all gross profits for sales "around the world," except on review and advertising copies. "Gross profit" is defined as the actual cash receipts received by the publisher, less $4.00 per book. The way the contract is written, the author can make a claim that he is entitled to gross profits on books he purchases for his own use. I'm sure that isn't the intent of the clause, but that is how it reads.

In section 5, "Accounting," Blooming Twig pays author royalties on a quarterly basis, and the author may hire a certified public accountant to look at the publisher records—but only going back two years prior to the examination date. If the accountant finds an error, the offending party will "pay for the amount of the error." What does this mean? It could be interpreted to say that if your accountant's examination yields no error, you could be required to pay the publisher's own accounting or legal fees to deal with the examination. This is a poorly written contract with many questions and holes. This section is one of them.

In section 6, "Representatives and Warranties," the author warrants that she has the right to enter into this agreement and that her book is not libelous, plagiarized, or obscene and does not otherwise violate anyone else's rights. The publisher also warrants that it is free to enter into the agreement and that "it has and will maintain the right and authority to grant to Author the rights granted herein." These are reasonable.

In section 7, "Indemnification," the author and the publisher agree to hold each other blameless, legally and financially, if litigation arises from a breach of the warranty on either of their parts. This section also includes a clause that says that both parties are obligated to let each other know if they enter into a lawsuit; that the non-involved party will be of reasonable help in such a case, at the expense of the involved party; and that neither party will settle a lawsuit against the cause or without permission of the other. The actual legalese is much more daunting, but that's what it says.

In section 9, "General," subsection A prohibits either party from assigning their rights without the written permission of the other, except that it gives the publisher the right to assign its rights upon sale of the company, etc. While technically the author has the same assignment rights, they would only be applicable if the party signing the contract on behalf of the author is a legal entity. Again, the intent is probably not to be so restrictive for an author, but that's what it says.

Subsection B says the agreement is subject to the laws of the State of New York, and any dispute will be litigated in Suffolk County, New York. This is a reasonable clause

AUTHOR-FRIENDLY RATING: To be fair, while we were working on this overview the publisher was in the middle of revamping its services and agreement, and that state of flux made it difficult to get concrete information.

Perhaps because of that, in its current incarnation the website is relatively disorganized, with links either misapplied or leading to pages with very little information. Although prices are listed, there's no detailed explanation of what they actually include, and the publisher seems disinclined to concretely determine what they include. I think the publisher is trying to create a foundation upon which he can tailor publishing packages for the individual author's needs. To that end, I had the sense that he was open to modifying the contract and the packages.

The publisher exchanged quite a few informed, genuinely friendly, low-key e-mails with me and had no problem sending over a contract.

While I don't think this publisher is out to cheat anyone, the whole thing is just too messy; there are simply too many problems with the contract (like a 2-year term), and service descriptions are murky.

BOOKSURGE PUBLISHING

http://www.booksurge.com

FORMAT OF BOOKS: paperback and hardcover

GENRES ACCEPTED: all

PUBLISHING FEES: BookSurge offers four publishing programs ranging from $99 for a book already formatted in a press-ready PDF to $3,000 for the Premium Publishing Program.

Author's Advantage Publishing Program: This package (http://www.booksurge.com/category/1272438201/1/Authors-Advantage-Black-White.htm) is $499 and is for authors with unformatted manuscripts looking to publish a black-and-white, paperback book. For hardcover, add $199; for color, $200. Much of the list below was not included in the description of the program but was discovered as I pecked around the BookSurge website:

- Choice of 11 cover templates (author provides graphics for templates)
- Bar code
- Choice of eight interior templates, with additional charge of $100 for 10 photographs
- Choice of trim size:
  5.25" x 8"
  6" x 9"
  7" x 10"
- ISBN
- R.R. Bowker's Books In Print registration
- Distribution through Baker & Taylor on a non-returnable basis
- Listing with online booksellers: Amazon.com, Alibris.com, Abebooks.com, Borders.com, and Target.com (Includes access to BookSurge's proprietary Internet-based sales monitoring system.)
- One complimentary marketing session with a BookSurge publicist
- PDF proof of the formatted book, with 50 free corrections, after which an unspecified fee applies

Total Design Freedom Program: Priced from $699 to $3000, this package (http://www.booksurge.com/category/1227567761/1/Publishing-Options.htm) is said to provide customized one-of-a-kind books, but that appears to apply only to the interior of the book; the covers are still template-based. It's unclear from the website, but presumably, this package includes everything in the Author's Advantage Publishing Program, with the following upgrades:

- Five interior options of varying complexity:
  - Level 1: No graphics, consistent page format

· Level 2: No graphics, varying page format
· Level 3: 20 images
· Level 4: 21–40 images
· Level 5: 41–60 images

Choice of six plain text and background cover templates, including author photo and back cover copy

OTHER SERVICES OF INTEREST: Like most publishers, BookSurge offers a full course of editing, design, and marketing services that can be purchased à la carte or paired with the publishing programs in a package. An overview of the packages is provided at http://www.booksurge.com/category/1227568961/1/Publishing-Packages.htm. This section is misleading, not only because BookSurge's numbers don't add up, but also because the packages appear to be tailored by genre; yet with the exception of the children's book offering, the packages are only subtly and arbitrarily different, as shown in this chart. Why is BookSurge's listed retail price on the Fiction Writer Package $898 more than the Expert Package when both offer the same exact features? Why does the Spirituality Package cost the same as the Fiction Package yet offer one less service? It's crazy.

	Kid's Choice	Fiction Writer	Spiritually Speaking	Your Life, Your Story	The Expert	Express PDF
Authors Advantage $499		x	x	x	x	
Authors Advantage w/color $899	x					
PDF Publisher $99 w/color $299						x
Comprehensive Copy Edit $3,600		x	x	x	x	

Basic Copy Edit $450 for up to 20,000 words	x					
Advance Copy $199	x	x	x	x	x	
Publicity Kit $499	x	x	x	x	x	x
Press Release $199 plus distribution $399	x	x	x	x	x	x
Hardcover $199	x					
X and Y Amazon ad $1,000	x	x	x		x	x
Signature Cover Design $999		x		x	x	
Color Illustration $4,200	x					
BookSurge Retail Total (Actual Total*)	$8,119.00 ($8,044.00)	$6,794.00 ($7,394.00)	$6,794.00 ($6,395.00)	$6,745.00 ($6,394.00)	$5,896.00 ($7,394.00)	$2,196.00 ($2,196.00)
Discount Price	$6,899.95	$5,759.95	$5,795.95	$5,720.75	$5,759.95	$1,991.00

* BookSurge's retail package prices do not necessarily equal the sum of their à la carte services—in some cases retail is more, in others less. In the end, however, the publisher's discounted price is the only one that counts.

All of the services included in the chart are available à la carte:

Custom covers: BookSurge offers two options:

> · Unique cover selection: For $499, a BookSurge designer chooses and arranges images and graphic elements of your cover. Includes five hours of design time, bar code, author

photo, and back cover text placement.

· Signature Cover Design: For $999, a BookSurge designer works with you to create a custom cover. Includes 10 hours of design time, appropriate images, bar code, author photo, and back cover text placement.

Custom illustration: For $4,200, a BookSurge illustrator provides up to 12 illustrations (including the cover). Each additional illustration is $400.

Advanced marketing/cover copy: For $199, this includes book description, one-sentence description, and author biography.

Publicity kit: For $499, this service includes 500 postcards, 500 business cards and 500 bookmarks.

Press release: For $199, this service provides one press release written by a BookSurge public relations professional.

Press release distribution: For $399, this distribution includes at least 50 media outlets tailored to your genre or topic.

Buy X get Y advertising on Amazon.com: For $1,000, this service pairs your book with another for compatible sales for one month.

Comprehensive copyediting: For $3,600, this service includes three rounds of edits for grammar, style, and content. This price is for manuscripts under 100,000 words. Individual rounds are priced at $.018 per word.

Basic copyediting: At $.015 per word, this includes one round of editing for grammar, punctuation, syntax.

Author domain service: For a $150 setup fee and a $39 yearly fee, this service provides you with a personalized domain name that points to your book's sale page on Amazon.com. This price is outrageous. You can go buy a domain name for about $8.00 and point to your Amazon.com page on your own.

Library of Congress Control Number (LCCN): For $75, this includes facilitation of your application for a LCCN and the addition of the control number to the copyright page of your book. FYI, the LCCN is free. The Library of Congress does not charge a fee for an LCCN.

Return program: For a $600 annual fee, this includes a one-year contract with Baker & Taylor, in which your book will be stocked at Baker & Taylor warehouses. You will have the opportunity to purchase returned books at a 50% discount.

RETURN OF DIGITAL COVER AND INTERIOR FILES:
BookSurge does not give departing authors their files, neither press-ready PDF nor production files, not even for a fee. When asked why, a BookSurge sales representative said:

> *We usually don't share our print files because they are specifically designed to work with our machines and manufacturing system. I could provide a PDF of the formatted book; however it would not be the print file.*

As you know, a PDF of the formatted book is useless unless all you want to do is read the book. A printer can't use it. As for the production files being formatted for BookSurge's machines, unless they are using some super-secret computers and software not used by any other publisher, this is a line of B.S.

RETAIL PRICE OF AUTHOR'S BOOK: BookSurge does not publish its retail book pricing, but the publisher's representative suggested a retail price of $15.99 for a 200-page, paperback book.

PRICE AUTHOR PAYS FOR BOOKS: I couldn't find the author discount on the BookSurge website, even with the aid of the search feature. However, after I e-mailed the publisher, a representative sent me a PDF with the author discounts, which are based on a sliding scale ranging from 30% for 1–9 books to 70% for 1000+ books. Here's what that math looks like for a 200-page, paperback book:

$15.99	retail price
– $4.80	30% author discount

$11.19   author price per book

Since we know the book costs $3.90 to print and since BookSurge does its own printing at a lower cost, one might wonder why the publisher is marking up the book by $7.29, especially since the publisher is also making a 35% royalty on retail sales. Now, if you are supplying BookSurge with a press-ready PDF with the intention of publishing the book yourself, you can buy 1,000 books at a 70% discount, or $4.80 each, which is a great price. At that price, you can sell the book for $11.80 and still make a $7.00 profit.

ROYALTIES PAID TO AUTHOR: BookSurge royalties are as follows:

- 35% of the retail price for paperbacks sold via Amazon.com and the BookSurge website
- 15% of the retail price for hardcover books sold via Amazon.com and the BookSurge website
- 10% of the retail price on bookstore and library orders

So, for a BookSurge sale on the same 200-page, paperback book, the math would look like this:

$15.99	retail price
x .35	author royalty percentage
$5.60	author royalty

$15.99	retail price
– $3.90	printing cost
– $5.60	author royalty
$6.49	BookSurge profit

NOTABLE PROVISIONS OF THE AUTHOR AGREEMENT: BookSurge's author agreement can be found at http://www.book-surge.com/category/1227573561/1/Author-Resources.htm. This is an excellent contract for authors.

In "License to Publish," the author gives the publisher a nonexclusive license to publish the book during the contract term.

"Term" makes it clear that the contract term lasts until the author terminates it with a 30-day written or e-mail notice.

"General Provisions" could cause a problem for the author. It states, "This Agreement may be modified by the Publisher giving 30 days notice to the Author of the proposed change." If the author disagrees with the change, the author must promptly terminate the contract. For example, if BookSurge decides to change author royalties from 25% to 20%, the author must cancel the contract before the change goes into effect. Otherwise, the author is deemed to have agreed to the modification. Of course, you can always terminate later by giving 30 days notice. However, if the publisher decides to change the contract, and gives itself exclusive worldwide rights for X years and prohibits the author from terminating the contract until that period is over, the author could be stuck if he fails to cancel the contract before the change goes into effect.

AUTHOR-FRIENDLY RATING: BookSurge gets a 10 for its contract, but a –5 for its average royalties, for its grossly inflated printing markups, for withholding production files from its departing authors, and for its confusing, at best, website. BookSurge.com provides very little information regarding up-front fees and the author's book price, and what information it does provide is often conflicting (i.e., the package prices). That said, since Amazon.com bought the publisher in 2005 it has added a bookstore to its website and includes distribution in its offering. Although $499 is decent for a basic publishing fee, it is a pretty bare-bones offering, and at $11.19 for a 200-page paperback, the books are expensive—unless you plan to buy 1,000 books and sell them yourself. In that case, the cost of books goes down to 70% off the retail price of $15.99. If you pay $4.80 a book, you can sell them for $12 and still make a reasonable profit.

There's no "Contact Us" link or phone number for BookSurge listed on the website, so to get more information you are forced to hit a "Ready to Self-Publish" button, which doesn't actually offer to answer your questions but instead asks you to fill out a contact sheet and questionnaire about your project. The good news is that if you fill out the form a screen will pop up with the company's phone number: 1-866-308-6235.

Here's a question: if it's nearly impossible to contact BookSurge in order to find out about their services, then where are they going to be after you've bought them?

Frankly, I'm surprised that Amazon's involvement has made Book-Surge less author-friendly. I've always wondered why BookSurge didn't take advantage of being owned by Amazon and offer its authors something special in terms of sales and marketing on Amazon.com.

There is more to being a good publisher than offering a decent contract. A first-time author would be best served by another publisher.

BOOKSTAND PUBLISHING
http://www.ebookstand.com

FORMAT OF BOOKS: e-book and paperback

GENRES ACCEPTED: all

PUBLISHING FEES: Bookstand Publishing offers two paper-back packages, and prices vary depending on the size of the book. Pricing for hardcover and color books is separate and will not be discussed here. A full pricing description is available at http://www.ebookstand.com/pricing.htm.

Jump Start Package: This package is priced at $295 for a standard 5.25" x 8.25" or 6" x 9" paperback and includes:

- One copy of your book
- Choice of eight basic cover templates and interior layout
- Non-optional Bookstand Publishing logo on back cover
- Electronic proof including one round of changes (An additional round of changes is $60.)
- ISBN
- Bar code
- E-commerce webpage for your book, which includes one static page on the Bookstand website with author and book information
- Electronic proof
- PDF e-book available for sale

Trade Paperback Publishing Package: For this package, the price is determined by the length of the book. For a standard 5.25" x 8.25", prices are:

Number of pages	Retail price
25–100	$499
101–200	$599
201–300	$649
301–400	$749
401–500	$849

This package includes everything in the Jump Start package, plus the following upgrades:

- A total of 52 copies of your book
- Unlimited photos, tables, and charts
- Choice of 11 deluxe template covers; you must provide the imagery and copy
- Listing with online booksellers: Alibris Channels, Amazon. com, and BarnesandNoble.com
- R.R. Bowker's Books In Print registration
- Printed proof, which does not include changes due to author errors. Each additional proof is $140.
- PDF e-book available for sale
- Option to remove Bookstand logo

OTHER SERVICES OF INTEREST: As with most self-publishers these days, Bookstand provides a myriad of editing, marketing, and design services. Here are a few of the more useful offerings.

Custom cover art design and creation: This service, at $499, does not include commercial artwork that may need to be purchased, such as stock photo art, but unlike many cover packages, there is no charge for the designer to work with the image. The custom cover includes one design, which will be reworked according to your comments. According to Bookstand support, there is no limit to design time; the designer works on the cover until it's right.

- Custom illustrations (interior or cover): Bookstand does not have in-house illustrators but, for $125 per hour, will help you find a freelance illustrator that works in various mediums, including sketches, water color, oil, digital, etc.
- Basic edit: For $.02 per word, this includes spelling, grammar, and punctuation.
- Distribution of press release: For $399, this includes:
  - Two free photos or logos
  - A variety of formats (PDF, plain text, etc.)
  - Sending the press release to media outlets, including newspapers, magazines, television, online news sites, and radio. The distribution lists do not appear to be targeted, which means this is likely just a spam blast.
- Press release preparation: For $269, a Bookstand publicist will prepare a 700–800 word, press release to announce your book. Preparation includes an author interview and two drafts.

RETURN OF DIGITAL COVER AND INTERIOR FILES: Bookstand offers a CD-ROM archive of the final press-ready files for $75. Although it is not stated on the website or in the contract, the publisher's support desk assured me that Bookstand keeps all of the production files on hand and, if need be, will send them to you without a fee. Remember that without getting this in the contract, such easy promises remain just that.

RETAIL PRICE OF AUTHOR'S BOOK: For e-books, the publisher suggests a price of less than $10, but the author sets the final price. For paperbacks, selling price depends on the page count and the trim size.

For a 5.5" x 8.5" and a 6" x 9" book, the prices are:

Number of pages	Retail price
101–200	$19.95
201–300	$24.95
301–400	$29.95

PRICE AUTHOR PAYS FOR BOOKS: Bookstand offers author discounts of up to 70% for 25 books or more. The discount is based on the book's page count and trim size. For example, for a 5.25" x 8.25" book, prices are:

Number of pages	Author price per book
201–300	$6.85
301–400	$9.25

If you print a 200-page book, the math looks like this:

$5.4	author price per book
– $3.90	printing cost

$1.55   Bookstand profit

That's a pretty reasonable markup, but remember, the publisher is also taking a royalty.

ROYALTIES PAID TO AUTHOR: Bookstand pays 50% of the purchase price of an e-book, 30% of the purchase price of each paperback sold through the Bookstand website, and 10% of the retail price of books sold through third-party retailers (e.g., BarnesandNoble.com).

For a 200-page, 5.25" x 8.25" paperback, the author royalty on an Amazon.com sale looks like this:

$15.95	retail price
x .10	author royalty percentage

$1.60   author royalty

Meanwhile, Bookstand makes:

$15.95	retail price
– $1.60	author royalty
– $6.38	40% Amazon.com discount
– $3.90	printing cost

$4.07   Bookstand profit

For this same 200-page, 5.25" x 8.25" paperback sold from ebookstand.com, the author royalty looks like this:

$15.95	retail price
x .30	author royalty percentage

$4.79   author royalty

Meanwhile, Bookstand makes:

$15.95　retail price
− $4.79　author royalty
− $3.90　printing cost
──────────────
$7.26　Bookstand profit

NOTABLE PROVISIONS OF THE PUBLISHING AGREE-MENT: Bookstand's publishing agreement is short and to the point and written in plain terms. The complete contract is at http://www.ebookstand.com/register.htm.

The author guarantees that the work is original and doesn't libel or violate the rights, including copyright, of anyone else. If it does, the author agrees that Bookstand will not be held legally responsible.

The author grants nonexclusive rights to the publisher and can terminate the contract in writing at any time and for any reason. If the author terminates the contract after acceptance but prior to fulfillment, the publisher returns the fee less a $75 processing charge.

The author gives Bookstand permission to keep 50% of the purchase price of an e-book, 70% of the purchase price of a paperback sold through its website, and 90% of a paperback sold through a third-party bookseller. Note that on some places on the website the publisher claims that authors receive a 15% royalty on hardcover sales from third-party retailers, like Amazon.com and BarnesandNoble.com (see http://www.bookstandpublishing.com/perfectbound.htm). This differs from the actual royalty page on the website (and the author agreement page), which states that the royalty for such third-party sales is 10% (http://www.bookstandpublishing.com/royalty.htm).

Unless an author purchases the publisher's editing services, the publisher provides no editing whatsoever but maintains the right to change minor, obvious spelling and grammar mistakes.

Bookstand will pay the author monthly, provided royalties amount to $25 or more.

Bookstand will consult the author on the retail price of a book but maintains the right to set the final price.

If the author's book makes no sales after 18 months, the publisher may remove the book from its website.

The contract is subject to the laws of the State of Washington, but it does not specify that litigation will take place in Washington. Further, the loser pays everyone's legal fees.

This is a case where a really short contract can hurt an author (although not intentionally). The contract doesn't address the process, turnaround times, definitions of what constitutes revisions to the layout, etc. Extremely short contracts are good because they are fast to read and not bogged down with a lot of legalese. The downside is that, if you're getting bogged down in the publishing process with regard to timelines, there is nothing that spells out each party's expectations and responsibilities. This is a problem with short contracts in general.

AUTHOR-FRIENDLY RATING: If your main goal is to publish a book for friends and family, the publishing packages offered by this publisher are reasonable. But if your goal is to have a bookstore quality product, you will at least need to add a custom cover design for $499. If we assume you'll publish a 200-page book, the addition would mean paying a publishing fee of $1,058. That's not unreasonable, but you need to balance that cost against royalties and printing markups. Suddenly, a good deal isn't looking so good anymore. The printing markup is about 30%, which is actually better than most other companies. The paperback packages do include 52 copies of your book, which softens the blow a bit.

It's the royalties that really hurt this publisher's ranking. In the examples I've discussed, Bookstand makes almost a 46% royalty on every book sold, and that's after subtracting printing costs.

The final problem area is the retail pricing. A book that is 200 pages or less is overpriced by $2–$3 at $15.95. The inflated retail price is only done to maximize the publisher's profit margin. True, the author's profit margin increases, too, but the result may be an over-priced book that people won't be willing to buy. (However, if the book is how-to nonfiction, for example, such a price may be justified).

We e-mailed the publisher several times and never received a reply. But, when I called, the support desk was extremely helpful and friendly.

This is one publisher that is truly on the fence between being ranked "Good" and "Just OK." The low royalties and the publisher's failure to respond to e-mails push it toward a "Just OK" ranking, but it's still treading water on the good side of the self-publishing pool. So, it's one you should look at, but when your choices are narrowed down to a few, compare the printing markups and royalties against the others you may be considering.

CREATESPACE
http://www.createspace.com

FORMAT OF BOOKS: paperback

GENRES: CreateSpace, an Amazon.com company, operates much the same as Lulu.com and is more of a content manager and printer than a publisher. Therefore, it does not discern genres or quality of writing; it only asks that you not use the site to print books that are disturbing (i.e., pornographic or hateful).

PUBLISHING FEES: CreateSpace does not require a setup fee of any kind; however, it offers few services beyond printing and distribution, instead pointing authors to its sister company BookSurge for those services. Complete details are available at http://www.createspace.com/Products/BooksOnDemand.jsp.

When you upload your content for printing, you receive:
- ISBN
- Bar code
- An electronic proof at the same price as 1 copy of your book
- Amazon.com's Search Inside feature
- The ability to sell your book on CreateSpace.com and Amazon.com

RETURN OF DIGITAL COVER AND INTERIOR FILES: You might assume that this is a non-issue because, in the CreateSpace model, you provide all of the files and the book prints exactly as you submitted it. However, the CreateSpace agreement seems to say that while the author owns all the rights to his content, the publisher owns all of the files created using its proprietary templates, including "source files, future-proof archive files, and packaging materials."

However, when I asked the CreateSpace help desk if I would own the source files created using CreateSpace templates, I received this answer: "The files are yours (as you retain all rights to your book) and you will not be charged to keep them. You should keep a copy of your files for your records."

That being said, if you want to sell your book outside of CreateSpace. com and Amazon.com, you'll need to purchase your own ISBN; CreateSpace owns the ISBN it offers with printing, and its contract states that you can only sell books imprinted with its ISBN on Amazon.com affiliated sites.

RETAIL PRICE OF AUTHOR'S BOOK: CreateSpace allows authors to set the price for their books, with the caveats that authors may not sell books on CreateSpace.com or Amazon.com for more than they charge elsewhere and that Amazon and its affiliates have the option to reduce the price of the book. In general, I think a 200-page paperback book should sell for around $13.95.

PRICE AUTHOR PAYS FOR BOOKS: Author discounts are based on the CreateSpace base price ($3.15 + $.02 per black-and-white page) and the number of books purchased. In the case of your 200-page, paperback book:

Number of books	Discount	Author price per book
1–49	None	$7.15
50–99	10%	$6.98
100+	20%	$5.72

We know the book actually costs $3.90 to print, so an almost 200% markup seems like a raw deal, but without charging you a setup fee, this is how CreateSpace makes its money.

ROYALTIES PAID TO AUTHOR: CreateSpace royalties are dictated by the retail price the author puts on the book and by what CreateSpace charges for its printing services. For each sale, CreateSpace deducts $3.15 + $.02 per black-and-white page + 20% or 30% of retail (for books sold on CreateSpace or Amazon.com, respectively). For example, if your book is 200 pages and you sold it on Amazon. com for $13.95, you'd make:

$13.95   retail price
– $7.15   CreateSpace.com "printing cost"
– $4.18   30% Amazon.com discount
_____

$2.62   author profit

Again, CreateSpace and Amazon.com are making the lion's share of the royalty simply for printing your book, but since you've not paid them a thing to do so, this is how they make their money.

Note: Although CreateSpace does reserve the right to lower the retail price of an author's book, the author's royalty is always based on the retail price set by the author. So, if CreateSpace lowers your book's price, the royalty will still be based on the original retail price—But if you lower the book price, your royalty will change accordingly. More information is available here: http://www.createspace.com/Products/BooksPrices.jsp;jsessionid=2F4F1ED90DBC47C7DC0687A18277E063.cspworker01.

NOTABLE PROVISIONS OF THE PUBLISHING AGREEMENT: The publishing agreement can be found at http://www.createspace.com/Help/Rights/MemberAgreement.jsp.

Section 1 says that CreateSpace can change the terms of the agreement, its policies, and its service offering at any time. It will post a notice of changes for up to 30 days, but it's up to the author to check the site for changes; the author's continued use of the site after the changes take effect signifies agreement.

Section 2 deals with content delivery. It basically states that the author agrees to abide by CreateSpace policies and guidelines, which include restrictions on publishing hateful, destructive, pornographic, stolen, or otherwise illegal content.

Section 3 outlines the services authors are eligible for once they have registered on the site, including book order fulfillment and a listing on the CreateSpace E-Store, Amazon Properties, and other sales channels. It also says that CreateSpace has the ultimate say on bar code placement.

Section 4 deals with how CreateSpace handles titles. Basically, it says that if an author violates the company's guidelines, it can remove the content and he or she will still be held responsible for any outstanding fees. It also says that the author can remove content at will; however, CreateSpace has 30 days after the notice to remove the content and can continue to fulfill any orders that are placed up to the end of that 30 days.

Also included in that section is subsection 4.2, "Pricing; Legal Title," which says that CreateSpace is the "seller of record" for the author's book. This means that it ultimately has the power to set the selling price. It also says that while the author sets the price, it must be set at or below the price the book is selling for elsewhere. This clause is bad if you intend to sell the book from your own website, which you could do for less than on CreateSpace since you'd not be losing any part of the royalty (and would be smart since you'd make more money). This clause can limit some of your sales avenues. However, you could always terminate the contract and publish elsewhere.

Subsection 4.4, "Customer Returns and Refunds," allows CreateSpace to handle returns in several ways, on a case-by-case basis:

1. The company can resell a returned book, with no additional royalty to the author.
2. The company can destroy the book.
3. The company can refuse all returns.
4. The company can accept the return and, if it has already paid the author a royalty, charge the return against future royalties or bill the author for the royalty amount.

Section 5 deals with taxes and fees, and states that CreateSpace will pay author royalties within 31 days of the end of the month in which the book was sold, provided the author has earned:

- $20 or more (if paid via direct deposit)
- $28 or more (if paid via paper check)
- $45 or more (if paid via wire transfer)

Section 5 also holds the author responsible if a buyer uses a fraudulent credit card to purchase his or her book, meaning that the amount of that sale will be deducted from future sales. This can be a problem since you are relying on CreateSpace's credit card processing system to detect fraud. However, it's not unreasonable.

Authors are also responsible for paying their own taxes on royalties; CreateSpace will not withhold a deduction.

Section 6 covers content, licenses, and feedback. In part, it allows CreateSpace to create digital versions of your book for the purpose of advertising and display, and to allow its customers to look at your content via Amazon's Look Inside feature.

Subsection 6.5, "Ownership," says that while you, the author, own all the rights to the content, CreateSpace owns all of its own templates and the resulting files it creates, including source files, future-proof archive files, and packaging materials. This would seem to mean that if you use the template to create a book and layout the cover, you do not own the files the template creates (i.e., the final, formatted, print-ready file for your book). However, as I have already noted, a CreateSpace representative told me that this is not the case, that in fact the author does own the files and should be sure to keep a backup of the file for his or her records. But the contract always prevails. You cannot rely on a customer service representative's word on this.

Sub-section 6.6, "Feedback," says that if the author sends CreateSpace information or a suggestion, all rights to that information or suggestion belong to CreateSpace, even if it leads to a change in the way the company provides service. That means that if you send them a great idea and they implement it, you won't get paid. But again, this is not unreasonable.

Section 7 has to do with representation and warranties, and basically is the standard language stating that your content is not breaking any laws—you didn't steal it, it isn't libelous or otherwise injurious to someone else, and as far as you know it is based on fact (where appropriate).

Section 8, "Indemnification; Maintenance of Rights; Copyright Infringement," basically states that CreateSpace will not be held responsible if a claim is brought against the author for his or her book, including attorney's fees. Further, it states that if the author learns of a claim against her title, she will remove the title from the site and accept financial responsibility for any books that are returned as a result of the claim.

The title of section 9, "Disclaimer of Warranties; Limitation on Liability," is written in full capitals to show importance, one presumes, and states that CreateSpace makes no guarantees that your content or the site will always be available. It also protects the company from damages if it should lose any hard copies of your content; if it does lose content, the author is only entitled to the lesser of $100 or the cost to replace the disk or other media the content was stored on. The lesson here is: don't ever send a publisher the only copy of your book.

Section 10 gives both CreateSpace and the author the ability to terminate the contract at any time by giving each other written notice. Upon termination, the author must pay any outstanding fees, and CreateSpace is obligated to fulfill any outstanding book orders.

Section 15 states that the agreement is governed by the laws of the State of Washington and that any disputes will be settled in Seattle, Washington. However, CreateSpace reserves the right to seek relief in Any court in the State of Washington if the author violates its intellectual property rights.

Section 16, "Miscellaneous," allows CreateSpace to sublicense any of its rights per the agreement, but it specifically states that the author may not assign any of her rights. Again, this can be a problem if you want your business to own the copyright to your book and assign any royalties to the corporation. It also states that CreateSpace will not be held responsible if anything, such as an act of God or foul weather, keeps it from fulfilling its responsibilities per the contract. That means that if a hurricane wipes out the printing press on the eve of a book signing and your books are not delivered, you cannot hold CreateSpace liable for any money you lose as a result. This is a standard clause.

AUTHOR-FRIENDLY RATING: CreateSpace is definitely gunning to be Lulu's strongest competitor. So far, it can't compete with Lulu's easy-to-use tools, hosted chat rooms, live-help (instant message style) operators, service boards, and noncorporate creative vibe.

I tried to load a book onto CreateSpace, but the process stalled midway through when its downloadable cover template, which is made to be used in Word Paint, would not interact with my Paint program. I e-mailed the help desk. Thirty minutes later, I had loaded a new book onto Lulu, and I still hadn't heard anything from CreateSpace. And 24 hours after that not a word from CreateSpace. The company may have copied Lulu's "Dashboard," where authors monitor their projects, but it forgot to take notes on usability and customer service.

CreateSpace's book prices are competitive. There are no setup fees, but authors pay for that in the printing markups. For an author to purchase copies of his 200-page, paperback book, the cost is $7.15 (about 80% higher than the actual print cost). But, it's much cheaper than Lulu ($1.38 per copy), and you automatically get a free ISBN for your project. Yet, for its $100 distribution fee, Lulu will give you everything that Create Space gives you, plus it will put your book in R.R. Bowker's Books In Print and make it available on Amazon.com and Barnesand-Noble.com. And you won't be limited to selling on websites affiliated with Amazon.com. Plus, quantity discounts will get you a better price on Lulu faster than they will on CreateSpace, and Lulu takes only a 20% cut of the profits as opposed to CreateSpace's 70%. So, on the Amazon.com sale of that same 200-page book, Lulu pays $4.34 and CreateSpace pays $2.62.

Both Lulu and CreateSpace have clauses in the contract to keep the author from selling books on their respective websites at a higher price than authors sell them. Again, this can be limiting, and you should be aware of this clause before signing up.

Whether you pay up front or through royalties and high book prices, you will end up paying to publish your book one way or the other (and don't forget, neither CreateSpace nor Lulu provides book cover art or editing services, so you will have to find people to provide those services and pay for them separately). CreateSpace and its competitors are best for authors who have completed files and don't care if they sell a lot of books. Yes, you don't pay anything up front, but if your book starts selling, you'll need to find a publishing solution with lower printing costs and higher royalties.

There is no such thing as free self-publishing. Don't be fooled by the hype.

LLUMINA PRESS

http://www.llumina.com

FORMAT OF BOOKS: e-book and paperback

GENRES ACCEPTED: all (accepts between 70%–80% of all submissions)

PUBLISHING FEES: There are three publishing packages: $799 for paperback, $899 for hardcover, and $999 for paperback and hardcover. If you want to sell your book as an e-book, add another $65 to any package.

All packages (http://www.llumina.com/prices.htm) include:

- ISBN numbers for paperback and/or hardcover editions
- Library of Congress Control Number (LCCN)
- Bar code
- R.R. Bowker's Books In Print registration
- Listing with online booksellers: Amazon.com, Barnesand-Noble.com and more
- Typesetting, including seven interior graphics. Extra graphics are $5 each.
- Four-color cover design, for which a designer will create up to two design options that use either author-supplied art or an image in the public domain. Includes two rounds of revisions. If neither of the options suit, the author can pay for another cover design at $75 an hour with a one-hour minimum.
- Choice of trim size:
  - Paperback:
    5" x 8"
    5.5" x 8.5"
    6" x 9"
    7.5" x 9.25"
    7" x 10"
    8.25" x 11"
  - Hardcover:
    5.5" x 8.5"
    6" x 9"
    7" x 10"
- Distribution through Ingram and Baker & Taylor
- A webpage on the publisher's website (see http://www.llumina .com/store/god.html for an example) with an additional yearly maintenance fee of $20

OTHER SERVICES OF INTEREST:

Marketing and Promotional Packages: All packages include 24 review copies of your book, a press release with an e-mail blast of the release to thousands of media, a sell sheet, and a list-

ing in Llumina's e-zine. To review the packages, visit http://www
.llumina.com/marketing.htm. Prices range from $529 to $599.

Bookstore Distribution Program: This isn't really so much
a distribution program as it is an assurance by Llumina that
if a bookstore agrees to take a chance on your book, it can be
returned if it doesn't sell (http://www.llumina.com/bookstore
_returns.htm). This program costs $500 for the first year and
$140 for each thereafter. All it does is cover the cost of making
your books returnable through Ingram, so you don't have to give
up the royalty on returned books. It includes a listing in a catalog
that Llumina sends to 2,500 book retailers. This is different than
having your book distributed by a distributor that actively mar-
kets the book to the book trade. But, if your books aren't marked
as returnable, virtually no retailer will buy them.

RETURN OF DIGITAL COVER AND INTERIOR FILES:
There is nothing in Llumina's contract or on its website regarding the
ownership of the working files, but the publisher replied to an e-mail
query thusly: "We do own the high resolution files at the end of the
contract; however, we will sell them for a fee of $300. Frankly, we
can probably get better pricing for books than you can and it may be
advantageous to print through us anyway."

This statement is only true if you can't get printing for any less than
200% more than the actual printing costs.

RETAIL PRICE OF AUTHOR'S BOOK: Llumina's book prices
are based on page count. A calculator is available here: http://www
.llumina.com/calculator.htm. A 200-page, paperback book, regardless
of trim size, will cost $15.95, which is a couple bucks higher than
average.

PRICE AUTHOR PAYS FOR BOOKS: Author discounts are
based on quantity. A calculator is available here: http://www.llumina
.com/calculator.htm. For a 200-page, paperback book, author discounts would look like this:

Number of books	Discount	Author price per book
1–24	30%	$11.17
25–199	45%	$8.77
200+	50%	$7.98

$11.17   author book price
– $3.90   printing cost
_____

$ 7.27   Llumina profit

As for the publisher's statement that it can get better pricing than an author could for book printing, I doubt it—unless the best price you could get is 200% more than the actual printing costs.

ROYALTIES PAID TO AUTHOR: For paperback and hardcover books, the royalties are:
30% of retail for copies sold through the publisher
10% of retail for copies sold through third-party retailers
For e-books, the royalties are:
60% of retail for copies sold through the publisher
40% of retail for copies sold through third-party retailers
So for that same 200-page, paperback book, the royalty for a book sold on Amazon.com would be:

$15.95   retail price
x .10   author royalty percentage
_____

$1.60   author royalty

Llumina's profit on each book sold on Amazon.com or other third-party retailer is as follows:

$15.95   retail price
– $6.38   40% Amazon.com discount
– $3.90   printing cost
– $1.60   author royalty
_____

$4.07   Llumina profit

For sales on the publisher's website of that same 200-page,

paperback book, the royalties would be:

$15.95 retail price
x .30 author royalty percentage

$4.79 author royalty

Llumina's profit on a sale of this book through its website:

$15.95 retail price
– $4.79 author royalty
– $3.90 printing cost

$7.26 Llumina profit

A complete description of the royalty structure can be found in the "Print Royalties" and "Electronic Royalties" sections of the author agreement at http://www.llumina.com/agree.htm.

NOTABLE PROVISIONS OF THE AUTHOR AGREEMENT: The complete author agreement is at http://www.llumina.com/agree.htm.

"Term of License" calls for a three-year term, which starts from the date the book is first released for publication, not the date you sign the contract. The contract will automatically renew for a one-year term if the author doesn't give a 30-day cancellation notice.

The author only grants nonexclusive print and electronic rights (see the "License to Publish" section) and can terminate at any time with 30 days written notice (see the "Author Cancellation" section).

The "Author Cancellation" term needs to be understood for what it is—a way for Llumina to keep your money if you cancel your contract before the book is published. It states that all fees received will be refunded, less the cost of the work already completed, which is billable at $50 an hour. The publisher's personal time bills at $100 an hour. This clause is fair because this publisher, like many others, spends a lot of time working with authors upon commencement of the publishing process. However, the clause seems to indicate that if you cancel before substantial work is done (e.g., cover design, layout design, etc.), you will get most, if not all, of your money back. But that's not what's going to happen. You will get some back, but there will be charges for the time the staff and publisher have spent working with you. Again, I don't think this is unreasonable; you just need to be aware of it. From the e-mail response below, it appears that this cancellation policy only covers situations prior to the actual publication of that book. When I asked the publisher what the fees were based on, I received this response, which is fair and reasonable:

> The [$50] an hour fee is for administrative, formatting, and design services that may have taken place prior to your notification to cancel. If our publisher, Deborah Greenspan, works on the project herself, her time is billable at $100 an hour. We reserve the right to deduct a reasonable fee for services already rendered if you cancel the contract prior to the publication of the book. Once the book has been published and this fee settled, you can cancel anytime with 30 days written notice, and no further costs would be due. However if you cancel once the book has gone to publication, no publication costs would be refunded to you because the book would be finished. "Subsidiary Rights" confirms the author's rights to all film, television, and other rights.

"Royalties" states the terms I've outlined, adding that royalties will not be paid on returns.

"Author's Copies" gives the author a 30% discount for an order less than 25 books, 45% discount for an order of 25-199, 50% discount for an order of 200-499, and 55% discount for an order of 500 or more.

"Publisher Termination" gives the publisher the right to terminate the agreement at any time without refunding the author's publishing fees if the book has been printed.

"Author Warranties" and "Indemnification" are standard and reasonable.

"General Provisions" contains no language requiring that lawsuits and arbitration proceedings be held physically in Florida. The language, "This Agreement is governed by the laws of the State of Florida," only requires a court or arbitrator to refer to Florida case law and statutes when interpreting the contract and its terms and to resolve other\similar issues.

AUTHOR-FRIENDLY RATING: While writing the last edition of this book, I sent the publisher three e-mails and never received a response. During the writing of this edition, my editor e-mailed the publisher and had a response in under 10 minutes. That's a good thing.

The prices of the publishing packages are acceptable, but the "custom" covers leave a lot to be desired. Of all the publishers reviewed in this book, Llumina produces the least impressive covers, some bordering on amateurish. Although the up-front fee includes cover art, you may be disappointed with the product.

The retail book prices are outrageous. In order to remain competitive, a 250- to 300-page paperback generally should retail for no more than $15 or $16. One book, a 272-page paperback called *Stay Dead!*, retails at $17.95 plus $5.50 in shipping charges. A 312-page, nonfiction paperback called *America's Trading Partners* retails at $24.95, plus $6.00 in shipping charges.

The retail price of the book directly affects what the author pays for copies. For orders of up to 25 copies of a $17.95 book, the author pays $12.57 per book. Don't forget shipping charges. How will the author ever sell the book for $15?

Despite the unfavorable prices, the publisher's contract is author-friendly and easy to cancel. The contract provides royalties that border on generous, but these pluses are lost in the sea of poor cover art and overpriced books.

VIRTUALBOOKWORM.COM
http://www.virtualbookworm.com

FORMAT OF BOOKS: e-book, paperback and hardcover

GENRES ACCEPTED: VirtualBookworm.com accepts all genre of books but those that deal with New Age, the occult, eroticism, or promote hate or violence.

PUBLISHING FEE: VirtualBookworm.com offers 11 publishing packages.

Paperback Package A: This package (http://www.virtualbookworm.com/podsoftcover.html) costs $360 and includes:

· Choice of trim size:
5" x 8"

5.25" x 8"
6" x 9"
8.25" x 11"
- Full-color cover
- Template-based cover design, including author bio and photo
- Electronic proof, including 15 free corrections (after that it's $50 for a block of 30 corrections)
- ISBN
- U.S. Copyright Office application kit
- One copy of your book
- Book page on publisher's website
- Bar code
- 15 internal graphics or images (must be submitted to specs; additional graphics are $2.50 each)
- R.R. Bowker's Books In Print registration
- Listing with online booksellers: Amazon.com and Borders.com

Paperback Package B: This package is offered at $440 and includes everything in Package A, plus a Library of Congress Control Number and a total of three copies of the author's book.

Paperback Package C: This package costs $495 and includes everything in Package B, plus a professional book cover and a total of five copies of the book. The professional book cover includes a consultation with the designer and one design. When asked about the design, the publisher's representative wrote to us:

Most of the time we obtain a stock image photo or have one taken. We don't normally create more than one version unless the author absolutely hates the first creation. But we do try to work with every author until they are satisfied with the cover (within reason).

Paperback Package D: Priced at $790, this package includes everything in Package C, plus the professional editing package, which includes grammar, spelling, and syntax.

Paperback Package E: This package is offered at $1,110 and includes everything in Package D, plus the Bronze Marketing Package, which includes:

· A professional press release
· 100 business cards
· A "personal storefront" template-based website for two years, including a single static page and links to a PDF excerpt of the book and the press release (Bookworm administers the domain name, but according to the company's representative, "It is yours whenever you choose to leave." See a sample at http://www.lorenlocknerbooks.com)

Paperback Package F: This package costs $1,395 and includes everything in Package E, plus the Silver Marketing Package, which includes:

· Distribution of the press release to over 200 media outlets (according to the Bookworm representative, media lists are compiled "through feedback from media outlets with their contact information and interests")
· Review copies and distribution to 10 "major" reviewers (these "major" reviewers are undefined)

Paperback Package G: For $1,950, this package includes everything in Package F, plus the Gold Marketing Package, which includes:

· 15 review copies
· Three years of the personal storefront
· Placement in Ingram's Advance Magazine
· 500 four-color postcards
· 1,000 business cards and bookmarks

Paperback Package H: At $2,350, this package includes everything in Package G, plus the return program, which allows booksellers to return unsold books to VirtualBookworm.com without affecting your royalty. The program includes a full year of returns after which the fee to maintain the program is $140.

E-book Package: This package costs $99 but is lowered to $65 if purchased with a print package. Details can be found at http://www.virtualbookworm.com/ebookpublishing.html.

Hardcover Packages: The price ranges from $430 to $2,100 for a hardcover print package. Details can be found at http://www .virtualbookworm.com/podhardcover.html.

Hardcover and Paperback Combo: The price ranges from $590 to $2,225 for a combo hardcover and paperback package. Details can be found at http://www.virtualbookworm.com/podcombo.html.

RETURN OF DIGITAL COVER AND INTERIOR FILES: Although it is not listed on the website or in the contract, a Bookworm representative assured me that authors may take their digital cover and interior production files with them, for a fee of $75, whenever they choose to part ways with the publisher.

Although the representative probably knows what he's talking about, one might want to get this promise written into the contract. Even though the contract does not contain any language stating that only the written terms of the contract are binding, it does contain language making the author liable for any legal fees regardless of the outcome of arbitration.

RETAIL PRICE OF AUTHOR'S BOOK: Prices are based on the page count of the book, and for paperback books are as follows:

Number of pages	Retail price
108–175	$12.95
176–250	$13.9
251–325	$14.95
326–400	$15.95

For paperbacks over 400 pages, prices are determined on a case-by-case basis.

For hardcover books, the price is that given for a paperback plus $5.00.

The price for case-bound books is the price given for a paperback plus $6.50

For a hardcover book with dust jacket, the price is that given for a paperback plus $7.25.

PRICE AUTHOR PAYS FOR BOOKS: The publisher gives the author a 50% discount on the first order of paperback books and a 30% discount on all subsequent orders. For hardcover books, the author receives 35% off the cover price on the first order and 30% off on subsequent orders. So, a 200-page, paperback book will cost you:

$13.95	retail price
– $4.19	30% author discount
$9.76	author price per book

As we know, the book costs $3.90 to print, so Bookworm makes $5.86 each time you buy a copy of your book.

ROYALTIES PAID TO AUTHOR: Bookworm pays royalties based on the net sales, which is defined on the publisher's FAQ webpage as the retail price less the bookseller's discount and printing costs. So for a 200-page book, the royalty for a book sold through Bookworm's website would be:

$13.95	retail price
– $3.90	printing cost
x .50	author royalty percentage
$5.03	author royalty

For a book sold through a third-party bookseller, the royalty would be:

$13.95	retail price
– $3.90	printing cost
– $4.19	30% bookseller discount
x .50	author royalty percentage
$2.93	author royalty

The royalty explanation in the publishing agreement is somewhat more ambiguous: "Author 50% royalties based on 'Net Publisher Print Receipts,' which equal the payments the Publisher receives from sales of the Work, less credit card charges, shipping and handling charges, chargebacks, discounts or disputes."

All royalties are paid monthly so long as they exceed $25; otherwise, they are held until royalties reach $25. The main complaints posted against Bookworm have revolved around royalty payments not being made on time, but the publisher says it has worked to correct that issue and, indeed, the complainants posted updates to that effect (see post at: http://www.absolutewrite.com/forums/showthread.php?t=962&page=2).

NOTABLE PROVISIONS OF THE PUBLISHING AGREEMENTS: There are two publishing agreements, one for POD and one for e-publishing. The POD contract is at http://www.virtualbookworm.com/infopackets.html, and the e-publishing contract is at http://www.virtualbookworm.com/infodocs/2005ebookcontract.pdf. The agreements are nearly identical. Unless otherwise noted, the provisions discussed are in both agreements.

The introductory portion sets the contract term to two years, beginning on the date the contract is signed. It also states that the contract is exclusive, but paragraph 3 allows the author to terminate by giving 90 days written notice. There is a $50 cancellation fee.

Paragraph 1 allows the publisher to seek injunctive relief if, prior to contract termination, the author enters into another agreement , which conflicts with the publisher's rights. Injunctive relief as a remedy allows the publisher to impose a court order that forces the author to stop selling the book elsewhere. The author also agrees to pay the publisher's legal fees and court costs.

So, if you choose this publisher, make sure you give 90 days written notice prior to executing any other publishing contract. Still, any clause that automatically makes an author pay a publisher's attorney's fees is bothersome. A more reasonably drafted attorneys' fees clause directs the losing party to pay the winning party's fees. It keeps everyone honest. So if you enter a publishing agreement with this publisher, insist that the last sentence in paragraph 1 be changed from "Author will also reimburse VirtualBookworm.com Publishing Inc. for all court costs and legal fees incurred" to "Author will also reimburse VirtualBookworm.com Publishing Inc. for all court costs and legal fees incurred, only if VirtualBookworm.com's claims against the author are upheld by a court; otherwise, VirtualBookworm.com will reimburse the author for all his or her court costs and legal fees."

Paragraph 3 allows either party to terminate the contract with 90 days written notice. There is a $50 fee if the author terminates prior to the expiration of the two-year term. No big deal. That's fair.

Paragraph 5 of the POD Publishing Agreement allows the author to search for a traditional publisher that will print at least 1,000 copies of the author's book in the first printing. Other than that exception, this paragraph prohibits the author from contracting with another POD publisher during the term of the contract (which can be canceled with 90 days notice). This clause protects the author who has an opportunity to sign with a traditional publisher but who hasn't given the 90 days notice of termination. So, if Random House wants to sign you, you can do so before formally terminating the agreement.

Paragraph 6 of the Publishing Agreement states that the publisher will pay the "Author 50% royalties based on 'Net Publisher Print Receipts,' which equal the payments the Publisher receives from sales of the Work, less credit card charges, shipping and handling charges, chargebacks, discounts or disputes."

Paragraph 5 of the Electronic Publishing Agreement prohibits the sale of the author's e-book on the author's website unless it is linked to the sales page on Virtualbookworm.com. This prevents the author from cutting out the publisher and making 100% of the royalties from each book sale.

AUTHOR-FRIENDLY RATING: Knowing what it costs for custom cover design, layout, and professional editing, I can't imagine how Bookworm can produce a high-quality product in the first four packages. For example, the $790 package includes editing of up to 75,000 words. If you have a 75,000 word manuscript, just a basic edit by a real editor is going to cost around $675, so there is no way you can get a professional book cover design, layout, and editing for $790. The problem with the other packages is that, while you're paying more, the actual value of what you're getting doesn't go up much. The storefront website is not going to help an author sell books. It's basically a template-based page with a book cover and link back to Virtualbookworm.com. That's not a website I'd want.

As long as you accept the printing markups and are OK with the publisher making more than you every time you sell a book, the royalty structure is acceptable.

My guess is that this publisher is a one -or two- person operation and isn't able effectively to handle all facets of book publishing. For example, we contacted the publisher with a question on August 21 and did not receive an answer until September 7. However, once we got one, the response was friendly and pretty thorough. And a second query, regarding royalties, was answered the day it was sent. It appears from the message boards on at least one publishing site that the publisher was slow to pay royalties and to respond to questions.

VirtualBookworm.com has been around a long time. I think it's trying to keep up in a business that makes it hard for mom-and-pop operations to compete. I don't believe it can deliver what it claims it can for the prices listed—not because it doesn't want to, but because a professionally designed cover, layout, and editing can't be done for that price.

I believe this publisher will attempt to deliver what it claims. I don't know if it can.

WHEATMARK PUBLISHING
http://www.wheatmark.com/index.cfm

FORMAT OF BOOKS: paperback and hardcover

GENRES: all

PUBLISHING FEES: Wheatmark offers seven packages, including specialized packages for poetry and for picture books (children's) and for printing press-ready books. Complete details and a comparison of the packages are available on the Wheatmark website at http://www.wheatmark.com/bookpublishing.cfm. The following overview covers only the four standard packages.

Basic Package: This package is priced at $1,299 and includes:

> · Cover design: The author must provide cover images or illustrations; otherwise a Wheatmark editor can find one

for the author for an additional fee of $299.
- Choice of trim size:
  - Paperback:
    5" x 8"
    5.5" x 8.5"
    6" x 9"
    7.5" x 9.25"
    7" x 10"
    8.25" x 11"
  - Hardcover:
    5.5" x 8.5"
    6" x 9"
    7" x 10"
- Interior layout design
- Cover copy tune-up, which includes a round of style edits
- Electronic proof, including up to 10 text corrections. Additional changes are charged at a rate of $60 an hour (a representative told me that about 100 changes can be made in an hour; If the publisher makes a mistake, of course, no fees apply)
- ISBN
- Bar code
- R.R. Bowker's Books In Print registration
- Distribution through Baker & Taylor and Ingram
- Listing with online booksellers: Amazon.com, BarnesandNoble.com, Borders.com, and more
- Marketing and sales sheet, which is basically a one-page description of the book with ordering information and, in some cases, an author biography
- Five copies of your book

Level 1 Package: This package costs $1,999 and is for authors whose books do not include a lot of interior graphics. It includes everything in the basic package, plus:

- Four-color, custom cover design, including images and an unlimited amount of design time (within reason)
- Editorial analysis: An editor will read your manuscript to

determine what level, if any, editing your book needs. The editor will look at character, content, and story development, as well as spelling, grammar, punctuation and syntax
- Printed proof
- Up to three interior graphics, including charts or tables
- U.S. Copyright Office registration
- Internet domain name: A customized URL that points to your book's page on the Wheatmark website
- Inside Search package, which allows visitor to browse your book before purchasing it
- Ten total copies of your book

Level 2 Package: At $2,999, this package is for nonfiction books, which may include more tables or graphs and may require an index. It includes everything in the Level 1 Package, plus:

- Up to 25 interior images or tables
- Footnotes and endnotes
- Index inclusion, which means that you create the index and the publisher formats it for inclusion in the book
- Cataloging-in-publication (CIP) data
- 10 author review copies

Level 3 Package: This package costs $3,999 and is for authors who would like a non-standard interior layout and who require an even greater number of interior images or graphics. It includes everything in Level 2, plus:

- Up to 100 interior images or tables
- Complex interior layout, including varying paragraph styles
- 15 author review copies

OTHER SERVICES OF INTEREST: Wheatmark provides a variety of à la carte marketing and editing packages for its authors.

Copyediting: Wheatmark will provide all levels of editing for a fee as follows:

- The basic edit is for common punctuation, spelling, grammar, syntax, and usage errors. This service costs $.02 per word and takes 2–3 weeks.

- Light copyediting is the same as the basic edit but applies to books that require less editing. It costs $.015 per word, and the service takes 2–3 weeks.
- Heavy copyediting is for books that contain frequent, serious syntactical errors (i.e., sentences that need to be rewritten). This edit includes minor fact-checking, and the editor will pay closer attention to plot, character development, continuity of voice, etc. This service costs $.024 per word and takes 2–3 weeks.
- A developmental edit is for books that require more, well, development. The author and her editor will work together for 6–8 weeks to "convert" the manuscript into something that can be published. A heavy copyedit is included in this package. The service costs $.054 per word.

Proofreading: For finished manuscripts. Once a book is laid out on a page, a proofreader will check for spelling errors and formatting mistakes, looking at font, spacing, the table of contents, etc. A prerequisite for this package is that the author must have paid for another editing package. This service is $.009 per word and takes 1–3 weeks.

Bookflash online press kit: For $499, the author gives Wheatmark all the necessary materials—press releases, book summary, author biography, photographs, cover image, news, reviews, etc.—and the publisher turns them into a website with a personalized URL. This service includes one year of hosting, and for every year after that, there is a $50 fee. For an example of the kit websites, see http://www.bookflash.com/press_kit/lock/rangers/index.cfm.

RETURN OF DIGITAL COVER AND INTERIOR FILES:

According to a Wheatmark representative, the author retains the copyright for his work as well as the work Wheatmark does for him.

However, that does not mean he automatically gets a copy of his design files. Here's what the rep said, via e-mail:

If you'd like to buy electronic files of your book that you can manipulate (say, add your own logo to and then sell it on your own), you may do so for $199 (basically, the labor that it costs to have your editor go in there and remove our ISBN, logo, and barcode).

RETAIL PRICE OF AUTHOR'S BOOK: The author is free to set the price of the book, so long as it meets Wheatmark's minimum price, which is based on the book's length. See a pricing chart at http://www.wheatmark.com/assets/infopacket.pdf. According to the chart, the minimum price for a 200-page paperback is $16.95, which is about $3 more than you will find generally, so I would not recommend trying to sell it at a higher price.

PRICE AUTHOR PAYS FOR BOOKS: Wheatmark gives its authors a 40% discount on the suggested minimum retail price. However, deeper discounts are available on volume sales. For 100–499 copies, the discount is 50%, and for over 500 copies, the discount is 55%.

So, if you purchase 25 copies of a 200-page, paperback book, your price would look like this:

$16.95	retail price
– $6.78	40% author discount
$10.17	author price per book
– $3.90	printing cost
$6.27	Wheatmark profit

At $10.17, the author price per book is one of the highest I have seen, and can hardly be called a discount when the publisher is marking up the book by almost 300 %.

ROYALTIES PAID TO AUTHOR: At Wheatmark, the author makes 40% of the retail price for books that sell on the publisher's website and 20% of net (defined here as the retail price less the 55% discount given to Ingram or Amazon.com) for books sold through other booksellers.

So, if that same 200-page, paperback book sells via the Wheatmark bookstore, the math is as follows:

$16.95   retail price
x .40   author royalty percentage
——————————————————————
$6.78   author royalty

On that same sale, the publisher makes $6.27. In this case the author actually makes more than the publisher, which is a rarity, but since the book is overpriced, the author may have a hard time selling it.

For books that sell on Amazon.com, the author makes:

$16.95   retail price
– $9.32   55% Amazon.com discount
——————————————————————
$7.63   net profit
x .20   author royalty percentage
——————————————————————
$1.53   author royalty

On that same book, the publisher makes:

$7.63   net profit
– $1.53   author royalty
– $3.90   printing cost
——————————————————————
$2.20   Wheatmark profit

NOTABLE PROVISIONS OF THE PUBLISHING AGREEMENT: The publishing agreement can be found at http://www.wheatmark.com/agreement.cfm.

In section 1, "License of Rights," the author gives the publisher nonexclusive, global rights to publish, advertise, and sell the book but retains the sole right to the film, radio, and television options of the book.

Section 2, "Editorial Control," states that the author has ultimate responsibility for the quality of the finished work even if she or he has paid the publisher for editorial services and that the author must approve the cover and any other work provided by the publisher prior to printing.

Section 3, "Copyright Notice," states that the book will be copyrighted in the name of the author.

Section 5, "Fees," basically states that the publisher's fees are as published on its website and may be changed at any time. It also says that if the publisher establishes a fee based on information it receives from the author and then later finds that information to be inaccurate, it may revise the fee and receive the difference from the author.

Section 7, "Style of Publication," gives the publisher final say over the design and formatting of the author's book. Even though the publisher will consult with the author on the design and style, it can override the opinion of the author. Further, it explains that the retail price of the book will be based on its page count and format, as published on Wheatmark's website.

In section 8, "Registrations," the publisher agrees to provide an ISBN and LCCN and to list the book in R.R. Bowker's Books In Print.

In section 9, "Distribution," the publisher agrees to distribute the book on online bookstores, its own bookstore, and through Ingram and Baker & Taylor, for a period of three years, after which it will charge the author $30 for each edition of the book printed. These fees may be deducted annually from the author's royalties.

In section 10, "No Guarantee of Minimum Sales," the publisher states that it cannot guarantee that the book will sell.

Section 11, "Royalty Payments," defines royalty percentages as the payments the publisher receives, less any returns. As I discussed earlier, the author receives 40% of receipts when the book is sold through the Wheatmark bookstore and 20% of receipts on all other sales. Further, it states that the publisher will make royalty payments on a quarterly basis provided they add up to $30; when less than that, the balance will be carried forward and added to the next quarter's royalty payment.

Section 12, "Sample Copies for Author," states that the author will receive sample copies, the number of which will be determined by the publishing package the author chooses. The publisher will pay all shipping costs.

Section 13, "Author Discount," states that the author will receive a 40% discount on his or her books with further volume discounts starting at 100 books.

Section 15, "Author's Warranties," states that the author has not misrepresented the fact that she wrote the book, that it does not libel or otherwise violate anyone else's rights, and that she has the right to publish it. Further, it says that the publisher will not be held legally or financially responsible if the book draws any legal claims. It also says that the publisher has the right to choose its own counsel if such a claim arises and that it will make sure the author receives her due share in any claims the publisher wins.

Section 17, "Suits for Infringement of Copyright," is along the same lines as Section 15. If the author's copyright is infringed and the author and the publisher prosecute together, both parties will share equally the expenses and recoveries of such a suit. If the publisher and author do not prosecute together, the prosecuting party will bear the expenses and the recovery. The author agrees that even if she does not want to bring suit, the publisher may bring suit in her name.

Section 18, "Term of Agreement," extends the agreement indefinitely until terminated by either party. It can be terminated at any time. If the author terminates before the book is printed or the publisher terminates before three years, the author will receive a refund less any fees she owes for work and services up to that point. This amount will be determined solely by the publisher.

Section 19, "Miscellaneous Provisions," states that any changes to the agreement must be made in writing and sent to both parties via certified mail. It also says that the agreement is subject to the laws of the State of Arizona and that all arbitration must take place in Pima County, Arizona. Plus, if there is arbitration, the loser must pay costs and reasonable fees for both sides.

AUTHOR-FRIENDLY RATING: Wheatmark gets a ho-hum and a shrug of the shoulders. It's not bad, but its cheapest publishing package is overpriced and both the retail and the author's book price are ridiculous—strong enough reasons to skip Wheatmark. But other than that, there isn't anything about Wheatmark that would come with a warning, and I don't think you'd have a terrible experience with them. Let's just say that there are better publishers out there.

Wheatmark's website is clean and easy to navigate. However, the online bookstore is basically a list, and while not as ugly as some, the thumbnails of authors' books are published at such a low resolution that they can be unrecognizable and therefore untempting for potential readers.

The Basic Package, at $1,299, costs way too much for what the company provides. The representative assured me that even in the least expensive packages the covers are all custom designed (though the website says something else). The best covers looked uninspired, though, and the worst looked template-based—although it's a little hard to say because of the image resolution.

On the customer service side, I sent the company an e-mail with some publishing questions and had a friendly answer within two hours. In the world of self-publishing, responsiveness is nothing to take lightly.

Paying $199 to keep your production files is not as bad as what other companies charge.

The bottom line is that there are many better and many worse publishers than Wheatmark.

CHAPTER 9

PUBLISHERS TO AVOID

If you choose to publish with any of the companies listed here, picture me whispering in your ear, "I told you so." It is harder to make the "Avoid" list than it is to make the "Outstanding" list, because I am not in the business of ruining people's livelihoods, but these publishers will make the process of self-publishing frustrating and financially unviable. I spent a lot of time trying to get these publishers to answer my questions, provide copies of their contracts, and explain why they do what they do. You will see the results of my efforts as you read this chapter.

Any publisher that refused to provide me a copy of their publishing contract automatically ended up on this list (except Wings Press because the owner provided me with detailed information about the contract). If they don't want prospective authors to see their contracts, there must be a good reason. Perhaps there's something in it that's not author-friendly, and they assume that, by not providing a copy, they are insuring the bad contract terms will never be discovered.

Other publishers ended up on this list because clauses in their contracts were absolutely horrible. Some clauses required authors to give up rights for many years, to give up their ancillary rights to movies and television, or to engage in other unsavory practices.

I have no vendetta against these companies. I know how important your book is to you, and my goal is to assist you in having a positive publishing experience. If you want to increase your chances of having a positive experience, go with one of the publishers described elsewhere in this book. If the only publisher who will take your work is in this category, it's time for you to consider if publishing your book is the best option for you.

ARBOR BOOKS INC.

http://www.arborbooks.com

FORMAT OF BOOKS: e-book, paper and hardcover

GENRES: all

PUBLISHING FEES: Arbor Books is both a self-publishing and ghostwriting service. The publisher's website does not provide detailed information about its services or fees. However, I filled out Arbor's "request a quote" form and received the following information regarding a 200-page, paperback book.

There are three packages: (1) for $3,800, the author gets 100 copies of the book; (2) for $4,500, the author gets 250 copies; and (3) for $6,500, the author gets 500 copies. All three packages include:

- Ten hours of phone or e-mail consultation, after which representatives bill at $110 an hour
- Custom-designed cover, which includes up to three rough drafts
- Typesetting (add $10 for every photo, graph, etc.)
- ISBN
- Bar code
- Library of Congress Control Number (LCCN)
- U.S. Copyright Office registration
- Printing, for the number of books of your choice, plus shipping
- Editing for an additional fee: A "commercial" edit (which is undefined), costs an extra $.05–$.10 a word, and proofreading costs an extra $.02–$.04 a word. This is quite high.

Distribution is not included unless you pay for the optional Marketing & Publicity Program, which costs an additional $2,000 dollars and includes:

- Promotional kit with the following parts: cover letter, press release, talking points, cover letter for speaking

> engagements, and back-cover copy, which includes a blurb, a biography, and "other elements"
>
> · Outreach to 150 retail distributors; library distributors; national book chains, including Borders and Barnes & Noble; Internet booksellers, including Amazon.com, Borders.com, Target.com, VirginMega.com, and Waldenbooks.com; book clubs and other specialty organizations and their catalogs; and key reviewers and media outlets, including *Kirkus Reviews, Publishers Weekly, The View, The Oprah Winfrey Show, Good Morning America, The Today Show, Live With Regis and Kelly, USA Today Book Club, C-SPAN, Imus in the Morning, New York Times Book Review, Time, Newsweek, Library Journal*, and many more.

Note: What this really means is that your book will be carried by at least one wholesaler that makes your title available from Internet retailers and makes it available to some traditional retailers. This does not mean that your book will be in bookstores. While the list of media outlets to which a press kit is sent looks impressive, keep in mind that anyone can send a book to these outlets. Arbor Books sending your book to Oprah probably doesn't mean much more than you sending the book.

OTHER SERVICES OF INTEREST: Arbor Books is a jack-of-all-trades, but of its many services, perhaps the most interesting is that it will actually write your book for you for $8,000–$22,000.

RETURN OF DIGITAL COVER AND INTERIOR FILES: A query to the publisher's representative asking who owns the working files elicited this response: "You can use freely as you wish." That is a bit too vague for me.

RETAIL PRICE OF AUTHOR'S BOOK: The author sets the price of the book. "We recommend pricing it in the middle of the market," said the publisher's representative.

PRICE AUTHOR PAYS FOR BOOKS: In the sample contract we received, reprints were listed as:

Number of copies	Author total price	Author price per book
100 copies	$950	$9.50
1,000 copies	$3,500	$3.50
3,000 copies	$7,500	$2.50

At the $9.50 book price, Arbor Books makes:

$9.50	author price per book
– $3.90	printing cost

$5.60	Arbor Books profit

If you buy 100 books, Arbor makes an additional $560.

ROYALTIES PAID TO AUTHOR: Arbor Books does not pay author royalties, because it doesn't actually sell books. Although it does include distribution in its marketing program, that program doesn't include fulfillment, and the company does not have a bookstore, nor does it provide its authors with websites to sell their books. If you go with Arbor Books and you don't buy the marketing program, you are on your own; however, that does mean you make 100% of the profits. If you buy the marketing program that includes distribution, you will make 100% of what's left after the trade discount (i.e., the fee taken by the wholesaler, by Amazon.com, etc.).

So, it appears that after the initial books that come with the package, you would need to order more from Arbor Books and then have them sent to a wholesaler (if you have the marketing program), to yourself, or to whomever you have fulfilling the books for you). Assume you sell your first 100 and order more for you to sell yourself. The 100 books would cost $950, or $9.50 per book (more if you factor in the shipping costs to you). If you charged a reasonable $13.95 for a 200-page book, you'd make a respectable $4.45. Assuming those 100 copies are printed digitally, Arbor Books is making $5.60 on each book.

The real problem here comes in when you have to price your book to sell on Amazon.com and other online retailers. Since Arbor inflates the printing costs (especially in low quantities), you'll have to price your 200-page book at $22 just to make $.40 per copy. The math is not pretty:

$22.00   retail price
– $9.50   author price per book
– $12.10   55% Amazon.com discount
_____

$.40   author profit

**NOTABLE PROVISIONS OF THE PUBLISHING AGREE-
MENT:** Arbor Books does not post its author agreement on its website
but readily presented one with the price quote.

The "Ownership of The Work; Author's Grant" clause says that
the work belongs to the author but that she grants the publisher the
nonexclusive right to print, publish, and distribute the book globally.
It also states that the publisher has not read the book and is relying on
the author's representation with regard to the author's ownership, right
to publish it, etc.

The "Production, Manufacturing, Design and Delivery" clause says
that the author must send all the necessary content to the publisher and
that the publisher is not responsible for returning it. It also outlines the
proofing and printing process, most notably stating that the author has
three days to review the printer's proof, which may vary from the design
proofs, and that the author will be charged 80% of the per-copy book
price for an over-run. This seems unfair since an overrun is generally
the fault of the printer. Plus, given that the printing costs are already
so inflated, it behooves Arbor Books to print more than you need and
make you pay for it. The author will receive a complete refund of books
that are not printed in the event of an under-run.

The "Marketing, Distribution and Sales" clause reiterates that Arbor
Books will not be responsible for marketing, distribution, or sale of the
work unless the author pays for the marketing package. In no event, it
says, is Arbor Books responsible for the success of the book. It does not
pay royalties.

In the "Representations, Warranties, and Covenants" clause, the
author agrees that she is the owner of the book and that she has the right
to enter into this agreement. Further, she warrants that the book is not
libelous or scandalous and does not infringe on anyone else's rights.

In the "Indemnity" clause, the author agrees not to hold Arbor
Books or its employees responsible, legally or financially, in the event of

a lawsuit resulting from any alleged breach of a representation or warranty by the author.

The "Term and Termination" clause states that the agreement is effective until the book has been delivered unless Arbor Books has agreed to market the book, and then it lasts until completion of those services. Either party may terminate the agreement for any or no reason with 30 days notice. Upon termination, the author must pay all outstanding fees. If the publisher terminates, it will account for the time spent on production and refund the author the difference between the amount paid by the author and the value of any time Arbor Books spent on the project, at a value of $95 an hour.

The "Pricing" clause says that the prices quoted in the agreement are good for only 180 days after the effective date.

In the "Non-compete" clause, the author basically agrees to pay $75,000 if she hires any of Arbor Books' editors, typesetters, or other staff outside of the contract during a 10-year period. This is a ridiculous clause, and the long time period probably makes it unenforceable.

The "Notices" clauses states that all notices, requests, and demands under this agreement must be made in writing and delivered via a tracked system (i.e., registered mail).

The "Governing Law, Jurisdiction and Venue" clause simply states that the agreement is governed by the laws of the State of New Jersey and that any litigation must be brought in Newark or Bergen County.

The "Miscellaneous" clause says that the agreement can only be amended in writing, and any amendments require a signature from both parties. It also says that while Arbor can transfer all rights, interests, and obligations stated in the agreement, the author may not.

AUTHOR-FRIENDLY RATING: When I look at this site, I feel like I'm in the middle of Times Square outside Crazy Eddie's Electronics Store and some guy wearing a huge gold chain is trying to entice me to come inside. The website is stuffed with content, images, words and dozens of links, but no useful information such as what the publisher's packages include, fees, or service descriptions. Most of the books posted on the home page were published by other companies, yet the intent (at least as I see it) is to make you think Arbor Books was somehow involved.

From a services standpoint, this publisher charges way too much. For $3,800, all you get is cover design, typesetting and 100 copies of your book. For $5,800, you get distribution but no fulfillment other than through online retailers. Sure, you get 100 books, but that's worth about $390 (assuming it's a 200-page, paperback book).

I have a feeling that Arbor Books is sort of a money pit where you keep paying in but not getting anything out of it. For $5,800, you get what most other companies reviewed in this book provide for about $1,000–$1,500. The grossly inflated printing markups further reinforce why this publisher should be on any writer's avoid list.

One humorous and revealing story about Arbor Books is a post by a blogger who was dismayed to find that the publisher was telling its authors to buy advertisements in the New York Times Book Review—for the sole purpose of then quoting their own ads on the back of their books and attributing the quotes to the *New York Times* as if the book had been reviewed! For this post, see http://robnyc.blogspot .com/2007/07/grab-your-credit-card-and-buy-glowing.html. His post prompted the publisher to remove those instructions on how to do that, and what remains is much subtler (see http://www.arborbooks.com /index.php?id=getreviewed.html).

AUTHORHOUSE
http://www.authorhouse.com

FORMAT OF BOOK: e-book, hardcover and paperback

GENRES ACCEPTED: all

PUBLISHING FEES: AuthorHouse offers two publishing packages. One is for black-and-white; the other is for color.

Standard Paperback Publishing: This package (http://www .authorhouse.com/GetPublished/StandardPaperbackPublishing. asp) costs $698 and includes:

- Custom-designed, full-color cover design, including two hours with the designer and, according to the Author-House representative, unlimited comps (meaning that

AuthorHouse's designer will work on the cover until you are happy with it; however, this promise is not in the publisher's standard agreement, so protect yourself by asking for the specifics to be added to your contract.

· Layout and design for interior, including 10 images and your choice of fonts and type size
· One paper review galley (this galley is intended to correct AuthorHouse typos or formatting issue; there is an unspecified fee for author changes)
· Author page on AuthorHouse website, including order info, book excerpt, and author bio (you have the option to purchase a domain name that points to your book page for $75 the domain name belongs to AuthorHouse initially but can be purchased for $75)
· One copy of the book
· The option to publish as either an e-book for $100 or hardcover for $350
· Distribution through Ingram
· Listing with online booksellers such as Amazon.com, BarnesandNoble.com and Borders.com
· Access to AuthorHouse web-based reporting
· Channel availability for a minimum of two years
· ISBN
· Bar code

Color Paperback Option: This package (http://www.authorhouse .com/GetPublished/ColorPaperbackPublishing.asp) costs $999 and includes everything in the Standard Paperback Publishing Package, plus:

· Layout and design for full-color cover and interior, which includes two hours of design time
· Up to 50 image insertions
· One PDF, rather than paper, galley
· Choice of trim size:
    8.5" x 8.5"
    8.5" x 11"

OTHER SERVICES OF INTEREST: AuthorHouse offers a host of optional services, including everything from copyright registration to editing and marketing services, but at a higher price than you'll find elsewhere. For a complete list of services, see http://www.authorhouse. com/GetPublished/Agreements.asp. For the sake of comparison, here are a few of the services:

Standard copyediting: Includes grammar, syntax and spelling for $.018 per word. This is almost double what a basic edit should cost.

Content editing: Includes grammar, syntax, and spelling, plus an in-depth review of the work's character development, content, and flow. The editor works closely with the author during the course of the editing process. This service costs $.06 per word, which is double what such an edit should cost.

Custom cover illustration: The author works with a design consultant and illustrator to create original artwork for the book's front and back cover. This service includes up to five hours of design time for $499.

Stock art placement: $8 per image.

Image scanning: $5 for black-and-white images, $8 for color images.

Image insertion: $10 per image.

U.S. Copyright Office registration: At $170, this is overly expensive. Even the AuthorHouse representative advised looking on the Internet, where the same service is available for around $100.

Web marketing service: This service includes domain name, website templates, placement of author-generated content, and updates for up to one year. The initial cost is $499. The domain name belongs to AuthorHouse but can be purchased by the author for a $75 fee. Another year of management can also be purchased for $300. The fact that AuthorHouse charges authors $75 for an $8 domain is bad enough. Then it charges $499 for a template-based website? This would almost be acceptable if the author then owned the website, but that's not the case. Plus, AuthorHouse makes it very difficult to transfer a domain. Last year, I helped an author get her domain name back from AuthorHouse. It wasn't easy.

RETURN OF DIGITAL COVER AND INTERIOR FILES: The AuthorHouse contract states: "You acknowledge that you may not utilize the formatted work and cover with any other publisher if we cease publication of this book." When asked whether a departing author could pay a fee for the files, the AuthorHouse representative said that she thought that would be possible but later e-mailed me this:

> We do not (typically) sell the production files. I apologize if I was misleading…I guarantee that a traditional company will rebrand your book and will not relaunch it with the same AuthorHouse look. Furthermore, the spine and the back near barcode and ISBN number our logos are present and so the printing (weight of stock, pics, etc.) must be high quality…Our image can't be associated with just any print job.

The representative is correct about a traditional publisher picking up an author's book. But if an author leaves to seek a more affordable and profitable self-publishing alternative, then the author will have to pay to have everything recreated even though he or she has already paid AuthorHouse to create these files. Yes, the author would want to remove AuthorHouse's ISBN and logo from his or her book, but with the production files in hand (or even a press-ready PDF) that would take a graphic designer a matter of minutes. Otherwise, the author will have to pay to have the book and its cover laid out again.

RETAIL PRICE OF AUTHOR'S BOOK: AuthorHouse does not publish the exact pricing chart for its books, although it has a sample structure here: http://www.authorhouse.com/GetPublished /BookSales.aspx.

AuthorHouse allows its authors to set the royalty for their books at 5%–50% for books sold via retailers like Amazon.com or 10%–50%

for books sold via AuthorHouse's online bookstore, and books will be priced accordingly. AuthorHouse has a minimum price scale, and obviously, a low-priced book equals a low royalty.

Although the sample chart would place the retail price of a 200-page, paperback book sold on AuthorHouse.com (where, one should note, the online bookstore does not publish the page count of books!) at $10.75 for a 10% royalty to $17.75 for a 50% royalty, the actual price is determined once the author agreement has been signed. That said, an AuthorHouse representative quoted me a spread of $12.30 for a 10% royalty to $19.70 for a 50% royalty. While a 50% royalty sounds swell, it's doubtful a 200-page paperback will sell for $19.70, especially one written by an unknown author.

PRICE AUTHOR PAYS FOR BOOKS: Author discounts are based on quantity and size of books. While no pricing chart is available on the AuthorHouse website, the representative told me that for a 200-page, 6" x 9", paperback book, the discount would be:

Number of books	Author price per book
1–99	$9.83
100–249	$8.85
250–499	$8.75
500–999	$8.50
1,000	$7.45
5,000	$4.00

So, if you buy at the lowest quantity discount, here's how much you're overpaying:

$9.83	author price per book
– $3.90	printing cost

$5.93 AuthorHouse profit

Now you know why AuthorHouse doesn't have the pricing chart available on its website. If I were marking up printing costs nearly 175%, I would make sure authors didn't know it, too.

ROYALTIES PAID TO AUTHOR: AuthorHouse calculates its paperback and hardcover royalties from the retail price of the book and allows authors to choose a royalty rate between 5% and 50% for books sold on retailers like Amazon.com and between 10% and 50% for books sold on the AuthorHouse website. The author can also choose to set the royalties at different percentages for sales on the AuthorHouse website versus third-party sales. Authors receive their payment scale, which is determined by the size of the book, after they sign the publisher's contract. The royalty for e-books is 25% of the purchase price.

For a 200-page, 6" x 9" paperback sold on the publisher's website, an AuthorHouse representative informed me, the author makes the following royalties (remember, the actual manufacturing cost for the book is $3.90):

Retail price	Royalty	Author royalty	Author House profit
$12.30	20%	$2.46	$5.94
$14.10	30%	$4.23	$5.97
$19.70	50%	$9.85	$5.95

For books sold through third-party retailers, the book prices go up to accommodate a 40% wholesale discount, and the breakdown is as follows for the same 200-page book:

Retail price	Royalty	Author royalty earnings	Author House profit
$15.49	5%	$.77	$4.62
$17.49	10%	$1.75	$4.85
$18.49	15%	$2.77	$4.43

The AuthorHouse royalty structure is explained at: http://www .authorhouse.com/GetPublished/BookSales.aspx. You don't need to visit this link unless for some reason you think it makes sense that AuthorHouse makes the lion's share each time your book sells. What is AuthorHouse doing to sell your book? Nothing. Any sales that result will be because of your efforts. So, when you get someone to purchase your book, why on earth should this publisher make almost triple what you do? Or, in the case of sales through Amazon.com, almost seven times what you do?

NOTABLE PROVISIONS OF THE PUBLISHING AGREE-MENT: A copy of the contract can be downloaded at http://www.authorhouse.com/GetPublished/Agreements.asp.

There's an old saying that you can't dress up a pig. With that, let's look at some of the highlights (or lowlights) of this contract.

Sections 1.3 and 1.5 make it clear that the author will not receive the production files (the book cover, layout, etc.) from the publisher upon termination, stating "You acknowledge that you may not utilize the formatted work and cover with any other publisher if we cease publication of this book."

Section 1.6 gives AuthorHouse 180 days from the date on which it receives your work to have your work published, which does not include the time that the work is in your hands for any reason or copyediting time.

Section 1.7 waives the author's channel access fees for the first year but then charges $20 annually, per format, for all subsequent years.

Section 1.8 makes it clear that AuthorHouse provides no promotional assistance unless the author purchases those additional services.

Section 5.6 is particularly troubling. AuthorHouse will not allow the author to transfer ownership interest or royalty rights to someone else without the express, written permission of AuthorHouse, which can be withheld at its "sole discretion for any reason." My guess is that this clause exists to prevent disgruntled authors from transferring their rights, including the right to sue, to a third party and is held like a club over the disgruntled author's head.

Section 6.1 is also fierce; it severely limits the author's legal remedies. You will either allow AuthorHouse to fix the problem ("use commercially reasonable efforts to cure") or to return your fees for the service at issue. Any author claim must be made within 30 days of the problem occurring. An author who is ready to make a claim or threatens legal action probably wants to get his money back and walk away from the publisher. My guess is that in 99% of the cases, AuthorHouse will "fix" the issue instead of refunding you a dime. If you plan on signing a contract with AuthorHouse, reread this paragraph many times. The drafter of this contract has anticipated author lawsuits and has tried to prevent the types of suits and claims authors were making.

Section 7.2 is the bright spot in an otherwise dismal contract. It allows the author to terminate the contract with 30 days written notice.

The author, however, won't be entitled to a refund or to the book's interior and cover production files.

Even if you are unhappy, the most you will ever get back is what you paid for the services. You will not receive lost profits or damages for pain and suffering (see section 4, "Disclaimer"). Such a clause is standard. The author who decides to sue, however, must file the claim for arbitration in AuthorHouse's hometown of Bloomington, Indiana. The prevailing party will be awarded legal fees.

AUTHOR-FRIENDLY RATING: If you are considering Author-House, it is probably because you've signed up for some information and now an AuthorHouse rep is calling you relentlessly. If after reading this book you are still considering AuthorHouse, then I can only shake my head in bewilderment.

While the publishing fees are not unreasonable, if you want a custom designed cover, you will need to add $499 to the price you pay. A review of AuthorHouse's à la carte prices, which are substantially higher than other self-publishing companies, reveals much. The printing markups and low royalties are egregious. However, the best example of the fleecing authors take here is found in something as simple as buying a domain name. The publisher charges a $75 fee to register an author's domain name for one year and then charges the author $75 to buy it back from them. This is ridiculous considering that you can register your own domain name on the Internet for around $8 a year.

Further, any disagreement with AuthorHouse is a lost cause. The publisher's contract makes it difficult to complain and see results. In fact, nothing about the AuthorHouse contract favors the author.

If you don't mind a 175% markup on printing and small royalties, then AuthorHouse is probably OK for you. But before you choose this publisher, rent the movie *Boiler Room*. Just like the shady stockbrokers in *Boiler Room*, AuthorHouse reps relentlessly call prospective authors and use the same pressure techniques employed by the best penny-stock hawkers.

Don't be fooled by the hype and slick sales techniques; I've worked with authors who've experienced AuthorHouse. Watching them get unstuck from that web has not been easy.

THE BECKHAM PUBLICATIONS GROUP

http://www.beckhamhouse.com

FORMAT OF BOOKS: e-book, paperback and hardcover

GENRES: all

PUBLISHING FEES: Beckham does not publish its packages but instead provides package details to individual authors after having read the author's manuscript. For submission instructions, see http://www.beckhamhouse.com/jointventure.html. Notice that Beckham refers to self-publishing as "joint venture publishing," which is somewhat misleading because a joint venture suggests that both parties are investing money into the project. Under the Beckham model, the only investor is the author. Beckham gets all the benefits of being in a joint venture, but with zero risk. Don't be fooled by the terminology; what Beckham offers is not a joint venture.

An author who submitted a 51-page book of poetry to Beckham provided us with the following details of Beckham's publishing package. It costs $1,965 and includes:

- ISBN
- Library of Congress Control Number (LCCN)
- U.S. Copyright Office registration
- Bar code
- Listing with online booksellers, including Beckhamhouse.com, BarnesandNoble.com and Amazon.com
- Custom cover design, which includes working with a designer to formulate an idea, illustration, and as many drafts as it takes to get it right
- 100 copies of the book
- Proofreading, which includes editing for punctuation, grammar, and spelling
- Page layout and typesetting, including unlimited interior graphics

· Listing in the Beckham catalog, including an online author page (for an example, see http://www.beckhamhouse.com/title_mloonaa.html)

· Optional e-book version for an additional $200

RETURN OF DIGITAL COVER AND INTERIOR FILES: Beckham will provide authors with print-ready PDFs of their books. Unfortunately, those will not do you a lot of good if you decide to publish elsewhere. If you leave Beckham (or any publisher that only provides print-ready PDFs) you will need to hire someone to redesign the book because it is not possible to remove the copyright page (the one with the old publisher's info, ISBN, etc.) or the back cover (which has the old company's logo and bar code) from a print-ready PDF. Beckham does not provide the working or design files for the books, not even for a fee.

RETAIL PRICE OF AUTHOR'S BOOK: Beckham quoted the aforementioned author a retail price of $9.95, which is reasonable for a slim volume of poetry. Otherwise, prices on the Beckham website and Amazon.com tend to vary. For example, the retail prices for a paperback fiction novel are as follows:

Number of pages	Retail price
264	$15.95
300	$14.95
308	$13.95

These prices are in general lower than you might see elsewhere in self-publishing.

PRICE AUTHOR PAYS FOR BOOKS: Beckham told our poet that she could buy books at 40% of list price. Take the 264-page paperback, and the math is as follows:

$15.95	retail price
x .40	author discount percentage

| $6.38 | author price per book |

The cost to print this book is $4.86, so Beckham makes $1.52 profit for each book the author purchases for his own use.

ROYALTIES PAID TO AUTHOR: Beckham's royalty schedule is complex and varies depending on where the book is sold. When asked, the publisher declined to specifically define what it costs to print a book, instead providing ballpark estimates. When the aforementioned poet asked via e-mail how she was supposed to figure out her royalty without specific numbers, publisher Beckham sent this very thoughtful, honest response:

The simplest approach is to consider your income will be with us about $2.00 or so a book. I don't use the term royalty because that connotes a payment based on the list price of the book and is a standard 7.5 percent for paperback and 10 percent on hardcovers with a possible sliding scale. Moreover, no publisher I know shares the pod (print-on-demand) income so that the writer gets 60 percent of the proceeds. But if you calculate the $2.00 or so as a royalty, it represents at least a 20 percent royalty on a $10 book.

I can certainly appreciate your wanting to calculate your income, but since I've taken all of this time to answer so many questions, I may as well continue. You would be much better served if you concentrated more on marketing. How many books of poetry actually sell? How many books of poetry have you purchased in the last year? What were the best sellers last year, and what were their special angles? Do you know that very very few books of poetry sell more than 1,000 copies, and that when June Jordan had a best seller about a decade ago, it was literary history? I'll leave it to you to discover how many she sold. Who is your likely reader? How do you reach the reader? What is your special uniqueness that will attract a media interviewer?

These are issues that you would find more profitable to explore. Let's face it, if you sell 1,000 copies, you may earn about $2,000. That may cover one mortgage payment in the Midwest. But if you spend more time doing the same research on marketing, you have a better chance of beating the odds so that there is enough income to be worth worrying about. Further, I can not give you a budget for a marketing plan because I don't have enough infor-mation to determine strategies. But you will find template packages from other publishers that will have no special slant for your title: book marks [sic], press releases, flyers. They all add up to nothing really, since they never spend enough time to answer the question, where is my likely reader and how do I reach her with my special message? In fact, one of my authors just today said that she wants to be on Oprah. What a surprise! But she hasn't done any research to find out how to get on to Oprah, like, what are the last 12 titles and how did those authors get to Oprah. What was different about each title? But she does ask for sales reports for January.

So a long answer with a simple message—be realistic and learn as much as you can about marketing (assuming you have studied poetry seriously—something few writers have bothered with). Best, Barry

Hmm, and this is from the author's supposed "joint venture" partner? Sounds like the only one making money in this "joint venture" is the publisher.

Based on Barry's cryptic message, here is the Beckham royalty schedule for print-on-demand sales as I understand it: the publisher pays the author 60% of the retail price less expenses. According to Beckham, this applies to sales on the Beckham website and Amazon.com. In the following example, I am using the 51-page poetry book that was submitted to Beckham House. For sales through the Beckham online bookstore, the royalty is calculated as follows:

$9.95	retail price
− $1.65	printing cost

$8.30	net profit
x .60	author royalty percentage

$4.98	author royalty

Assuming no other expenses are deducted (which I'm not certain is true because Beckham wouldn't give the author the cost of the book and said that shipping expenses would also be deducted from the net profits), Beckham's profit is $3.32.

For sales through Amazon.com or other online retailers, the royalty is calculated as follows:

$9.95	retail price
− $1.65	printing cost
− $3.48	35% Amazon.com discount

$4.82	net profit
x .60	author royalty percentage

$2.89	author royalty

Again, if there are other expenses deducted from the profit, this estimate may be high. If it is not, Beckham makes $1.93 for each sale of this book on Amazon.com or other online retailer.

For books sold via booksellers that require a discount of 40%–60%, Beckham offers a royalty of 7.5% of the retail price.

$9.95   retail price
x .075   author royalty percentage
_____

$.75   author royalty

For books sold via booksellers that require a discount of 61% or more, Beckham offers 5% of net sales, before expenses.

$9.95   retail price
– $6.07 61% bookseller discount
_____

$3.88   net sales before expenses
x .05   author royalty percentage
_____

$.19   author royalty

For books sold through a foreign trade publisher, the author receives 85% of retail.

$9.95   retail price
x .85   author royalty percentage
_____

$8.46   author royalty

For e-books, the royalty is 50% of the retail price. For the 51-page book of poetry, Beckham told the author she could expect to sell the e-book version for $5.95 to $10.95. Based on a $5.95 retail price, the royalty is calculated as follows:

$5.95   retail price
x .50   author royalty percentage
_____

$2.98   author royalty

NOTABLE PROVISIONS OF THE PUBLISHING AGREEMENT: Although Beckham does not provide a sample contract online, the publisher will provide one upon request.

In section 1, the author agrees to give the publisher "during the term of the copyrights in the work and all renewals and extensions thereof as presently in force or as hereafter amended by law" the exclusive right to publish and print the book, and the nonexclusive right to sell the work for a renewable term of "X" years. This clause makes Beckham's contract the worst in self-publishing. There is no reason to consider working with this publisher. If you sign this contract, Beckham will have the exclusive right to publish your book for the term of the copyright (your life plus 70 more years) unless the publisher breaches the contract. Further, section 9 of the contract reiterates that the author cannot publish or print the book without the publisher's written consent.

When I e-mailed the publisher to check on his intent with this clause, he e-mailed me back, saying, "I've changed that clause. It's now a two or three-year contract with automatic renewals." Then I e-mailed the publisher again asking to see the contract, and he told me to check the site in two to three weeks. If he changed it, why would I have to wait several weeks to see it? I then asked him why I couldn't just see a contract. We went back and forth a few times with him dancing around my request to see a contract. I'd put this entire exchange in your "Things That Make You Go Hmm" file.

In section 2, the author confirms that she has not taken the book from the public domain, that it is the author's original creation, and that she has acquired permission to publish anything that is not hers, and has not given the rights to the book to another publisher.

In section 3, the author warrants that her book does not contain any plagiaries or content that is defamatory, libelous, or otherwise illegal. If it contains any of the latter, the publisher is not responsible for any damages or legal fees. If a lawsuit arises because of the author's book, the publisher may withhold royalty payments in lieu of outstanding settlement payments.

In section 4, the publisher agrees to secure copyright of the book in the author's name. Don't be fooled by this clause. By giving the publisher the exclusive right to print and publish your book during the term of the copyright, it's irrelevant that the copyright is in your name.

Section 5 outlines the package price, which includes "rewriting, editing, proofreading, cover design, typesetting and interior layout, printing and binding, marketing described in the next paragraph, POD catalog, and shipping to one address." It also states the trim size and the number of perfect-bound books the publisher has agreed to create and provides the author's payment schedule. Note: There is no paragraph in the contract describing marketing services.

In section 6, the publisher agrees to sell the author's book to the author at 40% of the list price, provided the author buys 25 or more copies. Section 7 states that the publisher has the right to reprint and publish the book at its own expense and will pay the author the following:

a) 7.5% of the retail price for titles sold to trade bookstores and wholesalers who require a discount of 40%–60%.

b) 5% of the Publisher's net sales income before expenses for copies sold to wholesalers who require a discount of 61% or more. 85% of the royalties received by the Publisher from a foreign trade book publisher.

c) 50% of the sums received by the Publisher for e-book sales.

d) For print-on-demand sales, the Publisher shall pay the Author 60% of the net income received.

Furthermore, it states that the publisher will pay the author's royalty semiannually, in April and October.

In section 8, the author agrees that if another party infringes on the rights of the author or the publisher, the publisher has the option to participate in the suit and the right to half the net recovery. Not that it matters, but if you file suit against an infringer and the publisher decides to participate in the suit (presumably by paying part of the attorneys' fees), the publisher is entitled to half the recovery—but this clause doesn't require the publisher to pay half of the legal fees in order to share in half the recovery. Just stay away from this publisher.

In section 9, the author agrees that for the duration of the agreement she will not, without permission from the publisher, print or publish—or authorize the printing or publishing—any revised, corrected, enlarged, or abridged version of the work. P.T. Barnum once said, "There's a sucker born every minute." If you're still considering this publisher, that's you.

Section 10 says that if the publisher does not perform according to section 5, the author can terminate the agreement in writing and via registered mail and will receive all materials produced up to that point. This whole section is vague. There are no timelines built into the contract, so if it takes the publisher years to get your book out, can you really say the contract was breached? Again, go find another publisher.

In section 11, it states that outside of terminating the contract all communications can take place via regular mail.

Section 12 says that this is the entire agreement, and any changes must be made in writing. So, agreements made in e-mail or over a handshake are not legally binding.

Section 13 states that the agreement is legally binding for the author and her "assigns" and the publisher and his successors and assigns. So, if the publisher should sell his business or otherwise give up ownership, the publisher's exclusive right to publish the author's book goes to the new owner.

Section 14 states that disputes will be arbitrated in Maryland.

AUTHOR-FRIENDLY RATING: Although I initially found it hard to believe that the publisher actually intended to have a contract that gives it the exclusive rights to publish an author's book forever (essentially), that's what it says. It seems equally strange that the publisher would send an old and unfriendly version of the contract to a potential author and then claim to have rewritten it and to be unable to send it to me for several weeks (which by the way, he never did).

That being said, the poet who sent her book in to Beckham reported that the publisher exchanged several very friendly, informative e-mails with her and answered all of her questions.

In case you're actually considering Beckham and haven't heeded my warning about losing all your rights, the price authors pay for their own books is a little high—given the actual cost to print the book—and the royalties are a little low. But neither of these is really out of the ordinary for the market in general. The publisher also made it impossible to get an actual royalty calculation.

Overall, you need to run as fast as you can from any publisher who engages in this type of behavior. The publisher didn't know I was writing this book and just assumed I was a newbie author, so your chances of being treated differently are next to nil.

DORRANCE PUBLISHING
http://www.dorrancepublishing.com

FORMAT OF BOOKS: paperback and hardcover

GENRES: all

PUBLISHING FEES: Dorrance has been around since the 1920s and offers both traditional subsidy and self-publishing packages. The difference, according to the publisher, is that traditional subsidy means the publisher will keep your book in stock and provide marketing, distribution, and fulfillment. Self-publishing means the company will produce and print your book, and you will be responsible for storage and sales. Package details are not available on the website, which also looks like it has been around since the 1920s.

The following prices and terms were for a 52-page, perfect-bound, paperback book of poetry my editor submitted to Dorrance.

Subsidy Package: This package costs $7,500 and includes:

- Basic editing for grammar, spelling and punctuation, etc. Dorrance will perform "no rewriting, reorganization, or suggestions for improvement of presentation, content, literary expression, or style of writing of the manuscript"
- Book cover copy
- Custom cover: When asked what the custom cover included, we received the following reply via e-mail:

We will never send anything to the printer unless you are satisfied with it. There is nothing worse than a book that the author is unhappy with that has their name on it. We ask that you be as specific as possible for your idea about the cover so we can make you happy the first time. If you have a photograph or know an artist that will design it for you, that is completely acceptable. Again, this is your book.

- Interior typesetting and style, including images, charts, and illustration fee
- 500 books to be stored and distributed by Dorrance, plus 50 additional books for the author
- U.S. Copyright Office registration

- Book warehousing, fulfillment, and distribution for two years (it is unclear if this includes an ISBN and bar code)
- $1000 worth of promotion, which includes:
  - 500 copies of a direct mail piece
  - 75 review copies, mailed to local media; includes a clipping service
  - Press release, sent to 25 local media
  - Press release, sent to 100 wholesalers, jobbers, and distributors
  - Book announcement, sent to 25 local bookstores and 50 libraries
  - Inclusion in Dorrance catalog

If that seems like a lot of bang for a thousand bucks, I thought so, too. When we queried the publisher as to whether that $1000 covered everything on the list or applied against the list (which would mean the publisher would stop providing services when it hit $1000), the representative replied via e-mail:

The $1,000 budget covers everything listed there. The most expensive aspect is the actual review copies of the book. However, these copies are pulled from the initial print and bind. Another important fact about the promotion budget: we can allocate it any way you would like. If you would like more attention to be placed on one aspect than another, we can do that.

RETURN OF DIGITAL COVER AND INTERIOR FILES: When we queried Dorrance about their policy regarding ownership of the working cover and typesetting files, we received this answer via e-mail:

You can definitely have the files for your book. We do not want any of the rights to your book. The only thing we want to be able to do is publish it in the English language for the duration of the contract. If the book is still selling well after two years, we would like to continue publishing it for you, but this is your choice.

That's great, but the contract does not address this issue. The representative suggested that the author send the company a letter requesting the files, just to get it in writing. The contract does specify that all requests for materials to be returned must be made in writing and sent by certified or registered mail within 30 days of the author signing the contract.

RETAIL PRICE OF AUTHOR'S BOOK: According to the aforementioned author's contract, a 52-page book of poetry would retail for $8.

PRICE AUTHOR PAYS FOR BOOKS: The author receives 50 books as part of the package's purchase price. If the author exhausts that supply, he or she may purchase additional copies at 45% off the retail price.

$8.00	retail price
x .45	author discount percentage
$3.60	author discount per book

$8.00	retail price
−$ 3.60	author discount per book
− $1.68	printing cost
$2.72	Dorrance profit

ROYALTIES PAID TO AUTHOR: For up to 3,500 copies sold, the author royalty is 40% of retail price or 25% of retail price if the wholesale discount is greater than 40%. For sales outside of the U.S., the royalty is 25% of retail. For over 3,500 copies, the royalty is 25%.

Note that if your book really takes off, if you are successful, you will be penalized with a lower royalty.

So for the 52-page book, the author would make:

$8.00	retail price
x .40	author royalty percentage
$3.20	author royalty

Since the author's original package fee paid for the first 450 books, Dorrance makes $3.12 on each book ($8 − $3.20 − $1.68). After the 450 books are gone, the contract states that the publisher will pay to print subsequent books, in which case sales out of the second run would garner Dorrance the same $3.12 per book sold.

**NOTABLE PROVISIONS OF THE PUBLISHING AGREE-
MENT:** Dorrance does not publish copies of its contract on its
website, but my editor was able to obtain one.

Section I gives Dorrance, for the full two-year term of the contract,
the exclusive right to publish the book and "all other right to and in the
work," which refers to subsidiary rights covered later in the contract.

Section III covers what and how the author will pay Dorrance for its
services, which in this case is three installments of $7,500. It also says that
Dorrance "makes no contribution to the cost of the initial publication."

Section IV states that Dorrance has 180 working days (nine months)
after the contract is signed to complete the book, unless prevented by
the author, acts of God, or other circumstances beyond its control. The
author agrees to review any edits or production proofs within six days
of receiving them.

Section V provides the technical specs for the author's book, and it
states that while Dorrance will consult with the author the publisher has the
ultimate say in how the book will be designed. It also says that the author
will pay for any changes made to the book after the author has approved the
proofs. In this section, Dorrance also states the level of editing provided.

Section VI says that if the author would like any of her materials
returned (i.e., any cover art she has provided) she must make a written request for it within 30 days of signing the contract. Otherwise,
the original manuscript and all other materials submitted will not be
returned. This is not the same as getting the original production files
returned. There is nothing in the contract that provides for that.

Section VII details the author's royalty and the retail price of the
book. Royalties are paid biannually, at January 31 and July 31. Dorrance has the right to change the retail price of the author's book; in
such a case, royalties would be adjusted accordingly.

Section VIII states that the publisher will warehouse the author's
work at no extra charge to the author.

Section IX states that the author's package includes 50 copies of the
work at no extra charge. This section also provides the author's cost to
purchase books at a 45% discount plus the cost of shipping.

Section X outlines the publisher's promotion plan, with a caveat
that the publisher will spend no more than $1000 or the equivalent in
labor on promotion (remember, the publisher stated at the beginning

of the contract that it was not contributing any money to the first print run). The details are listed in the package description of this review.

A paragraph in section X also states that the author must tell Dorrance when she is undertaking promotional efforts on her own and that any mass mailing to customers on the Internet will result in termination of the contract.

Section XI permits Dorrance to sell any subsidiary rights (which include book club, paperback, hardcover, reprint, serial, dramatic, motion picture, television, radio, translation, and other such rights) during the term of the agreement. Should Dorrance sell any subsidiary rights, the author earns 80% while Dorrance keeps the other 20%.

Section XII says that Dorrance will secure a copyright for the book in the author's name.

In section XIII, the author agrees that she has the right to publish the book, that it is her work, and that it is not libelous or fraudulent. It also says that Dorrance will not be held legally or financially liable if litigation arises due to copyright or other issues.

Section XIV extends the contract terms to the electronic form of the book, stating that the e-book will sell for $5.00 and that the author will receive 40% of the net price ($2.00) on each sale.

Section XV details the term of the contract, which is two years. It says that if, before the end of the contract term, all 500 of the author's books sell, the publisher will print more at its own expense. After two years, if the book isn't selling, Dorrance has the right to terminate the contract by notifying the author in writing.

Similarly, the author can cancel the contract after two years by notifying Dorrance in writing, "except in the case that Dorrance has produced a subsequent edition of the book at its own expense." This clause creates an abyss because suddenly there is no end in sight. If your book is selling well, Dorrance can simply come out with a second edition, and you're stuck in the contract for an undetermined length.

If either party should cancel the contract and the initial print run of 500 books has not sold, the author is entitled to keep the books but must request them within 30 days of the contract cancellation date. The author will be responsible for the shipping fees.

If the author fails to pay any of the fees outlined in the contract, the contract will be terminated and any fees that have been paid will not be returned.

If the author terminates the contract during the production process and Dorrance is not in breach of contract, then all fees will be forfeited.

If after publishing the book, Dorrance determines that the book is libelous, obscene, or otherwise injurious or unlawful, it can terminate the contract and the author must forfeit all fees.

Section XVII says that the contract is complete and that any additions must be made in writing and signed by both parties.

Section XIX says this contract is subject to the laws of the County of Alleghany and the Commonwealth of Pennsylvania. Any disputes will need to be settled there, and under no circumstance will litigation resolve with either party paying the other more than the payments made in the course of this contract. However, the non-prevailing party must pay all lawyers' fees.

If the author thinks the publisher has not performed its duties according to the contract, she must present her case in a certified or registered letter to the publisher and give the publisher an unspecified "reasonable" amount of time to correct its mistakes; otherwise, the author cannot claim a breach of contract.

Section XX says the contract applies to the heirs, executors, administrators, and assigns of the author and the successors and assigns of Dorrance. That basically means that if you die or Dorrance sells its business to PublishAmerica, the contract is still binding.

AUTHOR-FRIENDLY RATING: Just when I thought I've seen every bad deal out there, Dorrance restored my lack of faith in humanity. First, the package is $7,500 for a 52-page book of poetry. Yes, it includes 500 books, but that's only $840 (assuming Dorrance isn't paying less than $1.68 per copy to print). A basic edit of a 723-word book of poetry should cost less than $100.

Assuming you can get all of the marketing services promised for $1,000 (which I don't believe is possible), you are still left with $5,500 for publishing a 52-page book of poetry.

Then add on a two-year exclusive term and a clause that allows the publisher to extend the term indefinitely if it prints another edition of your book, and things start looking really ugly. Sprinkle in that Dorrance has the right to sell your subsidiary rights during the term of the contract, and it gets even worse.

At this point it's not even worth discussing the printing markups, royalty amounts, and the fact that for $7,500 it's not even clear if the author will get the production files returned.

Stay away.

E-BOOKTIME

http://www.e-booktime.com

FORMAT OF BOOKS: e-book, paperback and hardcover

GENRES: all

PUBLISHING FEES: E-BookTime offers two packages: one to print in paperback and another to print in both hardcover and paperback. Both are pretty basic, and the publisher doesn't offer any à la carte design, editing, or marketing services. This review covers the paperback-only package. Complete details are available at http://www.e-booktime.com/paperback.html.

Paperback Package: This package costs $395 and includes:

· Five copies of the book
· Listing with online booksellers: E-booktime.com, Barnes-sandNoble.com, Amazon.com and others
· ISBN
· R.R. Bowker's Books In Print registration
· U.S. Copyright Office registration
· The option to include interior images and graphics for an extra fee of $5.00 per graphic
· The option to register for a Library of Congress Control Number for an extra fee of $50
· Cover: E-BookTime does not offer custom-cover design. However, it does provide free cover templates (http://www .e-booktime.com/covers.html) to which the publisher's designers are happy to add a photograph that you provide. If you are going to go the template route, you will definitely want to submit a photograph, as E-BookTime's cover designs are pretty hokey. Alternatively, you may pro-

vide a press-ready cover as long as it meets the publisher's specifications.
- Interiors: E-BookTime will only print black-and-white interiors
- Choice of trim size:
  5.5" x 8.5"
  6" x 9"
- Inclusion in the E-BookTime catalog (if the book does not experience sales of at least $100 in the first year, you will need to pay a $12 fee to post the book for a second year on the E-BookTime site)

RETURN OF DIGITAL COVER AND INTERIOR FILES: E-BookTime does not include information about cover and interior files in its author agreement. I sent the publisher two e-mails and left a detailed message on its answering machine in regards to this question, but did not receive an answer.

RETAIL PRICE OF AUTHOR'S BOOK: E-BookTime allows authors to set their own retail price as long as it meets the minimum price, as listed at http://www.e-booktime.com/paperback.html. Under these guidelines, a 200-page paperback in either trim size will retail for at least $12.95.

PRICE AUTHOR PAYS FOR BOOKS: Author discounts are based on quantity purchased and the number of pages in the book. If you publish a 200-page paperback, your discounts will look like this:

Number of books	Discount	Author price per book
0–24	30%	$9.06
25–99	35%	$8.42
100–249	40%	$7.77
250+	50%	$6.48

If you purchase under 25 copies per order, the publisher makes a profit of $5.16 for each book you purchase, as the printing costs are no more than $3.90 per book.

ROYALTIES PAID TO AUTHOR: Royalties are based on the retail price of the book and where the book sells: 30% for sales via E-BookTime's bookstore and 15% for sales through other retail channels, such as Amazon.com.

So, on the same 200-page paperback the author profits from a book sold through Amazon.com as follows:

$12.95	minimum retail price
x .15	royalty percentage

$1.94	author royalty

On that same sale, E-BookTime makes an amount equal to the author's royalty:

$12.95	minimum retail price
– $1.94	author royalty
– $3.90	printing cost
– $5.18	40% Amazon.com discount (as stated in the contract)

$1.93	E-BookTime profit

That makes E-BookTime one of the few publishers who actually split the profits evenly rather than taking the lion's share.

For a book sold through E-BookTime, the royalty is calculated as follows:

$12.95	minimum retail price
x .30	royalty percentage

$3.89	author royalty

Based on this calculation, E-BookTime's profit per book sale will look like this:

$12.95	minimum retail price
– $3.98	author royalty
– $3.90	printing cost

$5.07	E-BookTime profit

NOTABLE PROVISIONS OF THE PUBLISHING AGREE-MENT: A copy of the E-BookTime agreement is available for download at http://www.e-booktime.com/orderformprint.pdf.

"Author's Royalties" explains that on paperback books, the author receives 30% of the retail price for all books sold from the E-BookTime website and 15% of retail for books sold through other booksellers, such as Amazon.com. On hardcover books, the author receives 25% of the retail prices for books sold on the E-BookTime website and 10% for all books sold through other retailers, including Amazon.com.

The "Payment of Royalties" section says that royalties will be paid by check on a monthly basis and that authors will receive a sales statement with the royalty check.

The "Retail Prices" section says that the author may set the price of his book as long as it is at or above the minimum price set by the publisher. It also asserts that the publisher can change the minimum price at any time.

The "Author Discount Prices" section states that the author discount prices are based on the minimum retail price but that if the author "sets a retail price different than the published price, the Author Discount Price will be that shown for the actual page count of the book." This is simply a very confusing way of saying that even if you set your book price higher than the minimum suggested book price for a 200-page book, you will still receive the same discount. That assertion is based on the chart provided at http://www.e-booktime.com/paperback.html.

In the "Revision of Published Work" section, the author agrees to pay a revision fee of $150.00 for any revision to a published paperback or hardcover book cover or text.

The "Catalog Fee" section says that the catalog fee for the first year of publication is included in the publishing fees but that if the author's book does not generate $100 annually, the author will be charged a $12.00 fee.

In the "Distribution" section, the publisher agrees to sell the author's book via its own site, Amazon.com, other retailers, and a book distributor with a 40% wholesale discount. It will not accept returns.

In the "Warranties" section, the author agrees that she is the author and owner of the book and that it does not contains pornographic, hate, or racist materiel and is not libelous or filled with plagiaries.

In the "Indemnities" section, the author agrees that neither E-BookTime nor its employees are legally responsible for any claims that arise because your book is libelous or contains stolen work. Further, the author agrees to pay all legal fees that might arise from litigation.

In the "Terms" section, both parties agree that the contract is nonexclusive and can be terminated at any time without cause. If the agreement is terminated before the book has been published, all of the publisher's fees will be returned. If it is terminated after the book has been published, the author will receive all outstanding royalties. Further, the author retains the copyright for the work. It also states that the agreement is subject to the laws of the State of Alabama and that all lawsuits will be brought to court there. That's not necessarily an unfair clause, but it will be inconvenient if the author decides to sue the publisher and does not live in Alabama.

AUTHOR-FRIENDLY RATING: A low-calorie and low-tech offering to be sure, but at the very least, it is an honest offering. The website is also straightforward and easy to figure out. It is disappointing, however, that E-BookTime doesn't offer custom cover design as the templates are pretty abysmal. If you decide to go with E-BookTime, you need to hire a cover designer and submit a real book cover; otherwise, you will never have the type of quality book that you desire.

Naturally, it is always annoying when the publisher declines to answer e-mails and phone calls, and it does make one wonder how responsive they are to the queries of their authors and those of readers attempting to purchase books off the site.

What this publisher offers is similar to many no-frills publishers. If I was in the market for such a publishing experience, I would choose a publisher that at least answers my e-mails and returns my phone calls.

HOLY FIRE PUBLISHING
http://www.christianpublish.com

FORMAT OF BOOKS: e-book, paperback and hardcover

GENRES ACCEPTED: fiction, nonfiction, poetry, devotions and youth books

PUBLISHING FEES: Holy Fire offers three packages.

50% Royalty Plan: This plan costs $899 and includes:

- Up to 70% author discount
- Choice of six template-based covers
- R.R. Bowker's Books In Print registration
- Bookstore and special order availability
- Listing with online retails: Amazon.com, Target.com, BarnesandNoble.com and Borders.com
- ISBN
- Bar code

100% Royalty Plan: This package is priced at $1,499 and includes everything in the 50% Royalty Plan, plus:

- Custom cover: A graphic artist works with the author to establish a design theme. Holy Fire provides the cover image unless the author has one. (This is an $800 value, and includes only one cover.)
- Ten free books

Color Interior (Children's Books) Plan: This package costs $1,599 and includes everything in the 100% Royalty Plan, plus:

- 50% discount on books
- 100% author royalty
- Choice of trim size:
    8.5" x 8.5"
    8.5" x 11"

OTHER SERVICES OF INTEREST:

E-book: For $199, this service includes PDF formatting and setup and listing on Amazon.com. (This service can be found for free with other publishers.)

Ingram Advance and Christian Advance: An advertisement in the distributors' catalogs for $249.

Press Release: For $249, the Holy Fire staff will write and post a press release so that the media can read it or the author can send it out.

Worldwide Newswire: The Holy Fire website says that for $249 the press release is sent to 60,000–100,000 media. When I asked the Holy Fire representative how it determines who to send the press release to, she answered:

…we take the press release and send it to our contacts with MSN, Google-news, online newspapers and freelance writers…we do not arrange additional things like book signings and speaking engagements as a publisist [sic] would.

The author must pay for the Holy Fire press release to participate. Basically, this is a mass press release that is spammed out over the Internet.

Returnable: The author's book is returnable through Ingram. All returns are deducted from future royalties. $69

RETURN OF DIGITAL COVER AND INTERIOR FILES: According to the Holy Fire representative, the publisher will give departing authors a PDF of their interior and cover files as they went to press. It might be possible to get a production file for the interior of the book, but the cover can only be purchased in a downloadable high-res TIF file (for $35). A working file of the cover cannot be purchased. "But," wrote the representative in an e-mail, "you can not [sic] purchase the working layered file because we can not allow the artist's work to be changed."

RETAIL PRICE OF AUTHOR'S BOOK: The retail price of the books depends on the page count (http://www.christianpublish.com/retail.htm):

Number of pages	Retail price
105–124	$10.99
200–249	$14.99
300–349	$16.99

PRICE AUTHOR PAYS FOR BOOKS: Author discounts are based on the quantity of books purchased and the retail price; the author can purchase copies for up to 70% off the retail price. A 200-page book retails for $14.99, so the discount would look like this:

Number of books	Discount	Author price per book
1–25	40%	$8.99
51–250	50%	$7.50
1000+	70%	$4.50

As I have already discussed, the cost to print a 200-page paperback is no more than $3.90 per copy, so on small orders of books for your own use, Holy Fire makes a $5.09 profit per book. Yet, as you will read in the next section, the publisher claims it pays $4.90 to print the book. That is not true—unless this publisher has no idea where to get books printed. But even if that were true, the publisher would still be selling it to the author at a markup of almost 100%. I asked the representative three times why the price markup was so high and finally got this answer: "The other $4.09 goes to HFP to pay for emplyees [sic], advertising, websiite [sic] and things to keep the business going." (But it doesn't appear they are spending any money on a spell-checker).

ROYALTIES PAID TO AUTHOR: Depending on which package the author buys, Holy Fire pays royalties of either 50% or 100% of the net profit. The net profit is based on this equation:

Net profit = Retail – Wholesale discount – Cost to print

(Cost to print = $.02 x Number of pages + $.90 Cover charge)

So, if you sold that same 200-page book on Amazon.com, the math would look like this:

$14.99	retail price
– $7.50	50% Amazon.com discount
– $4.90	printing cost
$2.59	net profit
x .50	author royalty percentage
$1.3	author royalty

Of course, Holy Fire makes $2.30 ($1.00 printing markup + $1.30 in royalties) on that sale, but that's not the worst of it. Holy Fire makes an additional $.60 per book when someone orders an author's book through its website. Holy Fire's online store is powered by Amazon .com, which means Holy Fire gets a referral fee of 4% for every sale made through the "store" in addition to the other monies it makes per sale of a book. Here's the math:

$14.99	retail price
– $7.50	50% Amazon.com discount
– $4.90	printing cost (inflated by $1.00)
– $.60	4% Holy Fire commission

$1.99	net profit
x .50	author royalty percentage

$1.00	author royalty

Holy Fire makes $2.60 as follows: $1.00 printing markup, $1.00 in royalties, and $.60 in Amazon commissions. So, Holy Fire is not really paying a 50% royalty but rather 50% on what remains after it backs out additional profits for itself.

NOTABLE PROVISIONS OF THE PUBLISHING AGREEMENT: The entire contract can be found at http://www .christianpublish.com/publishingagreement.html.

Under "Publisher," item 9 says the publisher can terminate the contract at any time, without notice, for any reason, and the author may be eligible for a refund, less a $50 fee and any costs incurred, as long as the publisher terminates prior to the author having given the approval to print.

Item 12 says that all returned books will be deducted from the author's future royalties.

Under "Author," item 1 says the author will pay an annual catalog fee of $19 but that the first year's fee is included in the setup costs. This is reasonable.

Item 6 says that the publisher is not responsible for content and that any changes that are, made after the publisher provides the author with a digital proof will cost the author $150 for the interior and $150 for the cover.

Item 7 says the author can terminate the agreement at any time with 60 days written notice.

AUTHOR-FRIENDLY RATING: Christian publishing is a booming business, and there are many legitimate Christian publishers. Unfortunately, I can't in good conscience recommend this publisher to anyone. It bothers me that companies use religion to cover up being less than forthright about their business practices.

On its homepage, Holy Fire tells authors, "We will not compromise core Christian beliefs for any amount of profit. All prices are up front with no gimmicks." Lying to authors about having to pay more for books and giving authors a false printing cost compromises core ethical business practices and surely any Christian beliefs. Marking up printing more than 100% seems to be a compromise of beliefs for profit and is certainly not "upfront" pricing.

From a moral standpoint, this publisher should be ashamed of itself. Enough said.

INDYPUBLISH
http://www.indypublish.com

FORMAT OF BOOKS: e-book, paperback and hardcover

GENRES ACCEPTED: all

PUBLISHING FEES: IndyPublish offers five publishing packages, which are described here: http://www.indypublish.com /publishingservices/sv_sc_index.asp.

Basic Package: This package is free and includes:

- Standard, text-only, template-based, four-color cover
- Up to five author corrections to the book (additional corrections are $49 for 25 changes, after which corrections are available on a $2-per basis)
- Both a 6" x 9" paperback and e-book
- ISBN
- UPC/EAN bar code
- R.R. Bowker's Books In Print registration
- Listing with online booksellers: Amazon.com, Barnesand-Noble.com, Borders.com and the publisher's online store

· Author website, including a unique URL. The publisher did not reply to an e-mail asking for an example of its websites. I did find this website for an author listed on the front page of IndyPublish's website: http://www.robertlskidmore.com /mywebsite1_001.htm. I think I know why the publisher didn't reply. The website I saw had no picture of the book cover and nothing about the author. Just black text on a yellow background.

Bronze Package: This package costs $189 and includes the features in the Basic Package, plus:

· The option to submit a picture or graphic for the cover
· Up to 25 corrections by author after submission
· 100 bookmarks, 100 postcards, and 100 business cards featuring the book
· One paperback copy of the author's book

Silver Package: This package is priced at $285 and includes everything in the Bronze Package, plus:

· Choice of 18 cover templates and 15 interior templates, including a choice of background colors and the option to submit 10 interior graphics
· Library of Congress Control Number (LCCN)

Gold Package: This package, which costs $575, includes everything in the Silver Package, plus:

· Choice of 36 covers and 15 interior templates, including a choice of background colors and the option to submit up to three cover images, an index, five table and 20 interior graphics
· Up to 50 corrections by the author after submission
· Option to print a 6" x 9" hardcover version of the book
· U.S. Copyright Office registration
· One hardcover copy of the author's book

Platinum Package: This package costs $999 and includes everything in the Gold Package, plus:

· The option to submit five images for the cover, an index, 10 tables and footnotes, and up to 30 graphics for the interior
· Up to 100 corrections by the author after submission
· Two copies each of the author's hardcover and paperback books

RETURN OF DIGITAL COVER AND INTERIOR FILES: It is not clear from the IndyPublish website what happens to the author's production files when the publishing contract expires. The publisher did not answer an e-mail query regarding the files and does not provide a phone number to call for information.

RETAIL PRICE OF AUTHOR'S BOOK: IndyPublish allows authors to set their price as long as it is at or above the publisher's minimum price for the book, as determined by the book's page count. For a price calculator, see http://www.indypublish.com /publishingservices/sv_p&r_calcul.asp.

For a 200-page book, IndyPublish suggests a minimum price of $10.61 for paperback, $15.31 for hardcover, and $5.30 for an e-book.

PRICE AUTHOR PAYS BOOKS: The author's purchase price is based on the quantity of books purchased and the retail price of the book. Yes, IndyPublish allows authors to set the retail price of the book, but if authors raise the retail price above the minimum, they'll pay for it, because it increases the price the author pays to buy copies of his own book.

So for a 200-page, paperback book:

Retail price	Number of books purchased	Author discount	Author price per book
$10.61	1–19	25%	$7.95
	20–99	30%	$7.43
	100+	35%	$6.90
$13.95	1–19	25%	$10.46
	20–99	30%	$9.76
	100+	35%	$9.07

If you stick to the minimum price, IndyPublish makes the following profit every time you purchase a copy of your book:

$7.95   author price per book
− $3.90   printing cost
_____

$4.05

That's a huge markup, considering how little the author makes in royalties.

ROYALTIES PAID TO THE AUTHOR: For e-books, the royalty is 50% of retail less a $.50 transaction fee per book. For printed books, it's 50% of retail less printing costs, discounts, and a $1.00 processing fee.

The same calculator used to determine the price of the book will tell you what the royalty will be on a 200-page, paperback book. Here's how it looks:

Retail price	Royalty on bookstore and online sales	IndyPublish.com sales
$10.61	$2.80	$1.21
$13.95	$4.48	$2.38

For each of these sales, IndyPublish is making $1 more than the author.

Note: IndyPublish is the only publisher in this book that charges a processing fee in addition to a publisher's royalty. Also, the publisher lists a royalty for direct sales, but it's unclear where those sales come from since IndyPublish does not sell books on its website.

When I e-mailed IndyPublish to ask about the $1 processing fee and the royalty on IndyPublish sales, I did not receive a response.

NOTABLE PROVISIONS OF THE PUBLISHING AGREE-MENT: Section 4 explains the royalty, as I've already discussed, but adds that those terms apply only for books that net $40 or less; for books that net more than $40, the author shall receive 50% of the net below $40 and 100% of everything above $40. It also explains that royalties are paid quarterly as long as they are equal to or more than $15.

Section 5, "Rights," makes it clear that the author only grants non-exclusive rights for both print and electronic books during the term of the agreement, which lasts until one party gives 30 days written notice. The last sentence clarifies that the author retains all subsidiary rights.

Section 6, "Author Warranties," and section 7, "Indemnities," are standard and reasonable.

Section 9, "Terms," clarifies that the "Author may enter into other publishing agreements for the same work." Authors who choose the Basic Package should direct their attention to the second paragraph. If the publisher lists the book for sale on its website and fewer than 12 copies are sold in the first year, the author must pay $50 to keep the book listing on the website.

Section 10, "Book Price Determination," allows the author to set the book's retail price as long as it exceeds the publisher's minimum price.

Section 12 provides that Virginia law is the operating law for contract interpretation, and any legal disputes will be heard in Virginia.

Section 13, "Notices," describes the procedure to give notice and terminate the contract.

AUTHOR-FRIENDLY RATING: If you want a book that won't scream self-published, this publisher is not for you. It's impossible to get a professional cover design and/or interior layout for most of the prices the publisher charges for its packages. If your goal is to get your book published and printed so that you can give it to friends and family, then this publisher's services might work for you.

However, there are some major issues with this publisher. The first is that I e-mailed them several times requesting information about the publishing packages and never got a response. For me, that's all it would take to find another publisher.

The second problem is the price the author pays to purchase his or her own books. It is simply too high. Based on a 200-page paperback, the price the author pays for under 20 copies of his or her own book is 100% more than the printing costs. Plus, the price breaks for purchasing larger quantities aren't much of a break. It is even more troublesome that, if an author chooses a higher retail price in order to make a higher royalty, he or she will have to pay a higher price for each copy of his or her book. This makes no sense. The cost to print the book is the same regardless of the retail price. Essentially, the author is punished for wanting to earn a higher royalty. This is reason enough to skip this publisher.

INKWATER PRESS

http://www.inkwaterpress.com

FORMAT OF BOOKS: paperback and hardcover

GENRES ACCEPTED: all

PUBLISHING FEES: The publisher does not publish information on its publishing fee structure. Authors are invited to submit their manuscripts; if the manuscript is accepted, an Inkwater Press representative will forward a recommendation for publishing and a basic fee schedule.

Short Package: This package, which is only for books up to 47 pages, costs $799 and includes:[3]

- Saddle stitching (staple binding); perfect binding is an additional $50
- Listing with online booksellers: Amazon.com, BarnesandNoble.com, Powells.com and Borders.com
- R.R. Bowker's Books In Print registration
- Template-based, full-color cover
- Two electronic proofs; (subsequent proofs for $30 each)
- ISBN
- Bar code
- One copy of book
- Sales availability for one year, renewable for $50

Standard Black & White Package: This package, which costs $999, is for books up to 700 pages and includes everything in the short package, plus:

---

3 An author, whose book was accepted by Inkwater, provided the $999 package price and features. I raised the Deluxe Package and Short Package prices $100.00 based on the fact that the Basic Package price had increased by that amount since the last edition of *The Fine Print*.

- Choice of full-color, template-based cover
- Choice of template-based black-and-white interior
- Perfect binding; trim size of 5.5" x 8.5"
- Two electronic proofs; (subsequent proofs for $30 each) The first 50 changes are free. After that, changes (up to 100) are $.50 each.
- Ten total copies of the book
- Option to purchase a LCCN for $150
- Optional customized interior or cover for $450 each (on the cover, Inkwater's graphic designer works with the author to come up with a design; although the author may request changes, it is not clear how many versions the designer will produce before more fees apply)
- Optional to include black-and-white interior images, charts, and tables at $12.50 each

Deluxe Package: This package costs $1,399 and includes everything in the Standard Package, plus:

- Custom-designed cover
- Fifteen total copies of the book
- More trim size choices

RETURN OF DIGITAL COVER AND INTERIOR FILES: The Inkwater print-on-demand contract states that the publisher retains the ownership of the book's cover design, not the author, and that the author will have "no rights to reproduce the book design created by the publisher." According to an Inkwater representative, the author may buy the rights and the files for the cover for a fee to be determined on a case-by-case basis.

RETAIL PRICE OF AUTHOR'S BOOK: The Inkwater website does not offer a pricing schedule and does not provide details on how the publisher determines the price of the book. The author who provided us with the author agreement was told her 64-page book of poetry would retail for $15.95, but I've seen books with varying prices on the Inkwater website:

Number of pages	Retail price
160	$17.95
184	$16.95
198	$19.95
224	$20.95

PRICE AUTHOR PAYS FOR BOOKS: The author's discount is based on the retail price and the number of books he or she purchases. So, the author can buy:

Number of books	Discount
1–19	0
20–99	25%
100+	40%

If the author bought 20 copies of the 198-page paperback, the math would look like this:

$19.95	retail price
– $4.99	25% author discount

$14.96	+ shipping author price per book

That's a markup of over 300%. Here's what Inkwater is making every time an author buys the book at that price:

$14.96	author price per book
– $3.87	printing cost

$11.09	Inkwater profit

ROYALTIES PAID TO AUTHOR: The Inkwater royalty is paid quarterly and is based on net income. The Inkwater representative told the author who provided us with the author agreement that she would receive a 30% royalty.

For sales through third-party booksellers, the net income is based on this equation: Retail – Wholesale discount – Printing cost = Royalty.

The representative defined the cost to print as $.015 per page + $.90, as we have seen throughout the book, and said that the wholesale discount is 40%–50%. Note: The contract says that net also includes a deduction for shipping, but the Inkwater representative said that that is not actually true, as the reader would pay for the shipping. The author only pays shipping if he or she buys the book.

Here's how that math works out for a 198-page book sold on Amazon.com:

$19.95	retail price
– $9.98	50% Amazon.com discount
– $3.87	printing cost
x .30	author royalty percentage

$1.83	author royalty

Inkwater would make $4.27 on that same sale.

The equation for books sold via the Inkwater website is: Retail – Printing cost = Royalty. Here's how that would look on the 198-page paperback:

$19.95	retail price
– $3.87	printing cost
x .30	author royalty percentage

$4.82	author royalty

Inkwater would make a whopping $11.26 on that sale; not only is Inkwater selling books to authors at a 300% markup, but it is also taking a 70% royalty.

NOTABLE PROVISIONS OF THE PUBLISHING AGREEMENT: The "Ownership and Liability" section says that the author's work is her own and that it isn't hateful, libelous, or slanderous, and gives all rights of ownership to the author.

The "Service" section says that the publisher will list the book in R.R. Bowker's Books In Print and will make the book available on its website, Amazon.com, and BarnesandNoble.com. It also states that the publisher owns the book design, which means authors who terminate their Inkwater contract will have to pay to have their books redesigned if they want to continue to publish their books.

The "Term and Payment" section says that Inkwater will provide publishing and distribution services for one year and that there is a $50 renewal fee for each subsequent year. It also says that royalties will be paid on a quarterly basis for the previous quarter's sale, which means authors must wait three months to receive payment. The royalties are based on net revenue after deducting for printing, discounts, and shipping. Authors receive a 25%–40% discount on the retail price of their books, and author book orders take two or three weeks for delivery. It also states that the author is responsible for all shipping charges, but an Inkwater representative said that applies only to the author's book purchases.

The "Deliverables" section states that the author must give the publisher his or her manuscript in a finalized form; the publisher is not responsible for content. If the author buys editing services from the publisher, he or she agrees to work from the edited manuscript. If the author then makes substantive changes, he or she agrees to pay the publisher $85 an hour, with a one-hour minimum, to edit those changes.

The "Indemnity" section states that the author agrees to hold the publisher and its employees harmless from any and all claims that may be made on the book, including legal expenses. However, if those claims cost the publisher money, the publisher can withhold the author's royalties.

The "Termination" section says that either party can cancel the contract at any time without cause and with only a written notice and proof of delivery. If the publisher terminates the agreement, all payments minus a 35% service fee will be returned, unless the author has breached the contract. If the author terminates, all payments minus any services rendered and the 35% service fee will be returned. It also says that if the contract is terminated the author will have no rights to reproduce the book design. Finally, this section has an exclusivity clause whereby the contract is considered terminated if the author decides to publish the same book with any other publisher (traditional or other self-publishing company) while working with Inkwater.

The "Jurisdiction" section states that the contract can only be changed in writing and that changes must be signed by both parties. It also says that any legal proceedings are subject to the laws of the State of Oregon and must take place in Oregon.

AUTHOR-FRIENDLY RATING: The publishing packages are too expensive for what you get (e.g., template-based cover designs and no customized layout). The printing markup is as bad as it gets, the royalty split is pathetic, and authors don't own the cover or interior layout despite paying to have them created. There is simply no reason to choose this publisher.

But, unlike every other publisher to avoid, this publisher was at least responsive and honest about how it conducts business. The publisher's template-based covers are no worse than many "custom-designed" covers I've seen during the course of my research, and I appreciate that they are honest about the fact that they use a template. I also appreciated the fact that the representative was very forthcoming about the net receipts formula, that she always responded promptly to e-mail queries (within a few hours of receiving them), and that her answers were generally pretty specific and informative.

However, honesty that reveals a lack of author-friendliness still leads to same the conclusion—skip this publisher.

ITHACA PRESS
http://www.ithacapress.com

FORMAT OF BOOKS: paperback

GENRES: unknown

PUBLISHING FEES: Ithaca Press does not publish its pricing schedule on its website. Further, it claims to base its pricing on the needs of the book, so an author cannot get information about the company until she submits her book and gets it accepted for publication. Red flag number one.

Although I e-mailed a query to the publisher, I did not receive a reply, and the publisher does not publish a phone number. Red flag number two.

It should already be obvious that you need to find a different publisher, but if you must persevere, here is what I was able to gather from various parts of the Ithaca Press website with regard to what services and features are included in its publishing program:

- · 20 books
- · Cover design (unfortunately, the website offers little information as to what is included in the cover design, and with no online bookstore, it is not possible to see samples of the

publisher's work)
· Interior design
· Author website, which includes a book overview, author biography, free e-mail addresses, a secure merchant account for credit card processing, web hosting for 1 year, and a custom URL (ithaca Press does not have an online bookstore and it does not offer examples of its author websites, so I have none to offer you)
· ISBN
· Bar code
· U.S. Copyright Office registration
· LCCN
· R.R. Bowker's Books In Print registration
· $50 renewal fee for each subsequent year
· Copyedit and proofreading, including spelling, grammar, and punctuation
· Professional overview of author's book: An Ithaca publicist will provide the author with a professionally written summary of his book, which can then be used to create press releases (Note: this is not the same as a press release and does not include media distribution or a distribution list)

RETURN OF DIGITAL COVER AND INTERIOR FILES: Unknown

RETAIL PRICE OF AUTHOR'S BOOK: Unknown

PRICE AUTHOR PAYS FOR BOOKS: Unknown

ROYALTIES PAID TO AUTHOR: Ithaca royalties are based on the retail price, wholesale discounts and the printing cost and generally range from 5%–20%. Without knowing the retail price, what sort of discounts Ithaca offers booksellers, or how the publisher determines the cost of printing, I can't calculate the royalty.

NOTABLE PROVISIONS OF THE PUBLISHING AGREEMENT: Unknown since, the publisher declined to provide one.

AUTHOR-FRIENDLY RATING: The Ithaca website does not include any pricing. Instead, the author is asked to fill out a "Request a Quote" form with contact information and their book details; in exchange, the instructions promise, Ithaca will contact you with "ideas for how to bring your book to market."

Ithaca does not provide a quote without first deciding to accept the book, so the purpose of the quote form is simply to get your contact information. To Ithaca's credit, it was one of only two publishers to reject a fake book that we created for this new edition of *The Fine Print*. We put together a book that no publisher that claims to be selective should publish—a book of poetry written by a dog—yet every selective publisher that we queried, other than BookLocker, Ithaca and Book-Pros, accepted it. It was nice to see that Ithaca rejected it because they could not "imagine a market for it," which of course is true.

However, I had my editor submit a bunch of publishing questions via the contact page, using her real name, and she never received a reply. Ithaca lost all the points it gained for rejecting a terrible book by not responding to our questions.

Besides the company's website, I can find no proof that it is actually publishing books. A search on Amazon.com only pulled up books published by a UK company that has an imprint called Ithaca Press and that specializes on books about the Middle East and Islam.

Everything about this publisher is too sketchy for me. Skip this one.

*i*UNIVERSE

http://www.iuniverse.com

FORMAT OF BOOKS: paperback, hardcover and e-books

GENRES ACCEPTED: all

PUBLISHING FEES: iUniverse has four publishing programs.
The Fast Track Publishing Package: This package (http://www.iuniverse.com/packages/fast-track.htm) costs $299 and includes:

- ISBN
- Webpage in the iUniverse online bookstore
- PDF proof and one round of corrections
- Delivery of books in 30 days or less

- No choice of format: 6" x 9" paperback only
- Template-based cover design
- Sales through iUniverse only; includes access to myuniverse.com, the publisher's online distribution and royalty monitoring system, and quarterly sales reports
- One free copy of the book

Select Publishing Package: This package (http://www.iuniverse.com/packages/select.htm) is $499 for an online submission and $599 for a paper submission. It includes everything in the Fast Track Package, plus:

- Custom, four-color cover
- E-book setup
- Distribution to wholesalers and booksellers
- R.R. Bowker's Books In Print registration
- Listing with online booksellers: Amazon.com, BarnesandNoble.com and more
- Five free copies of the book
- Volume discount for authors
- Listing in Google Book Search
- Marketing tool kit, which is a set of templates used to create bookmarks and press releases
- Choice of trim size:
    5" x 8"
    5.5" x 8.5"
    6" x 9"
    7.5" x 9.25"
    8.25" x 11"

The Premier Publishing Package: This package (http://www.iuniverse.com/packages/premier.htm) is $799 for an online submission and $899 for a paper submission. It includes all services or products in the Select Publishing Package, plus:

- Ten free books
- Eligibility for:
    - Editor's Choice: Your book is placed in the Editor's Choice section of the iUniverse.com bookstore.
    - Readers' Choice: Your book is placed in the Readers'

Choice section of the iUniverse.com bookstore.

· Star Program: To qualify, you need to sell 500 books, at least half of those through retail channels. The program is a repackaging of the book, with a professional copy-edit and a revision of your cover, cover copy, and author biography. Your book will have full return status, and retailers will be able to purchase your book at an industry standard discount (the book will be submitted to Kirkus Reviews, and you'll get a consultation with the iUniverse marketing team for the relaunch)

· Marketing Success Workbook, which is a guide to marketing your book (a $49 value)

· Eligibility for the Bookseller Discount, which lets you take a lower royalty so that booksellers can take a greater discount on your book

· Editorial evaluation (http://www.iuniverse.com/services/editorial-services/editorial-evaluation.htm), which is not editing but an assessment of how ready the book is for publishing, grammar to content and plot development (a $299 value)

The Premier Pro Publishing Package: This package (http://www.iuniverse.com/packages/premier-pro.htm) is $1099 for online submissions and $1199 for paper submissions and includes all services and products in the Premier Publishing Package, plus:

· Hardcover formatting

· One free hardcover book and 20 free paperback books

· Cover Copy Polish: An iUniverse copywriter will write your back and front covers, flaps, title, and author biography. ($149 value)

· Eligibility for the Pro Art Direction: With Editor's Choice designation, you are assigned an art director who translates your design idea and works with a designer to produce a cover for your book; you have the right to ultimate acceptance or rejection

OTHER SERVICES OF INTEREST: As you can imagine, a giant company like iUniverse offers a myriad add-on services. Here are a few worth noting:

Editorial services: All levels of editing are available, including basic grammar and spelling at $.018 per word; line editing, which covers syntax, word choice, and light structural changes for $.024 per word; and content editing, which focuses on plot and flow, at $.029 per word. These fees are almost double that of the industry standard, and you can find competent editors for much less.

Kirkus Discoveries book review: Universe charges $360 for this service. If you worked directly with Kirkus, you would pay $350, but you would still need to send it two copies of your book. Kirkus Discoveries is a respected publication. Its writers are the same folks who write the impartial reviews you'll find on Kirkus Reviews, which means your payment doesn't guarantee a stellar review. If you receive a bad review, you can decline to post it. Requesting a Kirkus Discoveries review lends your book legitimacy.

Ghostwriting: An iUniverse author takes your first draft and/or notes and writes a manuscript in consultation with you. There is a $299 fee for a cost estimate and writing sample. Why would you want an iUniverse author to consult with you instead of a publishing professional? I'd skip this service myself.

Developmental edit: This is a thorough reading of your book with feedback and constructive criticism intended to create a strong rewrite. For nonfiction writers, editors will look at concept development, organization, and illustration. Fiction writers will get feedback on plot, pace, characterization and dialogue. The fee is $.044 per word. You are paying a lot for something that doesn't include copyediting. A publishing-ready edit, which would include copyediting and notes like these with a second round of copyediting to look at the changes the writer made based on the initial feedback, can likely be found elsewhere for less.

Co-op advertising: Your book will be included in a group ad with other iUniverse authors. Journals include the New York Times Book Review, Poets & Writers, ForeWord Magazine, and

BookMarks Magazine. Prices vary from $250–$450 per book. This kind of advertising falls into the "Flush your money down the toilet" category. Your co-op ad will feature a number of other unknown authors, and industry "insiders" and literary enthusiasts are not going to pass on the ads for books by well-known authors and zero in on the tiny book cover and blurb about your book in an ad that everyone in the industry knows is from a self-publishing company. If you buy this service and make your money back from it, I will let you watch me rip out each page of this book and eat it.

RETURN OF DIGITAL COVER AND INTERIOR FILES: If you terminate your contract with the publisher, you will have "the right to purchase" your digital files in press-ready PDF format with the iUniverse logos and ISBN removed. The fee is based on when you terminate. If you terminate at 18 months or later, you'll pay $150 each for the cover art and interior files. If you terminate any earlier, you'll pay a whopping $750 each for the cover art and interior files. The problem is that you can't really sell your book anywhere without an ISBN, so you will need to have the entire cover and interior laid out again, even if all you want to do is insert an ISBN. You will have paid $1,500 for a set of worthless files.

When I asked iUniverse about the fees, the company responded that in most cases the only reason authors take the files is because they wish to publish the book themselves, which I doubt. If the author goes to a new publisher, the iUniverse rep asserted, that publisher will create new production files for the book. New production files wouldn't have to be created if iUniverse provided them to the author.

After a long conversation about why I couldn't have the production files, I asked why the PDF cost so much, and the iUniverse "customer service" rep had this snippy retort: "If you're looking for print-ready productions files to have set up with a printer, it may be better for you to work directly with a graphic designer instead of using our services."

Charging you $1,500 for the press-ready PDF is shady. Period. If you decide you want to publish your book with a company that offers higher royalties and lower printing markups, you should be able to take your production files to such a company. Otherwise, it's like publishing from scratch. You have already paid to have these production files created. They are of no use to the publisher if you terminate your relationship.

RETAIL PRICE FOR AUTHOR'S BOOK: iUniverse sets the price for all of its books, loosely based on a sliding scale. I say loosely because while the chart would dictate that a 200-page, 6" x 9" paperback would retail for somewhere between $15.95 and $19.95, it's possible to find a 410-page, 6" x 9" paperback selling on the publisher's website for $14.95 and another of 146 pages selling for $15.95. So it's anyone's guess how your book will be priced. The following is from the publisher's pricing chart:

Number of pages	Retail price
120 or less	$10.95–$13.95
180	$13.95–$16.95
240	$15.95–$19.95
300	$17.95–$21.95
360	$20.95–$23.95
420	$22.95–$26.95

PRICE AUTHOR PAYS FOR BOOKS: Authors may purchase their first 30 books at a 45% discount, and after that books are priced on a sliding-scale discount with a 30% discount for 1–5 paperback books, 40% discount for 20–99, 45% for 100–249, and so on. iUniverse also sets the retail price for all of its books on a sliding scale, so a 200-page book will retail somewhere between $15.95 and $19.95. Here's what the math looks like:

$17.95   retail price
– $5.39   30% author discount
_____

$12.56   author price per book

Here's another way to look at it:

$17.95   retail price
– $3.90   printing cost
– $5.39   30% author discount
_____

$8.66   iUniverse profit

When I asked why the cost of books was so high, considering the substantial fees authors pay to get their books in print and the low royalty, an iUniverse representative provided this response:

> As your publisher, we provide you with an ISBN and bar coding, list your book in Bowker's Books In Print, make sure your book appears on numerous Web sites and available for order from brick and mortar [sic] bookstores, distributors and wholesalers. We maintain your file at the printer and assume the cost of printing.

This answer is otherwise known as dodging the question. Some might even call it bull.

ROYALTIES PAID TO AUTHOR: iUniverse pays 20% of the sales price for print books and 50% of the sales price for e-books, provided the sales are made through iUniverse. Otherwise, for books not sold through iUniverse, royalties equal 20% of the retail price less the wholesale discount. Here's how that math works out on a 200-page paperback sold on iUniverse's website:

$17.95   retail price
x .20   author royalty percentage
———
$3.59   author royalty

Here's the math on that same 200-page book sold through Amazon:

$17.95   retail price
– $6.46   Amazon.com discount (36% at iUniverse)
———
$11.49   net profit
x .20
———
$2.30   author royalty

You already know that it costs $3.90 to print this book, so in this scenario, iUniverse makes a royalty of $5.29 per book.

A royalty of 20%, no matter where books are sold, is low by self-publishing standards. When you do the math, you should wonder why you pay them to publish your book and they end up making more on each sale than you do.

Note: iUniverse says that it gives all wholesalers a discount of 36%, which is lower, at least in the case of Amazon.com, than the standard 50%. This could mean that Amazon.com will not offer discounts (which come out of its profit) or engage in other activities to help sell your book. Also, iUniverse's schedule A addendum to its contract says that authors make 25% royalty on books sold through Barnes & Noble due to an exclusive partnership between the publisher and bookseller.

NOTABLE PROVISIONS OF THE PUBLISHING AGREE-MENT: The contract for each program can be found at http://www.iuniverse.com/packages/contracts.htm. With the exception of schedule A, the contracts and the paragraph numbers discussed below are the same regardless of the program.

Paragraph 2, "License to Publish," gives iUniverse nonexclusive print rights in English for three years from the book's release date (paragraph 5, "Term"). However, the author can cancel anytime during the term by giving 30 days notice. If the author does not give 30 days notice, the contract automatically renews for 30 days. This paragraph also gives the author the right to purchase the text and cover digital production files of their work in a PDF file (paragraph 6, "Author Cancellation").

Paragraph 11 allows the publisher 90 to 180 days to release your book.

Paragraph 12 gives the publisher total control over price, appearance of your book, and more. Prices for books can be found at http://www.iuniverse.com/how-we-work/pricing-royalties/book-pricing.htm, but as already mentioned, a book of 180–240 pages prices at $15.95–$19.95. What will the general public pay for a book by an unknown writer?

Paragraphs 19 and 20 cover author warranties and indemnifications, which are reasonable and standard.

Paragraph 21 explains the manner in which the author or publisher must give notice to terminate the agreement. These requirements must be precisely followed for the termination to be effective and valid.

Paragraph 23 used to prohibit the author from commencing a copyright infringement suit without the publisher's permission and gave the publisher the exclusive right to commence a lawsuit on your behalf. If you failed to participate monetarily in the case and iUniverse later received a monetary award from the defendant, the author had no right to a share in the proceeds.

Once I pointed out this unfair arrangement to iUniverse, it quickly redrafted this section with the following language, which is now a standard part of the contract:

If during the term of this Agreement the copyright in the work is infringed, author hereby authorizes publisher, at publisher's sole expense, to commence an action for copyright infringement in author's name. Any recoveries from such litigation shall be applied first to reimburse publisher for its expenses incurred in such litigation and thereafter any remaining balance shall be divided equally between publisher and author. Publisher shall have no liability to author if publisher elects, in its sole discretion, not to commence such an action. If publisher does not bring such an action, author may do so at author's sole expense. Any recoveries from such litigation shall be applied first to reimburse author for author's expenses incurred in such litigation and thereafter any remaining balance shall be divided equally between author and publisher.

Paragraph 24 is stuffed with legalese, but don't be intimidated. If a legal dispute arises, such as an issue over contract interpretation, the statues and case laws of New York will be used to interpret the provisions. It also prohibits the author from assigning rights in the contract to anyone else without the publisher's consent. For example, if you decide to incorporate a business, you must first obtain the publisher's permission before assigning the contract rights to your new corporation.

Paragraph 24 also addresses circumstances in which specific portions of the contract are judicially determined to be illegal or unenforceable. In such cases, the contract itself won't be invalidated or terminated. Rather, the problematic portion will either be deleted or modified to conform to the law.

The second to last sentence in paragraph 24 says that any promises or representations made to the author prior to signing the agreement are unenforceable if they are not mentioned in the agreement. If the written contract doesn't resemble the oral agreements you made, don't sign it. Once you've signed the agreement, the only way to alter it is in writing, or it doesn't count. An oral agreement that you and iUniverse made before or during the term of the contract is invalid unless it's memorialized in writing. This is not a negative. All agreements should be in writing.

In schedule A, found at the end of the contract, you'll want to note the following:

1. Section 1, "Royalties," outlines royalties for paperback and hardcover books, stating that on books sold through Barnes & Noble, the author will receive 25% of the sales the publisher receives from the book, less taxes, shipping charges, and returns. For all other books, the publisher will pay 20% of net sales, less any taxes, shipping charges, and returns. E-books garner 50% of the net sale, less distribution and technology fees, taxes, and returns. I would ask the publisher to define "technology fees" as it could be a way to whittle away at your e-book profit.

2. Section 4, "Free Copies," states that the author will receive a certain number of free copies of her book, as specified by the publishing package.

3. Section 6, "Title Maintenance," says the author agrees to pay an annual fee to maintain the book title, which is posted on the website. The fee is subject to change but will never exceed $25.

4. Section 7, "Production Files," states that the author has the right to purchase the text and cover digital production files of the work in PDF format upon the effective date of termination of the contract. The fee is based on when you terminate. At 18 months or later, you'll pay $150 each for the interior and cover art files; terminate any earlier and you'll pay a whopping $750 each. As I outlined previously, this is patently unfair and a strong reason for not doing business with iUniverse.

AUTHOR-FRIENDLY RATING: iUniverse is the 900-pound gorilla of self-publishing. In the last edition of this book, iUniverse was rated an "Outstanding" publisher. Oh, what a difference an edition makes. All the strides toward author-friendliness were wiped away when the publisher started charging authors the outrageous fee of $1,500 for a PDF of their digital interior and cover files.

Add in one of the lowest royalties in the business and high printing markups, and there isn't much left to do but shake your head. Plus, when asked about these issues, the response was nothing more than doublespeak.

If all of this wasn't bad enough, iUniverse was purchased by AuthorHouse. Talk about your Evil Empires.

I was disappointed when I discovered how far iUniverse has back-peddled into the murky swamp of self-publishing companies to be avoided.

LITERARY ARCHITECTS
http://www.literaryarchitects.com

FORMAT OF BOOKS: e-book, hardcover and paperback

GENRES: The Literary Architects website does not state a preference as to what genre it publishes, but all 10 of the books currently available on its website are nonfiction. As a "hybrid" of self- and traditional-style publishing, Literary Architects claims to be selective in accepting book projects and was quoted in Publisher's Weekly as saying that it only accepts 25% of submissions. Literary Architects books are printed and shipped through BookSurge.

PUBLISHING FEES: Literary Architects does not provide package details on its website. Instead, the publisher customizes its packages based on the author's book. Therefore, the author must submit his or her book before learning anything about the publisher's fee structure or contract. Nonetheless, the Literary Architects FAQ page indicates that its offering includes:

- Consultation: A Literary Architects agent reads the author's book and then partners with the author to come up with a publishing plan for the book.
- Editing: Books receive a developmental edit (organization, structure, clarity, salability), a copyedit (spelling, grammar, syntax), and a proofread (consistency within the layout and design).
- Custom cover
- Listing with online booksellers: Amazon.com, BarnesandNoble.com, BooksAMillion.com and other online bookstores. Amazon.com orders ship within 24 hours. Books are also sold through the publisher's website.
- Marketing campaign: Includes a publicist, targeted mailings (print and e-mail), e-mail buzz campaigns, blog marketing, press release mailings, distribution through specialist retail channels, library promotion, posters, postcards, bookmarks, flyers, letters to targeted professionals, a customized website for the book, and targeted podcasts.

Here is a sample of a customized website: http://www .thefaithequation.com.

RETURN OF DIGITAL COVER AND INTERIOR FILES: The publisher declined to furnish any detail regarding the publishing services without a book submission.

RETAIL PRICE OF AUTHOR'S BOOK: Here's what Literary Architects says about its pricing:

Unlike most self-publishers, we do not base your book's price solely on its page count or our cost for printing the book. We will not price your book based simply on a formula that calculates the unit cost, the royalty we pay you, and then adds a guaranteed profit for ourselves. This means we will never price your book at $35 when comparable books in your market are selling for $12.95.

In keeping with this non-formulaic approach, book pricing on the publisher's website appears to vary, with books ranging from $14.95 for a 16-page children's book to $18.00 for a 208-page how-to golfing book and $15.95 for a 300-page autobiography.

PRICE AUTHOR PAYS FOR BOOKS: Literary Architects gives authors a 50% discount off the retail price of the book. So if you published a 208-page, 6" x 9" paperback book, your prices would look like this:

$18.00	retail price
– $9.00	50% author discount
$9.00	author price per book
– $4.02	printing cost
$4.98	approximate Literary Architects profit

ROYALTIES PAID TO AUTHOR: Unfortunately, the publisher declined to provide this information without a book submission.

NOTABLE PROVISIONS OF THE PUBLISHING AGREE- MENT: The publisher declined to provide us with a sample copy of its agreement.

AUTHOR-FRIENDLY RATING: My researcher sent the publisher an e-mail with a book of poetry attached and received this reply from co-founder Renee Wilmeth: "Sorry, we do not publish any poetry." My researcher returned Ms. Wilmeth's e-mail, asking if the publisher could supply some basic information, such as what genre of books the company does publish, publishing fees, etc., so that she could take that information back to her (fictional) writing group and received no reply whatsoever.

A second query sent under my researcher's actual name garnered the following response:

While we are a hybrid publisher, we require titles to be submitted with a proposal and manuscript as a traditional publisher does including detailed information on the author platform. We do have a price sheet for participation fees or royalty data. If we accepted a project for publication, we proceed through a fairly detailed proposal process with the author which includes assessing a number of risk factors and market potentials which all affect what portion of the risk the author shoulders.

The author contract is the last part of the process and we do not release our contracts or terms to the public. (Nor do we allow our authors to. You'll find this is fairly standard procedure for publishers unlike print on demand printers or author services firms.)

I'm assuming that she meant to write "we do not have a price sheet for participation fees or royalty data," otherwise the sentence does not make sense, and furthermore, she didn't forward a price sheet.

The two founders, Bryan Gambrel and Renee Wilmeth, have 28-years' experience in the publishing industry between them, which bodes well. They seem to hold every position in the company too, so that makes me think they are a pretty small company. That may be the reason for the terse e-mails and a small book list. The latter can also be attributed to the company's selectivity.

If a company is open and up-front about its process, pricing, and contract terms, why not make a sample contract available to anyone? Why not discuss the process or fees? I'm sure this company is honest in its dealings, but I always advocate running from any company that doesn't provide publishing information before it gets your book. I practically begged for information—should any author really have to?

PAGEFREE PUBLISHING, INC.

http://www.pagefreepublishing.com

FORMAT OF BOOK: e-books, paperbacks and hardcover

GENRES ACCEPTED: all

PUBLISHING FEES: There are several pricing options for paperback and hardcover books. This review only covers paperback fees.

Basic Paperback Package: The pricing for this package is based on word count:

Number of words	Package price
Up to 70,000	$399
70,000–120,000	$459
120,000–150,000	$519

This package includes:
- Customized, full-color cover, using stock or author-provided art
- ISBN
- Bar code
- Library of Congress Control Number (LCCN)
- Choice of eight trim sizes
- Template-based interior; custom interior for $50
- Basic edit (This is truly basic. The company runs the equivalent of a spell-check on the manuscript.)
- Five graphic elements; additional images, drawings, graphs, etc., for $5 each
- Ten line corrections with electronic proof; additional corrections for $2 each, plus $20 for a new proof
- Paper proof for $50
- One copy of the book
- Distribution through Ingram
- Listing with online booksellers, such as Amazon.com and the publisher's online store (http://www.thegreatamericanbookstore.com)

· R.R. Bowker's Books In Print registration
· Option to make the book available as an e-book for an additional $25

Paperback for Bookstore Package: The pricing for this package is based on word count:

Number of words	Package price
Up to 70,000	$1799
70,000–120,000	$1949
120,000–150,000	$2099

This package includes everything in the Basic Paperback Package, plus:

· Fifty total corrections
· 10% discount on the In-Depth Edit, which includes story analysis, suggestions to eliminate run-ons, unnecessary words, and variance in tense; although it does not say so, one would expect it also includes spelling, grammar, and punctuation
· Advertisement in Ingram's Advance Catalog
· Returnability program: Books will be returnable through Ingram
· Ten total copies of the book
· Marketing Plan, which includes:
· E-book
· Press release
· Trade Distribution Acceptance Program: This program is undefined on the website.
· Mailing to 3,700 bookstores (mailing of what?)
· Half-hour marketing consultation

The Publisher 99 Package: The pricing for this package is based on word count:

Number of words	Package price
Up to 70,000	$4,599
70,000–120,000	$5,299
120,000–150,000	$5,999

This package includes everything in the Basic Paperback and Paperback for Bookstore plans, plus:

- 99% royalties (see details in royalty section of this review)
- Your own publishing company imprint (it's unclear what this means. A query to the publisher was returned with little additional info (we are able to offer you the ability to create your own imprint and, if you like, you can use a colophon/logo. "We would have no problem creating a simple logo for you.")
- Book available in paperback, hardcover, and e-book; a three bindings use the same trim size, text, and cover design
- Custom interior
- Fifty total interior graphics
- One-year archival
- Ten paperback copies or four hardcover copies
- Press release written by PageFree staff
- Premier presentation in Hidden Treasure Books Marketing Program: It's unclear what this program really entails. The website only lists inclusion in a CD catalog and having your book "discussed and promoted in detail…to booksellers and media." When I asked the representative what this program included, she said via e-mail:

We act as a publicist on behalf of your book. We contact bookstores whose customer demographic matches that of your ideal reader. If you desire, we can work to set up book signings for you. We do Internet marketing and when a book is stocked, we send a press release to local media for the purpose of bringing in traffic to that location. We also investigate corporate opportunities for a bulk purchase, when appropriate. In addition to bookstores, we contact non-bookstore related retailers whose customers match your ideal reader.

OTHER SERVICES OF INTEREST:

Marketing services: PageFree partners with sister company Hidden Treasure to provide marketing services, but the latter's website is poorly organized and its services ill-defined; Make sure that, if you contract Hidden Treausre's services, you get a clear definition of what it is going to do for you.

In-Depth edit: Includes story analysis, suggestions to eliminate run-ons, unnecessary words, and variance in tense. Although it does not say so, one would expect it also includes spelling, grammar, and punctuation. This service is $.015 per word.

Returns: Your book will be returnable through Ingram. The fee covers the cost of returns, and so returned books are not deducted from future royalties. This service is $500 annually for paperback books and $1,299 hardcover books.

RETURN OF DIGITAL COVER AND INTERIOR FILES: According to the PageFree author agreement, "any and all art or electric files created in part or whole by Publisher remains the property of the Publisher and may not be used by author without the express written consent of publisher."

However, if you purchase the Publisher 99 Package, the files will be given to you at no additional charge. Otherwise, according to the PageFree representative, the files may be purchased for the original setup fee of whichever package you choose. So if you go with the basic package, you will pay $459 to have the files created and then another $459 if you actually want to take the digital files with you. Why should you have to pay the same amount to get the files you've already paid to have created? They are of no use to the publisher. This is simply a way for the publisher to make money from departing authors. If I was signing a contract with PageFree, I'd try to negotiate something that would give me the original production files upon termination.

RETAIL PRICE OF AUTHOR'S BOOK: The author determines the retail price of the book and the wholesale discount. Although this seems like a flexible plan, the practical aspects make it not so (for details, see the royalty section of this review).

PRICE AUTHOR PAYS FOR BOOKS: PageFree's author book price is based on the page count. The publisher provides the following equation: $.025 per page + $1.90 cover. So for a 200-page book: $.025 x 200 + $1.90 = $6.90. That's less expensive than some publishers, but it's still a $3.00 markup from the actual $3.90 it costs to print this book.

ROYALTIES PAID TO AUTHOR: PageFree pays authors 75% of the net profit per book sold. "Net Profit" is defined as: Retail price – Wholesale discount – Printing cost = Net profit.

The publisher's schedule allows the author to calculate the cost of printing the book in the various formats, using the following formula: $.018 per page + $1.20 cover fee. So for a 200-page book, the printing cost is: 200 x $.018 + $1.20 = $4.80 (even though the actual cost to print this book is $3.90).

Typically, Amazon.com and other online retailers take at least a 50% discount, although a PageFree representative asserted that Amazon would be happy with a 40% discount. On its website, PageFree says: "note on discounts: The wholesale discount may be determined by the author. The discount is extended to Ingram as distributor and Ingram shares that discount to the bookstores. Thus, a 55% discount will result in a 40% to the store itself."

By setting the trade discount at 55%, an author would have to retail a 200-page book for $17.00 to make any money from a sale via Amazon.com.

$17.00	retail price
– $4.80	printing cost
– $9.35	55% Amazon.com discount
$2.85	net profit
x .75	author royalty percentage
$2.14	author royalty

Note that in this calculation, PageFree is reporting printing costs per book at $.90 higher than they actually are. So PageFree is making $1.61 per book sold.

The Amazon.com (third-party retailer) scenario isn't terrible since there is no getting around the third-party trade discount. So you'd think that for sales from the PageFree site, that huge trade discount wouldn't be an issue. But PageFree Publishing gives itself a trade discount for books sold on its website. The publisher's explanation for taking the same discount is that "any books we order for fulfillment are sold to us at a higher price than those ordered by Ingram to fulfill bookstore orders. We are also charged an additional handling fee, as well as our own administrative/credit card costs."

This is a lie. Publishers don't pay more for books that they fulfill. Yes, there may be some shipping fees to the publisher from the printer and the administrative costs of handling credit card transactions, but that's it. In fact, the publisher is at the most paying $.015 per page and $.90 per cover (for a paperback with black-and-white interior). Taking the same discount as Amazon.com is a shady practice because it misleads authors into thinking that with a 75% royalty they will take the lion's share of the profits, while in fact, PageFree makes more money on books sold from its website than the authors do.

This is not standard practice; I know of only one other publishing company that gives itself a trade discount. Here's what authors make on a book sold on the PageFree website:

$17.00	retail price
– $4.80	printing costs
– $9.35	55% PageFree discount

$2.85	net profit
x .75	author royalty percentage

$2.14	author royalty

PageFree is making an astonishing $10.96 for each of an author's books it sells (under this scenario). That is more than five times what the author makes. Guess who actually makes 75% of the profits?

PageFree is triple-dipping into the profits, marking up the cost of printing, and taking a wholesale discount and a royalty.

Note: There is an option wherein the author can pay an additional $400 publishing fee and take 99% of the royalty. However, that will only add about $.67 to the royalty. In order for the extra fees to pay off, the author would need to sell 598 additional books.

NOTABLE PROVISIONS OF THE PUBLISHING AGREE-MENT: The publishing agreement is at http://pagefreepublishing .com/PDFgallery.htm.

The first paragraph grants PageFree a nonexclusive license to sell the book in print or electronic formats during the term.

In the third paragraph under "Other Materials," the contract states that while the author owns the content of the book, all files created in part or in whole by the publisher belong to the publisher and cannot be used without written permission from the publisher. This means that if you decide to publish your book elsewhere, you will either need to negotiate to take the production files from the publisher at an additional fee equal to the price of your publishing package, or you will have to start from scratch and pay for the cover art and layout a second time.

In the middle of the third paragraph under "Accounting," the author can terminate the agreement at any time with 30 days written notice. The fourth paragraph under "Accounting" specifies Kalamazoo County, Michigan, or the federal court in the Western District of Michigan as the venue for any legal dispute.

AUTHOR-FRIENDLY RATING: What this publisher does by giving itself a trade discount, plus marking up the printing, and then taking a royalty to boot, is one of the worst things a self-publishing company can do to an author.

When you add to that the fact that the only way to get your original production files (which you will eventually want to do when you realize how much money you're losing here) is to buy them for what you paid to have them produced, I can't even think of one reason I'd consider using PageFree. While the publisher's representatives were very responsive to my queries and the royalty scenario for third-party sales isn't bad, everything else about this publisher's offering is terrible. From almost every angle, this is a bad deal.

PLEASANT WORD
http://www.pleasantword.com

FORMAT OF BOOKS: paperback or hardcover

GENRES: Only publishes Christian authors whose books do not contain objectionable material, such as unbiblical theology, challenges to the deity of Jesus Christ, offensive language, and indecent scenes.

PUBLISHING FEES: This publisher offers four packages. Complete details and a comparison of the packages are at http://www.pleasantword.com/default.asp?id=7959.

White Ribbon Package: This package costs $799 and is for authors who want their book published without marketing or distribution services and, therefore, does not include royalties. It includes:

- ISBN
- Bar code
- U.S. Copyright Office registration
- Library of Congress Control Number (LCCN)
- Interior formatting, choice of six trim sizes, and choice of four cover templates; includes one hour of design time

Yellow Ribbon Package: This package is $999 and includes every service in the White Ribbon Package, plus:

- Listing with online booksellers: Amazon.com and BarnesandNoble.com
- Distribution through Baker & Taylor (or a comparable company) so that your book is potentially available to 25,000 bookstores and libraries
- Ten free copies of the book
- Choice of 10 cover templates
- A website on Pleasant Word's website; for an example, see https://www.pleasantwordbooks.com/product.asp?pid=1323&search=&select=&ss=1.

Red Ribbon Package: This package costs $1,499 plus editing fees and includes every service in the Yellow Ribbon Package, plus:

- Customized cover: Authors have access to a tool that allows them to select fonts, colors, and more. A designer takes author's stock choices and creates a "custom" cover. Includes minimal photo editing and placement by a professional designer, three hours design time (additional time is $50 per hour plus an unspecified fee), and one initial design.
- Edit: Authors who choose this package are required to pay

for their manuscripts to be edited for an extra fee. Includes a choice of copyedit (grammar, spelling, syntax and punctuation at $4.50 a page) or a pre-typeset read (spelling and typos at $.50 a page). All Red Ribbon authors must pay for proofreading in addition to the copyediting after the manuscript is typeset, and the fee is $3.00 a page. Pleasant Word calculates 250 words a page if the author doesn't know the finished page count. This essentially means the author is required to pay $4.00–$7.50 a page for editing, which means that, for example, copyediting and proofreading a 200-page manuscript would add $800 to $1,500 to the cost of this package.

- Option to purchase marketing programs
- Fifteen copies of the book
- Listing on Pleasantwordbooks.com

Blue Ribbon Package: This package is priced at $1,999 plus editing fees and includes every service in the Red Ribbon Package, plus:

- Thirty copies of the book
- Custom cover, including five hours design time and two cover designs
- E-mail announcement to the publisher's trade list of 1,000 Christian bookstores
- Promotion at the Christian Booksellers Association convention
- Copyediting and proofreading are required at a total fee of $7.50 a page, which (as outlined in the Red Ribbon Package), will add $1,500 to the fee to publish a 200-page paperback
- Authors can purchase copies of their books for 62% off the suggested retail price (minimum order is 5 copies)

OTHER SERVICES OF INTEREST: Pleasant Word offers a variety of marketing and publicity packages, which can be found at http://www.pleasantword.com/default.asp?id=9681. The prices are not listed and appear to change with the package, but I was quoted $895 for the Start-Up Package as applied to the Red Ribbon Package, which includes:

- Press release written by a Pleasant Word publicist and distributed via a "national newswire," which means it's just e-mailed out to a list of some kind
- A "one sheet," which is a four-color sheet including author biography, book recap, and interview questions
- Five press kits, including the one sheet, press release, and a catalog
- A one-time listing in the Pleasant Word catalog
- Requirement for author to buy five books as review copies
- Requirement for author to purchase a back cover rewrite for $175

RETURN OF DIGITAL COVER AND INTERIOR FILES: Pleasant Word will not supply authors with their production files. However, in the first 90 days after the book is produced, authors are eligible to receive a PDF of their book as printed. After 90 days, the author will have to pay a fee for the files. When asked why that might be, a representative for the company answered:

You can get the PDF for free for up to 90 days (chances are, though, that you will not need it, as we already send you a PDF of the final version anyway) and you can get it after that, but then there is a fee because we'll have to "unarchive" it.

Seriously, "unarchive" it? Is it stored in Fort Knox or on a hard drive someplace? But, whatever. Get the PDF within the first 90 days while you still can.

RETAIL PRICE OF AUTHOR'S BOOK: Pleasant Word's retail prices are based on the page count, trim size, and cover of the book. A full discussion and examples of retail prices are available at http://www.pleasantword.com/default.asp?id=8316. A 200-page paperback will retail for $17.99 unless it is 8.25" x 11," and then it will retail for $19.99. This is way too high. A book that size should retail between $12.00 and $14.95. The high retail price means that the printing costs are greatly inflated.

PRICE AUTHOR PAYS FOR BOOKS: Author discounts are based on the retail price and vary from package to package:

Package	Author discount
White	50%
Yellow	58%
Red	60%
Blue	62%

If you publish a 200-page, 6" x 9" paperback under the Yellow Ribbon Package, your prices would look like this:

$17.99	retail price
– $10.43	58% author discount
$7.56	author price per book
– $3.90	printing cost
$3.66	Pleasant Word profit

Pleasant Word makes nearly a 100% markup!

ROYALTIES PAID TO AUTHOR: For details on retail pricing, handling fees, and bookseller discounts, refer to http://www.pleasantword.com/default.asp?id=8288).

Pleasant Word claims to pay the author 100% of the net profit. The publisher defines net profit as the retail sale price less the bookseller's discount, the author's discounted price (a.k.a., actual printing cost plus markup, disguised as actual print cost), and the handling fee of $1.95 per book sold on Pleasantword.com.

For the $17.99, 200-page, Yellow Ribbon, paperback book, the author makes the following for a book sold on Amazon.com:

$17.99	retail price
– $7.56	author price per book
– $9.90	55% Amazon.com discount
$.53	author royalty

That's a puny royalty, considering Pleasant Word is making $3.66 (the printing markup) on each sale, which is more than seven times what the author makes!

For the same book sold on Pleasantword.com, the author makes:

$17.99   retail price
– $7.56   author price per book
– $1.9   handling fee
———————————
$8.48   author royalty

Again, although Pleasant Word claims the author is making 100% of profits, it isn't true. The author makes 100% of the profits after Pleasant Word nearly doubles the printing price and adds a handling fee. The handling fee is acceptable. While I would never agree to a 100% printing markup, as long as the publisher discloses it and you can live with it, the royalty under this scenario is fine. Just keep in mind that for every book sold by an author, Pleasant Word is making $5.61.

Pleasant Word allows authors to give readers a 27% discount on books sold on its website, which may result in higher sales, but will also decrease the author's royalty per book.

$17.99   retail price
– $7.56   author price per book
– $4.90   reader's discount
– $1.95   handling fee
———————————
$3.58   author royalty

Note that Pleasant Word makes $5.61 on this sale too.

The 27% discount is a great feature and helps a slightly overpriced book get to a better retail price, but only for sales on the publisher's site. The author can take the 200-page book that retails for $17.99 and sell it for up to $13.09. But even with that discount, the publisher is still making more than the author is for each sale.

NOTABLE PROVISIONS OF THE PUBLISHING AGREEMENT: The publishing agreement can be found at http://pleasantword.com/default.asp?id=8211.

"Author Right to Ownership" grants to the publisher a nonexclusive right to print and publish the work. The author can sell and distribute the book while the contract is in effect and can also terminate the contract at any time. While the author owns the book and the cover concept, the publisher owns the print-ready cover and interior files:

Author has the right to make copies of the cover (front and back) for purposes including, but not limited to, advertising and promotional material. Author will be supplied, upon request, with PDF files of the final published version of the Work (including cover) within 90 days of publication. Author requests for files after 90 days will incur a fee for archive retrieval.

So while you're paying for these things to be created, you don't actually own any of them. If you decide to publish elsewhere at a later time, you will need to pay someone to recreate the interior and the cover.

"Copyright, ISBN / Library of Congress" states that the publisher will procure an ISBN, register the copyright in your name, and obtain an LCCN. These add-on services are a nice perk because the services alone are worth around $100.

"Publisher's Rights" outlines offensive materials that the publisher will not publish, such as books that promote the Word of Faith or Prosperity doctrine, the Brownsville/Toronto "revival," and women pastors in leadership over men. If an author submits other material, such as unbiblical theology, challenges to the deity of Jesus Christ, offensive language, indecent scenes, or suggestive dialogue, the publisher will allow the Author to modify the material. If the author refuses to change the objectionable material, the agreement will effectively be cancelled, and the publishing fees will be refunded, with the exception of all fees and costs incurred up to that point and a 10% cancellation fee.

"Term and Termination" allows three years for the publisher's non-exclusive license, although either party may terminate the contract with 30 days written notice.

"Dispute Resolution" requires parties to resolve disputes through arbitration in King County, Washington. If both parties agree, they may mediate instead of arbitrate a dispute.

AUTHOR-FRIENDLY RATING: I hold publishers who cloak their services around religion to a higher standard because many authors rely on such affiliations when deciding to trust a publisher, and that fact alone may deter authors from questioning a publisher's fees. Pleasant Word's "Why Publish With Us" webpage (http://pleasantword.com /default.asp?id=7952) lists these two points:

> *3. Pleasant Word is a Christian company in every sense of the word. Every part of what we do is focused on bringing glory to God first and foremost.*

Every employee of Pleasant Word is a committed Christian, so you can be sure we will serve you both professionally and spiritually.

4. As Christians and professionals, we have a responsibility to be honest and realistic. Our acquisitions editors don't work on commission. They'll be happy to answer any questions you have, and they won't give you false expectations or compromise on Christian values just to make a sale.

I believe it's a compromise of Christian values (and just about every other moral value I can think of) when a publisher leads authors to believe that its printing costs are 100% higher than they actually are. The "author's discounted price," can easily lead an author to believe that somehow this is the actual printing cost or close to it.

The packages aren't bad for what you get, but authors should skip over the packages that don't include a customized cover design—for $999 spent with Pleasant Word, the author only receives a template cover. An author whose book targets the Christian market may want to consider the Red Ribbon Package because it receives appropriate promotion in the Christian venues, but it still costs way too much.

The author royalties on third-party sales, such as those on Amazon.com, are horrible. In the example discussed in this review, the author makes $.53 per sale while Pleasant Word makes $3.66 through the extra padding it adds to the printing costs. The royalties for sales on the Pleasant Word website are better, but only in comparison to the royalties paid on third-party sales.

Although the contract is reasonable, authors should question the publisher's "objectionable material" clause; its language is broad and may allow the publisher to indiscriminately collect another $200 for work it deems "objectionable."

The only way to get a sample contract and learn more about the fee is to sign up for information. This is also misleading because the link tells you that you are only going through the "initial steps" of signing up for service, but in fact you have to give them your social security number and choose your service package and add-ons to get to the contract, at the bottom of which there is a link to payment. Should you want to get information, do not provide your real social security number. That's crazy.

When a publisher chooses to make religion a central focus of its service and writes copy that suggests that due to strong Christian principles authors "know they can trust us," the publisher has a duty to be over-the-top honest. Being less than forthright about the real printing costs, while advertising how honest and Christian it is, instantly makes Pleasant Word a publisher to avoid. Enough said. There are plenty of honest Christian publishers. Find one. Until this publisher actually practices what it preaches, you will be wise to avoid them. There are simply no pleasant words to describe the business practices of this publisher (I couldn't resist that pun).

PUBLISHAMERICA
http://www.publishamerica.com

FORMAT OF BOOKS: paperback

GENRES ACCEPTED: Fiction and nonfiction works about, for, or by people who are confronted with challenges, real or imagined, and are determined to overcome them.

Since most books deal with overcoming challenges, at some level, PublishAmerica considers most fiction and nonfiction, although it will not print theses, coffee table books, screenplays, textbooks, or books of quotations.

PUBLISHING FEES: PublishAmerica claims to operate like a traditional publisher and that, therefore, there are no publishing fees. However, the publisher's contract terms are so outrageous that, with the exception of not charging up-front fees, it really has little in common with traditional publishing.

According to the publisher's website and contract, the publishing package includes:
- Professionally designed cover and interior layout (it's unclear how much design time, how many designs, and what kind of art is included in the design)
- Professional edit, the scope of which is determined upon the editor's assessment of how much editing is needed
- ISBN
- Bar code
- Two complimentary copies of the book
- Assistance with marketing efforts for a direct-mail campaign

that, according to the PublishAmerica website, goes out to your friends, family, and undefined fans
· Distribution through Ingram, Baker & Taylor, and Brodart
· Listing with online booksellers: Amazon.com, BarnesandNoble.com and others
· Returns: PublishAmerica loosely claims that it returns "many books," but when the author who supplied me with the contract sent a query to the acquisitions editor asking: (1) how the publisher determines if a book will be returnable, (2) if returns would come out of her royalty (which is standard practice among self-publishers), and (3) what discounts booksellers get on returnable books (Internet rumor has it at 5%), this is the answer she received: "Our book is returnable only through Ingrams [sic] who deals with retailers." Basically, no answer.

RETAIL PRICE OF AUTHOR'S BOOK: The PublishAmerica website does not list the publisher's retail prices, but based on its online bookstore, a 200-page, paperback book would retail for $19.95, which is about $6 more than industry standard and quite expensive for a paperback by an unknown author.

PRICE AUTHOR PAYS FOR BOOKS: PublishAmerica extends its authors a 20% discount on purchases of 20 or fewer books and 30% on 21 or more books. Here's what that discount would look like on a 200-page, paperback book:

$19.95   retail price
– $3.99   20% author discount
_____

$15.96   author price per book

Since we know it costs $3.90 to print the book, this means PublishAmerica makes $12.06 every time you purchase a book, which is outrageous. One hundred books would cost you $1,397 which is close to or more than what you would pay at many self-publishers—meaning that you could take that money and spend it on another publishing firm that will give you a fair contract and a decent royalty.

ROYALTIES PAID TO AUTHOR: PublishAmerica's royalties are based on the number of copies sold:

Number of books sold	Author royalty percentage
Up to 2,000	8%
2,001–8,000	10%
10,000+	12.5%

It's unclear from the publisher's contract whether royalties are based on the book's wholesale or retail price, but an author's query to one of PublishAmerica's acquisitions editors resolved that it is based on the payment the publisher receives. For a book sold on PublishAmerica .com, the author makes:

$19.95   retail price
x .08   author royalty percentage
———————
$1.60   author royalty

In the meantime, PublishAmerica makes:

$19.95   retail price
– $1.60   8% author royalty
– $3.90   printing cost
———————
$14.45   PublishAmerica profit

For books sold through third-party retailers like Amazon.com, the author makes the same royalty, but PublishAmerica makes less than it does through sales on its own site.

The acquisitions editor would not tell me what the booksellers' discount is, but the PublishAmerica FAQ shows a 40% discount for Amazon.com:

$19.95   retail price
– $7.98   40% Amazon.com discount
– $1.60   author royalty
– $3.90   printing cost
———————
$6.47   PublishAmerica profit

It might be acceptable for PublishAmerica to make this kind of profit off your book if it was putting a lot of money into the marketing of it, but for a poorly-edited and seldom-marketed book, this borders on highway robbery—not to mention the fact that the book is so over-priced it will have a very hard time in the marketplace.

NOTABLE PROVISIONS OF THE PUBLISHING AGREE-MENT: PublishAmerica won't provide a copy of the contract until it has accepted your manuscript, but I was lucky enough to get a copy of one that was offered to a wary author.

After reading the contract, I know why this publisher doesn't want anyone to see it. The first clue that something shady might be going on is that the only address listed for the company is a post office box.

Section 1 grants PublishAmerica exclusive rights to publish the book in all formats for seven years worldwide. This seems reasonable at first glance because the publisher fronts all printing and publishing costs, but a closer look at the contract language makes it clear what's really going on here. Authors have a three-month window of time before the end of the first seven-year period in which they can terminate the contract; otherwise another seven-year term commences. Why is the seven-year term a big deal? Well, the only way an author is going to sell books is if that author is aggressively marketing his or her book. What happens if your book takes off and a big-time publisher approaches you? You're stuck in a seven-year contract. What happens if your book takes off and you realize that by publishing on your own you can make quadruple what PublishAmerica is paying you? You're stuck in a seven-year contract.

Section 8 breaks down the division of profits for the sale of a bundle of rights that the author owns for his or her published book, such as translations, book club sales, motion picture, radio, serial, and televi-sion. Should the author allow the publisher to sell any of those rights, the author will receive only 50% of any monies earned. These are rights that are typically negotiated for between a traditional publisher and an author. Authors don't just give away 50% of these rights for the honor of having a publisher print copies of their book. Again, if the author's book takes off and third parties want to purchase these rights, the author is stuck with PublishAmerica as a partner. PublishAmerica, per section 20, doesn't own these rights to sell them, unless the author specifically gives it the rights in writing. The only way an author's book will ever end up in a situation where these additional rights are even an issue will be if that author finds the opportunity. PublishAmerica is not out aggressively selling or promoting any of its authors' books. Why should you do all the work and give them half the money for the sale of any of the rights set forth in section 8 of the contract?

The author who provided me with this contract asked to change the language of section 8 to include a clause saying that if any additional rights—those not already owned by PublishAmerica under the terms of the sample contract—were sold, the publisher and author would negotiate the division of payment at the time of sale. She was told that "the language in the contract is non-negotiable."

Section 10 sets forth the price at which authors purchase copies from the publisher. The author receives a 20% discount of the retail price (which is set by the publisher) for orders fewer than 20. For orders of more than 20, the author receives a 30% discount. This sounds good until you realize that the retail price of PublishAmerica is grossly over-inflated. For example, there is a 209-page book published by PublishAmerica that retails for $19.95. As you know already, the cost to print one copy of this book is approximately $4.05 (209 pages x $.015/page + $.90 for the cover). So if the author of this book orders 20 copies of her book, she pays $15.96 per copy, which means that PublishAmerica makes a profit of $11.91 for each book the author orders. Purchase a hundred books and you've already paid more than you would to publish with many of the companies in this book. The difference is that with most every other company you can terminate the contract at any time and are making royalties of much more than 8%.

Section 12 of the contract explains that authors get royalty statements twice each year (February and August). While one might assume authors would receive royalty checks at that time (if royalties were owed), that isn't specifically stated. The contract simply says that authors will be notified as to what royalties (if any) are owed. This could be problematic. There is nothing set forth in this contract that tells you how and when you will be paid.

When the author who provided me with this contract asked the acquisitions editor when royalty payments would be received, she was told they would arrive with the royalty statements. When she asked to have that fact added to the contract, she was told "The language in the contract is non-negotiable." Big red flag.

Section 13 of the contract covers author-requested corrections to the electronic proof copy. Here is where we get into a black hole: if the author wants changes to the proof copy and those changes cost the publisher more than 15% of the original cost to create the proof, the author is charged against his or her royalties. The problem is that, while the contract offers to provide a receipt of the cost of corrections, authors have no idea how much it costs to create the electronic proof, so one may never get a straight answer here. It's like not knowing anything about a car and going to a mechanic who tells you your brakes are shot. How do you really know? When the PublishAmerica author asked the acquisitions editor what it cost to create a proof and how corrections would be charged, she received this answer:

> *Charging the author for corrections outlined in Paragraph 13 has never happened. This is a worse [sic] case scenario that would only be the case if a page proof was returned with questionable content that was not included in the original manuscript. Although it is rare, we will contact you with details of the cost of correction at that time should the need arise.*

Section 14 allows the publisher to edit an author's book as the publisher sees fit. This section of the contract actually makes sense since technically authors assign the rights to the book to PublishAmerica for seven years.

Section 16 allows the publisher to require an author to make revisions to the work as the publisher sees fit. If you sign this contract and PublishAmerica demands rewrites, either you do them or your book doesn't get published for seven years. A clause like this is reasonable if a publisher plunks down a healthy advance and is going to spend money promoting an author's book, but that is not the case here. Section 14 covers basic editing PublishAmerica may decide to do. Section 16 comes into play if PublishAmerica decides your book needs more than simple editing, such as substantial plot changes.

Section 17 gives the publisher the right to set up a website for your book with a domain name that PublishAmerica will own. Once your affiliation with PublishAmerica has ended that website goes away, and all the time and energy you spent trying to drive people there to buy your book is for naught.

When the author who provided me with the sample contract asked if she could retain the domain name at the end of the seven-year contract, here is the reply she received: "After the seven year contract is up, we will terminate the website set up for you. You are welcome to continue the website at your own cost."

Note: The contract says that the publisher may set up a website for the author's book, but it doesn't say it will nor does it define what the website will look like anywhere on PublishAmerica.com. I performed a Google search on the authors featured in "Up in Lights" on the homepage of PublishAmerica, and while five out of 13 of them had websites, only one (http://www.survivingintimateterrorism.com) appeared to have been generated by PublishAmerica. It was a single, static page with contact links. The other websites that turned up were owned and maintained by the authors.

Section 20 is very confusing. On the one hand, it states that PublishAmerica has the exclusive rights to contract for the sale of the author's literary work in all hard, soft, and reprint editions. On the other, it states that the author agrees that PublishAmerica has the exclusive right, for the duration of the contract, to negotiate all movie, television, radio, and other rights on the author's behalf, only if so instructed by the author in writing. Further, it requires the author to approve the negotiations. It states, "Approval of all terms, provisions and conditions of any and all contracts in connection with any such sale, lease, license or other disposition shall be given by the Author...." This means the author must approve any deal PublishAmerica negotiates, but only if the author has given PublishAmerica the exclusive right to negotiate those sales in writing. Under the contract, the author isn't permitted to negotiate with a movie producer. Only PublishAmerica has that right. The author has the right to instruct PublishAmerica to negotiate with this producer and to approve whatever PublishAmerica has negotiated. There's a lot of doublespeak and dependent clauses all over this section. Furthermore, the publisher need not pay the author her portion of the sales until 90 days after the monies are received by PublishAmerica.

Section 24 allows the publisher to stop publishing an author's book at any time. PublishAmerica will then sell the author whatever inventory, sheet stock, book plates, etc., it has remaining at half the list price.

Of course, you will never know the list price of that stock unless you only buy back the actual printed copies of your book.

Section 25 gives the publisher 365 days to publish the book despite assurances on the website that your book will publish in a matter of months.

Section 28 states that all arbitration will take place in the City of Frederick, Maryland, which is standard contract language, though it does benefit the publisher and likely makes arbitration more difficult and expensive for you.

AUTHOR-FRIENDLY RATING: Performing a Google search on PublishAmerica will call up several boards with ongoing discussion and criticism of the publisher. Check out the Writers Beware website, which provides a whole page devoted to the "PublishAmerica Hoax" at http://sfwa.org/beware/general.html#PA.

It's also worthwhile to check out the Wikipedia overview of PublishAmerica at http://en.wikipedia.org/wiki/PublishAmerica, which covers both authors' complaints and recent arbitration and provides links to news coverage of the publisher. For author case studies, check out http://www.wizardessbooks.com/html/PA_stories.htm.

Even had I not read these postings, it doesn't take incredible insight to see that the books are way too expensive and the royalties are shoddy.

For the price authors pay to buy their own books, they ought to go with a good self-publisher where they will at least get the services they've contracted.

The writer who forwarded me the contract on which much of this commentary is based could not get PublishAmerica to answer any questions about its services until she forwarded a copy of her book. Even after she submitted the book and it was accepted, the PublishAmerica acquisitions editor assigned to her book would only answer questions about the contract and insisted all other questions be forwarded to customer support. The author forwarded her questions to customer support, and the very day it received them, customer support e-mailed her query back to the acquisitions editor, who then took five days to answer the questions incompletely.

Hilariously, a month or so later, the author received a letter from the PublishAmerica Acquisitions Department stating that, having received her query regarding its publishing services, it would be happy to review her manuscript if she would simply forward it—this nearly two months after the manuscript had been accepted by the same acquisitions department. Obviously, there are some internal communications issues at PublishAmerica.

The website is so poorly written and misleading that it should serve as a warning to writers who think their book will get a strong edit from PublishAmerica. Also, the website explicitly states that the editor will determine if the book needs an edit and how much of one it needs and that, not surprisingly, in the interest of getting a book into print, the publisher sometimes will forego the edit. Never forego the edit!

One of the main complaints from PublishAmerica authors is the lack of marketing, but PublishAmerica doesn't promise to market the book. In fact, the website states that the author's best option is to promote locally, and PublishAmerica expects the author to provide a list of family, friends, and fans to whom it can send direct mail soliciting book sales.

If the author manages to hustle up a book signing, PublishAmerica may not be there with the books. One man successfully sued PublishAmerica because he spent thousands of dollars on publicity for his book, only to find out that bookstores were unable to order it.

One author who contacted me hired a lawyer and spent thousands of dollars to get out of her contract. She was more than willing to provide a copy of the contract and valuable information about the way PublishAmerica treats its authors. Shocking, disgusting, and despicable are just a few of the adjectives to describe this publisher's practices.

How this company keeps chugging along is beyond me. Don't be fooled into thinking that PublishAmerica is a "traditional" publisher and that its acceptance of your book is akin to acceptance by any other traditional publisher. It's not. If you don't have the money to publish your book and PublishAmerica is your only option, save up until you can afford a better option. You'll be glad you did.

PUBLISH TO GO
http://www.publishtogo.com

FORMAT OF BOOKS: e-books and paperback

GENRES ACCEPTED: Publish To Go accepts all books, operating more as a printing or e-book preparation company than as a publisher.

PUBLISHING FEES: A complete breakdown of the publishing fees is at http://www.publishtogo.com/prices.htm.
Paperback printing services and fees are provided on a quote basis only. Publish To Go is primarily an e-book publisher that also provides a few à la carte services.

> **E-book Package:** This package costs $225 and includes:
> - ISBN
> - Bar code
> - Submission to Amazon.com and Powells.com

OTHER SERVICES OF INTEREST:

PDF formatting: If your book is not already formatted as a PDF, prices for this service start at $75 (for up to 100 pages).

ISBN: A single ISBN number for $90

Bar code: $30

Copyright submission: $110

Library of Congress Control Number (LCCN): $50

RETAIL PRICE OF AUTHOR'S BOOK: Publish To Go does not offer pricing information on its website. The only way to guess is by looking at the books themselves, which is more difficult than it sounds because the "Hot Off the Press" link is located three inches or so below the main left-hand navigation (an American flag and a link to Amazon.com are given higher priority!). Once I clicked through to the "Hot Off the Press" page, I found that half the books were available only by sending an e-mail to the publisher or the author, a few had broken links leading nowhere, one led to a resort website, and another to an author's website with no contact information. Only one was actually available for immediate purchase (a 230-page paperback). In all other cases, the description of the book offered neither a page count nor a price.

The 230-page, paperback book I found is available for purchase through either the publisher or Amazon.com. The publisher offers the book at $11.99 and claims that it can also be found on Amazon.com for $14.99. In fact, Amazon was offering the book for $10.17.

If $14.99 is the actual retail price, the pricing is not wholly unreasonable, but would a reader really go to as much trouble as I did to find and buy the book of an unknown writer?

PRICE AUTHOR PAYS FOR BOOKS: Publish To Go offers paperback printing and publishing services on a quote basis. I queried the publisher to see what it would cost to print a 200-page, 6" x 9", perfect-bound, black-and-white, paperback book, but no one responded to my e-mails, and the website does not list a contact phone number.

ROYALTIES PAID TO THE AUTHOR: Publish To Go doesn't pay royalties because it isn't a publisher per se. The author keeps all sales monies unless he or she makes the book available under another publisher, and then, according to the author agreement, the author must pay Publish To Go 1% of the retail price.

NOTABLE PROVISIONS OF THE PUBLISHING AGREEMENT: The complete contract is in the scroll-down box at http://www.publishtogo.com/orderform.htm.

"Rights" makes it clear that the author retains all rights and can publish the book in any format *elsewhere but not under another publisher.* If the author sells the book under another publisher without Publish To Go's permission he or she must give Publish To Go 1% of the retail price. This section also makes it clear that the Publisher cannot be held liable for any delays in its services.

The "Warranties" section is standard and reasonable.

"Relationship of Parties" is standard in most commercial contracts where one party provides services to another. Nothing the author does can bind the publisher and vice versa.

"Term and Termination" indicates that the contract endures until either party submits a written or e-mailed notice. The termination is effective immediately. The clause also specifies that the publisher registers the ISBN and lists itself, not the author, as the "publisher." This means that if the author publishes the book elsewhere after termination, the author must obtain a new ISBN or pay Publish To Go a royalty to use the original ISBN.

"Limitation of Liability" is formatted in all capital letters, so the author can't deny its existence. It states that the publisher isn't liable for any amount that exceeds the original publishing fee.

"General" permits the publisher to change the contract terms by a posting on its website; such new terms become effective after 30 days. The onus is on the author to periodically check the website for relevant updates. An author who disagrees with any contract changes can always terminate the contract before the 30 days expire.

AUTHOR-FRIENDLY RATING: On the services side, Publish To Go's fees for e-book publication are too high, considering that all you get is an ISBN and bar code. The only reason the author needs an ISBN is so that the publisher can list the book on Amazon.com. Also, the author must already have a cover and layout to use this company.

However, I find it more worrisome that the company seems to neglect its business and its customers. Aside from the fact that the website hasn't been updated in more than a year, and many of its links no longer work, publishtogo.com is very outdated and rather frustrating in the way it provides (or doesn't provide) information. Also, the publisher does not provide any mode of direct contact—only a P.O. Box and e-mail address—and has a clause in its contract that says it is not liable for delays in providing its services. So hypothetically speaking, you could send your money to these folks and never hear from them again. Publish To Go does not provide any pricing information for its printing services, which is pretty annoying considering everyone in the universe is able to provide some kind of ballpark pricing at the very least. And the company did not respond to my query e-mails. If this is your only publishing option, don't publish your book.

SIRIUS PUBLICATIONS
http://sirius-books.com

FORMAT OF BOOK: e-book and paperback

GENRES ACCEPTED: Sirius accepts fiction (especially romance), nonfiction (especially how-to, writer's reference books, and self-help), short stories (5,000–50,000 words, especially science fiction). Sirius claims to only accept 20% of submissions and will not publish porn or religious material.

However, the submission page at http://sirius-books.com/ssubmissions.html states that Sirius Publications is only interested in previously published books or unpublished short story collections. It also states that, in late 2002 (this is not a typo), it will open submissions to unpublished, book-length manuscripts, which means the submissions page hasn't been updated in more than five years. As of October 2007, the site still says its bookstore will be closed from June 2–10, 2007. This company seriously neglects its website.

PUBLISHING FEES: The prices are: $0 for e-books, $199 for paperback, and $500 for paperback and e-book combined. All packages include:

- Basic editing
- Template cover
- Template interior layout
- ISBN
- One trim size: 5.5" x 8.5"
- An additional fee of $25 per year for hosting fee for all books

OTHER SERVICES OF INTEREST:

Custom cover: What exactly is included in the custom cover is unclear, as the website description is limited to this: "Designer uses existing graphics and artwork." This service is $99.

Custom cover with original artwork: $250

Editing: Includes spelling, grammar, punctuation, and syntax. This service is $3 a page or $.012 a word.

Advanced editing: Includes everything in the basic edit, plus clarity, logic, and content. This costs $5 per page or $.02 per word.

RETURN OF DIGITAL COVER AND INTERIOR FILES: Although I tried to contact Sirius Publications via e-mail, instant message, and voice mail, I never received an answer.

RETAIL PRICE OF AUTHOR'S BOOK: Sirius e-books sell for between $4 and $12. Although the website states that paperbacks are only available in 5.5" x 8.5" size, the section on paperback prices is based on page count and two more trim sizes:

Number of pages	Retail price for 5" x 8" trim	Retail price for 6" x 9" trim
Up to 100	$12.95	$15.95
101–200	$13.95	$16.95
201–300	$15.95	$18.05
301–400	$17.95	not found on website

PRICE AUTHOR PAYS FOR BOOKS: Sirius authors receive a 35% discount off of the retail price. Therefore, a 200-page paperback retails for $13.95 and costs the author $8.95. The retail price is reasonable. But the price the author pays for a copy of his or her own book is not, considering that at most the book costs $3.90 to produce. It breaks down as follows:

$8.95	author price per book
– $3.90	printing cost
$5.05	Sirius profit

ROYALTIES TO AUTHOR: Sirius royalties are based on whether the author signs an exclusive or nonexclusive contract. For an exclusive contract, the royalty is 20% of net profit, and for a nonexclusive one, the royalty is 15% of net profit. The net profit is the "retail price…less returns and discounts and overhead (including but not limited to credit card fees)." Plus, the publisher reserves the right to withhold 10% against returns.

For a 200-page, paperback book sold on Amazon.com under a nonexclusive contract, the royalty would look something like this (note that an exact amount is hard to determine because the publisher's terms are so vague):

$13.95	retail price
– $6.98	50% Amazon.com discount
– $1.40	return fee
– $3.90	printing cost

$1.67	net profit
x .15	author royalty percentage

$.25	author royalty

Because the publisher would not respond to requests for information, it was impossible to figure out how much authors can make from sales directly from the Sirius Bookstore. However, the sales pages on the site are not attractive. For an example, see http://www.sirius-books .com/otherness.html#buy.

NOTABLE PROVISIONS OF THE PUBLISHING AGREEMENT: There are five different contracts. The author's choice depends on whether the publisher receives exclusive or nonexclusive print rights and e-book rights or both print and e-book rights. Clauses found in all agreements are discussed at the end of this section. There are two e-book contracts (exclusive and nonexclusive) that can be found at http://www.sirius-books.com/ebnonex-contract2.html and http:// www.sirius-books.com/ebex-contract.html, respectively.

The nonexclusive POD contract is available at http://sirius-books. com/podex-contract.html. Paragraph I of this contract gives the publisher five-year, nonexclusive print rights, which means the author may still give nonexclusive print rights to others.

Paragraph XIII confirms that the author can still terminate the contract with 10 days written notice.

Paragraph II requires the author to pay a $199 fee to set up POD printing and a $25 per year maintenance fee. The author receives 60%

of the net revenues generated the first year or until the author earns $100 in royalties, whichever comes first. "Net revenue" is defined as the "retail price for the work…less returns and discounts and overhead (including but not limited to credit card transaction fees)." After that, royalties are 15% of the net revenue.

Paragraph IV gives the publisher the right to withhold a 10% reserve against returns.

The exclusive POD contract is available at http://sirius-books.com/podex-contract.html. Paragraph I of this contract grants to the publisher five-year exclusive print rights.

Paragraph III gives the author the right to terminate this contract at any time with 90 days written notice.

Paragraph V states that author royalties are 35% for the entire term of the contract.

The contract also states that the author must pay the $199 setup fee and $25 per year maintenance fee.

The exclusive e-book and POD contract is available at http://www.sirius-books.com/epex-contract.html. Paragraph I of this contract grants to the publisher one-year worldwide, exclusive print and electronic rights.

Paragraph XIII allows the author to terminate the agreement with 10 days written notice.

Paragraph IV states that author royalties are 70% of the net revenues from electronic sales and 80% of the net revenues from printed book sales for the first year or until royalties total $100. After that, print royalties are 50% of the net revenue of each sale. The publisher may withhold a 10% reserve against returns.

The contract also indicates that the author must pay the $199 setup fee and the $25 per year maintenance fee.

All contracts contain paragraph V copyright language, which states, "It is understood that all rights to print or publish electronically do hereby remain the exclusive rights of Sirius Publications." This statement contradicts the other language in the contracts. During the term of any of the exclusive contracts this sentence may be true, but it is never true for the nonexclusive contracts. The author should point this discrepancy out to the publisher and modify the contract accordingly before signing it. This inconsistency is probably either a misprint

("Sirius Publications" should be "author" in this section) or a leftover provision from an older version of the contract.

Paragraph XII of each contract has "other sales" clauses that address various sales avenues and the author's royalties in such circumstances:

1. The "Royalties On Books Sold at Conferences, Signings, etc., in stores, either online or physical" clause is an optional clause (the author can opt out) that allows the publisher to sell the book on Amazon.com and other online or offline retailers. The author's royalty is 25% of the "net retail price" after the store's discount. For example, if the book's retail price is $15 and Amazon.com takes a 50% discount, the author's royalty will be 25% of the net retail price of $7.50.

    There is no reason not to accept this clause, as its terms may only increase sales avenues. However, an author in a nonexclusive contract may want to avoid a situation where both the author and publisher send copies to the same seller, such as Amazon.com, at different prices. The author's decision to accept this clause depends on how aggressive he plans to be in selling the same version of the book that the publisher is selling under a nonexclusive contract.

2. "Author Initiated Sales" doesn't require the author to initial or agree to anything. If you initiate a bulk order for any version of the book other than the one for which the publisher has an exclusive right, there would be no reason to share your good fortune with the publisher, unless you didn't want to deal with the production and distribution of whatever version on your own.

3. "E-book Reader Companies & Their Sales Outlets" may not be acceptable to the author if he or she has specific plans for marketing or selling the e-version and has not already given the publisher exclusive e-rights. (This clause appears in the exclusive and nonexclusive e-books contracts, and the exclusive e-book and print-on-demand contract.)

4. "Short Run Printing Clause" allows the publisher to seek out short-term printing options without imposing any obligation on the author.

Paragraph XII (a) means that any disputes with the publisher relating to the contract will be governed by the laws of the state in which the publisher is located.

AUTHOR-FRIENDLY RATING: The Sirius website is ridiculously outdated, with old content and an amateurish structure and navigation. I had to work pretty hard to find the information I needed, and much of what I found was in conflict with information provided elsewhere on the site. The contracts are annoyingly complex for the simplicity of the fee structure and service offering. The books are too expensive, and the royalties are at best low and at worst ill-defined and misleading. The publisher did not respond to my e-mail, and I had a hard time finding a phone number. I can't think of a single reason why an author would use this publisher.

TATE PUBLISHING

http://www.tatepublishing.com

FORMAT OF BOOKS: e-book, audio, paperback and hardcover

GENRES: Tate is a Christian publishing company but does not specify that its books need be on Christian topics. Tate claims to receive 10,000 manuscripts each year for review and claims to accept anywhere from 4% to 6% of them for publication. Submission review takes 6–8 weeks.

PUBLISHING FEES: Tate bills itself as a traditional publisher and does not offer publishing packages, but rather asks the author to participate in a partnership in which both parties contribute funds towards the process of getting the book designed, marketed, and distributed.

The author is asked to contribute $3,985.50 for the marketing of her book, regardless of the size and design of the book (an author who submitted a 50-page book of poetry received the same deal). The publisher promises to pour $15,700 to $19,700 of its own resources into the book, saying "We pay for the production, printing and distribution and marketing of the books we publish." Tate also says that if the author sells 5,000 copies of her book, not only will her investment be returned, but also her next book will be published for free.

The author who submitted a 50-page poetry book provided me with information on Tate's publishing services. They offer:

- E-book and audio versions of the book
- U.S. Copyright Office registration
- Library of Congress Control Number (LCCN)
- UPC bar code
- Distribution through Ingram, Spring Arbor and Appalachian. Here is what the publisher says about its distribution services:

If we sign you as a Tate Publishing author, we will pay for all of the costs of printing, mailing, and distributing your book through our distribution system. This is important because if your book is a success and you publish with another publisher you need to be prepared to cover costs upwards of $20,000.00 - $30,000.00 in the first three to six months of release.

This is a scare tactic along the lines of "We fight the terrorists over there so we don't have to fight them here."

- Book sales and availability through 25,000 stores and libraries, including Amazon, Barnes and Noble, Borders, Wal-Mart, and Tate Publishing. Note: I chose a page of 5 Tate books at random and was unable to find any of the books on Amazon.com or BarnesandNoble.com. However, an Amazon.com search on "Tate Publishing" did turn up about six books that appeared to come from this publisher.
- R.R. Bowker's Books In Print registration
- Marketing: A representative told me that the bulk of its $20,000 investment in each author goes towards marketing, which would initially focus on local bookstores and media. A Tate informational e-mail says that the publisher promotes the book through catalogs, online promotion, publicity, and the annual CBA (Christian Booksellers Association) conferences.
- Twenty-five copies of your book

RETURN OF DIGITAL COVER AND INTERIOR FILES: A Tate representative told me that if the author should determine to leave Tate and publish elsewhere the book's design files would remain with Tate. When I asked if it would be possible to pay a fee for the files, the representative said that I would have to discuss that with the acquisitions editor and that, if it were possible, a clause stating the specific terms and price would have to be added to the contract.

RETAIL PRICE OF AUTHOR'S BOOK: Although pricing seems to vary, while scanning the Tate bookstore, I found a 208-page, fiction paperback for $13.95 and a 200-page, nonfiction paperback for $15.95. These prices seem in line with the rest of the industry.

One thing I found disturbing was that, in a Q & A sent out to potential Tate authors, the publisher wrote:

Q: How Many Books Will I sell?
A: It depends. A successful book will sell between 2,500 and 5,000 copies in a year. The true success depends upon the quality, layout and design, but most importantly the marketing and visibility of your book. We will make sure that the book is marketed and given the necessary visibility to succeed.

Of course, given your investment, it would be convenient if your book sold 5,000 copies, but how often does that happen? I asked one of the publisher's representatives who said that, while she would not tell me that selling that many books would be easy, Tate only accepts 4% of submitted manuscripts because "the minute we accept your book we are $20,000 in the hole, so we only take books that, we know are going to sell thousands of copies."

PRICE AUTHOR PAYS FOR BOOKS: Authors receive a 60% discount off the retail book price. If your 200-page, nonfiction book sells for $15.95, you can buy it for:

$15.95	retail price
– $9.57	60% author discount
$6.38	author price per book
– $3.90	printing cost
$2.48	Tate profit

As we have discussed throughout the book, a 200-page book costs $3.90 to print digitally, so Tate is marking up its books by more than 150% after the author paid $4,000 in partnership funds. So where exactly is the partnership?

ROYALTIES PAID TO AUTHOR: Tate's royalties are based on the retail price of the book. If the book is sold on Tate's website, the author earns 40% of the retail price; for third-party and wholesale sales, such as Amazon.com, the author earns 15% of the retail price. So for a 200-page, paperback book sold on Tate's website:

$15.95　　retail price
x .40　　　author royalty percentage

$6.3　　　author royalty

On that same sale, your partner, Tate, makes $5.70 after printing expenses.

For a sale on Amazon.com, that same book would earn you:

$15.95　　retail price
x .15　　　author royalty percentage

$2.39　　　author royalty

On that same sale Tate, makes $1.69:

$15.95
– $7.97　　50% Amazon.com discount
– $3.90　　printing cost
– $2.39　　author royalty

$1.69　　　Tate profit

NOTABLE PROVISIONS OF THE PUBLISHING AGREE-MENT: The publisher does not provide sample copies of its publishing agreement. If an author is accepted, she will receive a contract. The submissions process takes 6–8 weeks. The publisher refused to provide a contract, so I was unable to analyze it. Interpret that refusal however you wish.

AUTHOR-FRIENDLY RATING: While my book doesn't have an "Are you kidding me?" category, if it did, Tate would be the star. It says it invests $20,000 into each book, yet won't tell you how or where. But it asks you as a "partner" to put up $4,000 of it.

Tate is misleading its authors when it calls itself a traditional publisher. No traditional publisher asks an author for $4,000 up front. Only a few of the self-publishing companies covered in this book charge more than $4,000 for a publishing package.

That being said, there's not a lot of info on the various online author lists about Tate, except that everyone agrees that it seems crazy to spend $4,000 to self-publish a book. Not unlike PublishAmerica, negative comments about Tate are answered immediately by "happy authors" with nothing but good things to say about Tate. Some of their comments were fact-checked by other folks on the list, and in some cases the "happy authors" either appeared to not exist or misrepresented their success.

TRAFFORD PUBLISHING

http://www.trafford.com

FORMAT OF BOOK: paperback and hardcover (e-books are included with some packages)

PUBLISHING FEES: Trafford Publishing offers five publishing packages, including two for children's books, which will not be discussed here. Each package is offered either as a Classic or Plus. For the Classic option, the author has to submit a press-ready formatted manuscript. The Plus option comes with formatting, although the author still needs to provide detailed instructions and a physical example of how they'd like the book to look (i.e., taking a manuscript from a word processing program and turning it into a book). For more information about the packages, see http://www.trafford.com/1001.

Legacy Package: The Classic option is $697, and the Plus option is $1,397. They both include:

- ISBN
- Library of Congress Control Number (LCCN)
- U.S. Copyright Office registration
- Bar code
- Full-color cover: Although the website says that the Trafford staff will produce a cover, the caveat is that they will do so working from the author's files and artwork. The author gets two hours of the designer's time. That means the

author is responsible for submitting either a digital cover layout with all the required artwork or detailed sketches of the front and back cover, with all the necessary materials (photographs for scanning, illustration originals, text for the back cover, etc.).

· Typesetting/formatting (with the Plus option only): The author is responsible for providing detailed instructions and a sample of how the formatting should look.

· Book availability for author to purchase (book will not be available to the public)

· Two copies of author's paperback

Entrepreneur Package: The Classic option is $1,097, and the Plus option is $1,797. This package includes everything in the Legacy Package, plus:

· Webpage on publisher's website
· Listing through publisher's online store

Best Seller Package: The Classic option is $1,597, and the Plus option is $2,297. This package includes everything in the Entrepreneur Package, plus:

· Listing with online booksellers: Amazon.com, Borders.com, BarnesandNoble.com and Chapters.ca
· Distribution through Baker & Taylor
· R.R. Bowker's Books In Print registration
· Book made available for sale as an e-book
· Press release announcement to "thousands of book industry contacts," plus 250 bookmarks, 100 postcards, and five 11" x 17" posters of the book's cover
· Twenty total paperback copies of author's book

RETURN OF DIGITAL COVER AND INTERIOR FILES: File ownership is not covered on the Trafford website or its author agreement, but I e-mailed the publisher, asking who owns production files for the formatted book, and received this reply: "At Trafford, you always retain full copyright and control over the layout of your book and cover." This canned answer doesn't answer the question.

RETAIL PRICE OF AUTHOR'S BOOK: Trafford allows the author to set the price of her book as long as it is at least 2.1 times the printing cost. The printing cost for a single copy of a 200-page, 6" x 9", perfect-bound book is $8.37, and the Trafford calculator (see next section) told me the minimum sale price would have to be $17.59. (Yes, that's even though $8.37 x 2.1 is $17.58 if you round up.)

PRICE AUTHOR PAYS FOR BOOKS: Trafford offers a calculator to help authors figure out the price of their book. It is available at http://www2.trafford.com/calc/index.htm.

I entered a 200-page, 6" x 9", perfect-bound book and got the following discount chart:

Number of books	Discount	Author price per book
1–49	0%	$8.37
50–249	3%	$8.12
250–499	9%	$7.62
500–3999	12%	$7.37
4000+	30%	$5.86

If you buy 1–49 books without discount, here's what Trafford makes:

$8.37	Trafford "wholesale" price
– $3.90	printing cost

$4.47	Trafford profit

Trafford is located in Canada, so don't forget, there will be a hefty shipping fee too!

ROYALTIES PAID TO AUTHOR: Trafford pays 60% of the "gross margin," which is the retail price less the trade discount to booksellers and less the single copy printing cost. For the same 200-page book, the royalties would look like this if the book is sold from Trafford.com:

$17.59	retail price
– $4.39	25% Trafford.com discount
– $8.37	printing cost

$4.83
x .60   author royalty
_____

$2.90   author royalty

In this scenario, Trafford has triple-dipped into the profits:

$4.47   printing markup
+ $4.39   Trafford.com discount
+ $1.94   Trafford royalty
_____

$10.80   Trafford profit

If that same book sold on Amazon.com, the author would make:

$17.59   retail price
– $7.03   40% Amazon.com discount
– $8.37   printing cost
_____

$2.19   net profit
x .60   author royalty percentage
_____

$1.31   author royalty

In this scenario, Trafford only double-dips, making a profit from the sale of the book and its printing markups, for a total profit of $5.35.

Luckily, the ultra-shady practice of pocketing a discount, a printing markup, and a royalty from the sale of an author's book is not widespread, yet Trafford has perfected it. For a book sold through Trafford, the actual net profit on that book is $13.69. Trafford is making a whopping 79% of the profits.

NOTABLE PROVISIONS OF THE PUBLISHING AGREE-MENT: The publishing agreement can be found at http://www.trafford.com/downloads/contracts/PGContract-US-EN.pdf.

Section 14, "Accounting of Royalties," states that Trafford makes royalty payments on a quarterly basis. The royalty is defined as 60% of the gross margin.

Section 16 says that Plus package authors must provide scan-ready art, a digital file of their book, plus a sample and specific details as to how they want their book laid out. For the Classic package, the author must supply a PostScript file of the interior layout of the book and specifications for the book's appearance, including size.

Section 18 says that the agreement is nonexclusive and that either party may terminate it at anytime, without cause, with written notice. It also says that the agreement is subject to the laws of British Columbia, Canada, and that any arbitration will take place there.

AUTHOR-FRIENDLY RATING: The old adage "a fool and his money are soon departed" comes to mind when I think of the author who chooses this publisher—especially after reading this review. Triple-dipping is the scummiest thing a self-publishing company can do. If you pay thousands of dollars to publish your book, why should the publisher be making 79% of the profits on each sale? Why should you have to pay a printing markup of more than 100% to purchase copies of your book for personal use?

The Best Seller Package for $2,297 is what most publishers in this book provide for $1,000–$1,500.

On an annoying note, while trying to get a copy of the agreement, I clicked a link that said "Download our Publishing Guide," which instead led me to a form that asked for my name and address. When I hit the "Download Publishing Guide Now" button, it then launched a questionnaire, which asked me questions such as what other publishers are you considering and what is your yearly income. Then, for all that, I received a form letter in my e-mail inbox and no copy of the publishing guide! A return e-mail asking for the publishing guide elicited no response.

That being said, an e-mail query regarding file ownership, sent via the "Contact Us" page, was answered within 24 hours.

Trafford's business model will bury you and your book. You will pay more up front than you need to. The printing costs are so over-inflated that the retail cost of your book will make it uncompetitive. Finally, after all the money you paid to publish, Trafford will be making most of the money each time you sell a book.

WINGS PRESS

http://www.wings-press.com

FORMAT OF BOOKS: e-book and paperback

GENRES ACCEPTED: Wings accepts all genres of fiction with an emphasis on romance. Wings Press does not accept nonfiction, x-rated, erotic, or alternative lifestyle books or books with over 150,000 words. The rules about word count are fairly complex, so look for guidelines at http://www.wings-press.com/guideline.htm.

PUBLISHING FEES: The fee is $0 for e-books and $90 for paperbacks.

- Custom covers: An in-house designer works with the author to create a cover.
- Basic edit: Each manuscript goes through two readers, who edit for consistency with Wings' publishing guidelines; after the editor has addressed any issues raised in the initial edit, books are copyedited for spelling, grammar, punctuation, and syntax.
- ISBN

Print books are available for sale on Amazon.com, on Wingspress.com, and in brick-and-mortar bookstores via special order. However, the books on Amazon are actually available through Pawprints POD (the printer Wings uses) and not directly through Amazon itself. If you search for a Wings book on Amazon, you'll note that Pawprints POD turns up as the seller in the section on each book's page where it lists new and used copies for sale.

RETAIL PRICE FOR AUTHOR'S BOOK: E-books are all priced at $6, and paperbacks vary in price, based—it would appear—on page count. A 200-page book would cost $10.95, which is actually on the low end for self-published paperbacks.

PRICE AUTHOR PAYS FOR BOOKS: There are no author discounts at Wings Press, but according to a company representative, "The author is offered the option of taking their royalty up front as a discount." A query as to what that actually means went unanswered, but I assume it means the author pays the retail price less his royalty. The royalty on a book sold via Wings Press is $1.80, so the same 200-page book discussed previously would cost the author $9.15. Wings Press does not print through Lightning Source, but its printer Pawprints POD quotes a print cost of $5 a book on its website. Since they won't tell me, I have no idea if Wings gets a discount off that price:

$9.15   author price per book
– $5.00   Pawprints POD charge
_____

$4.15   Wings Press profit

Add in the additional $1.10 Wings is likely making on the printing, and the profit is $5.25 per book.

But, since Wings Press is printing books digitally, I don't believe it pays more than anyone else would to print the book. If Wings Press knows that it can print a book for $3.90 but chooses to pay $5.00, it's either because it's padding the printing and getting a kickback or it owns a piece of the printing company.

ROYALTIES PAID TO THE AUTHOR: The royalties are different for e-books and paperbacks.

E-book royalties are 30% of the download price, which is $6, so the author receives $1.80 per book.

For paperbacks sold through the publisher's website, the author receives $1.80 per book regardless of the book's retail price. On the $10.95 book discussed previously, that comes out to 16%.

The author will receive 30% of the net sales on paperbacks sold through any other venue, according to information provided by the publisher's president, Lorraine Stephens. However, it is impossible to know what the "net" is based on: the "author liaison" for the company told me she thought the contract was on the website, but when I couldn't find it and asked again, I received this reply: "I discussed this with the Exec. Editor and President. We do not publish our contract. If a manuscript is accepted, we send a contract to the author, who has the option of accepting or declining."

It's disconcerting to think the one and only author liaison at Wings does not know where the contract can be found and that the publishing company does not provide contract information informally. In fact, when I tried to find out what kind of discount Wings gives to Amazon. com, I received this answer from the liaison: "I'm not sure of the % because I am not the one who handles that." Since the rep couldn't take the time to find out the percentage, I'm going to estimate it. The books are sold on Amazon.com through the "Marketplace" by the company that prints the books for the publishers. One of the publisher's titles,

Clandestine Rendezvous (a 276-page paperback), sells on the publisher's site for $11.95 but is sold by Pawprints POD in the Amazon Marketplace for $17.95. Amazon takes about 37% for products sold this way. Remember, the publisher would not answer my questions about Amazon sales, so the figures below are my assumptions. Accepting that, here is what an author of a 276-paperback makes on Amazon.com sales:

$17.9   retail price
− $6.64   37% Amazon.com discount
− $9.15   author price per book (a.k.a., printing markup)

$2.16   net profit
x .30   author royalty percentage

$.65   author royalty

Pawprints gets some portion of the $9.15 obviously, so it's impossible to tell what Wings Press makes on such third-party sales, but rest assured it's more than $.65.

NOTABLE PROVISIONS OF THE PUBLISHING AGREEMENT: The publisher does not provide sample agreements. Authors will be offered a contract upon acceptance of their books. However, the last time around, President Lorraine Stephens informed me the contract is a two-year exclusive contract with one-year renewal periods.

According to Stephens, an author could terminate the contract at anytime (however, that's not what it says in the contract). Regardless of what any publisher tells you, if it's not in the contract, it's not enforceable. Period.

AUTHOR-FRIENDLY RATING: There is still very little information available about the publishing services Wings Press offers, and the author liaison did not provide more than cursory answers to my questions. (For example, she mentioned that there is a fee but would not state the amount. When I tried to nail her down on fees, she stopped answering my e-mails.) I'm still not clear whether this was because she was being less than forthcoming or she simply didn't know the answers—neither is great. Despite the fact that it charges for printing, hence the $90 fee (essentially what Pawprints POD charges as its setup fees) and the printing markups built in to each sale, the liaison said Wings Press considers itself an independent press rather than a self-publisher. However, that phrase is mentioned no where on the website, and indeed, there is little information on the website in general as to what qualifies her to say that or what the company does for paperback authors, so I have the feeling this is a case of self-inflation.

A two-year exclusive contract is never a good idea when choosing a self-publishing company unless that company is spending its own money to advertise and market your book. Running a website that sells the book if someone clicks on a link doesn't count. Remember, just because the publisher says an author can terminate at any time, it may be difficult to exercise this right if it's not in writing and in the publishing contract. Business contracts don't work that way. It's more likely the publisher will enforce contract terms and disregard anything outside its contract.

The $1.80 royalty for each book sale from the publisher's own site isn't favorable, especially for authors with long works. A 300-page book sells for about $12. The cost to print a 300-page book is about $4.80. Of the $7.20 that remains, the author receives $1.80 and the publisher makes $5.40. Under this calculation, the author only makes a 15% royalty. I couldn't get any answers about the Amazon sales, and I spent a long time trying to figure it out. If you have to guess at what you might make in royalties, find another publisher.

While I have no reason to question Wings Press's intentions, I would stay away from any publisher that refuses to provide a sample contract and won't tell you exactly what you would make from sales through other channels.

Without the benefit of examining the contract, I can only imagine how author-unfriendly its terms must be. Proceed with caution!

WORDCLAY

http://www.wordclay.com

FORMAT OF BOOKS: paperback

GENRES: all

PUBLISHING FEES: Wordclay is owned by Author Solutions Inc. (parent company of AuthorHouse and iUniverse). It is similar to Lulu and CreateSpace in its offering; authors pay nothing to upload to and sell their books from the Wordclay website. Unlike its competitors, however, Wordclay offers authors a host of publishing services, from editing and design to distribution. Complete details and pricing are available at http://www.wordclay.com/ServicesStore/ServicesStoreHome.aspx.

Softcover Distribution: This package is $99 for one year, $129 for two years, and $139 for three years. Wordclay's distribution service is for authors who want to sell their book on websites other than Wordclay.com, such as Amazon.com and BarnesandNoble.com. There is no difference, outside of term length, between the packages; all three include:

- ISBN
- Bar code
- Distribution through Ingram
- Listing with online booksellers, including Amazon.com, BarnesandNoble.com, and Borders.com

OTHER SERVICES OF INTEREST: The downside to the free-upload model is that the templates the publisher provides will only take authors so far, and then they need to find service providers to help them create a cover, edit content, etc. The Wordclay model is different than others in this category, such as Lulu and CreateSpace, in that it offers these services, for a price, in-house. Below is a sampling of the basic services needed to get a book out, but full service listing is available here: http://www.wordclay.com/ServicesStore/ServicesStoreHome.aspx.

Editorial services: Basic spelling, grammar, punctuation, and syntax editing costs $.02 a word and is generally completed in 60 days. For those in a hurry, Wordclay offers an Express Edit, which takes 1–2 weeks and costs $.04 a word. Content editing, which includes grammar, flow, content and organization, takes up to 75 days and costs $.06 a word.

Custom typesetting: Includes up to five hours of design time, font styles and sizes, chapter-start styles, table of contents design, running headers, page numbers, and images for a flat fee of $249.

Front cover design: Includes two hours of consultation with a designer, 14 hours of design time, and two proofs. The final cover may include photography or illustrations and may take up to 60 days to complete. This service is offered for a $999 flat fee.

Domain name registration: Wordclay will register a domain name of your choice, which will then point to your book page on Wordclay.com. Author pages look like this: http://www.wordclay .com/BookStore/BookStoreBookDetails.aspx?bookid=10005. Perusing the Wordclay bookstore, I did not find any author pages that had taken advantage of this offer. This service is offered for a $49 flat fee.

Retail return insurance: This service makes your book returnable via Ingram for one year without affecting your royalty. If you want brick-and-mortar bookstores to ever consider selling your book, making it returnable will certainly help, but it is no guarantee. This is offered for a $799 flat fee.

RETURN OF DIGITAL COVER AND INTERIOR FILES: A Wordclay representative told me via live chat that authors only own the files they create. Therefore, if you pay a Wordclay designer $999 to create a book cover for you, Wordclay owns the cover files, and they are not available for purchase. If after publishing with Wordclay you decide to publish your book elsewhere, you will have to pay yet another designer to create a new cover for you, despite the $999 already spent.

RETAIL PRICE OF AUTHOR'S BOOK: Wordclay allows authors to set their own price for the book as long as it is higher than the base price. I submitted a 56-page book of poetry and was told that the minimum price for the book would be $9.64.

PRICE AUTHOR PAYS FOR BOOKS: Author discounts are based on Wordclay's cost to print and a distribution fee. If you published a 56-page, 6" x 9", paperback book, the math would look like this:

$5.53   Wordclay "printing cost"
+ $1.00   distribution fee
_____

$6.53   author price per book
– $1.74   actual printing cost
_____

$4.79   Wordclay profit

When I asked the Wordclay representative how the company came to the $5.53, she answered: "We [sic: action verb missing] $5.53 from Lightning Source, our book printer. This amount is determined by the page count of your book."

Since it costs $1.74 (at the most) to actually print the book, I can't figure out how marking up the printing 350% has anything to do with the page count of the book. It's these types of fees, hidden in the crevices of the "free publishing" advertising that companies like Wordclay publish, that prove there is no free self-publishing.

ROYALTIES PAID TO AUTHOR: Wordclay allows the author to set the price of his or her book as long as it is over the base price and therefore the royalty, too.

So let's say you sold the 56-page, paperback book for $9.64 on Wordclay.com:

$9.64   retail price
– $5.53   Wordclay "printing cost"
– $1.00   distribution fee
_____

$3.11   author royalty

Keep in mind that Wordclay makes $4.81 off the book simply for printing it. Plus, when I asked the Wordclay representative about royalties on sales through Amazon.com, she initially told me that she couldn't tell me what it would be, and then, after much persuasion, ball-parked it at $.64.

How did she come up with that? We'll never know, but by backing out the number, it appears that Wordclay gives Amazon (and other retailers) a 25% trade discount. (In the example given, this would be

$2.47, which when deducted from the $3.11 royalty leaves $.64.)

NOTABLE PROVISIONS OF THE PUBLISHING AGREE-MENT: The publishing agreement can be found at: http://www.wordclay.com/TermsOfUse.aspx.

In the "Agreements" section, the author agrees to take full responsibility both for the content that is published and any materials used to create the content; if anything is misspelled, lost, or damaged, Wordclay will not be responsible.

Furthermore, Wordclay does not guarantee the quality of its printing (e.g., colors may appear differently between printings and from what you see online).

Pursuant to section 1.4 of the terms and conditions, any interior design and/or cover design you create either using Wordclay's templates or hiring its designers: "You acknowledge that you may not utilize the formatted Work and cover with any other publisher, if we cease publication of the Work." In other words, if you determine to print your book elsewhere, you will also have to pay to have it redesigned. So exactly what do you get for the $999 cover design fee if, in the end, you don't really own the cover?

The "Your Legal Responsibility" section says that Wordclay will not publish works that are plagiarized, libelous, illegal, or written in language that is pornographic, hateful, or obscene. This is reasonable.

In "Our Legal Responsibility," it says that Wordclay cannot be held liable for your work (i.e., if you get sued for something you publish, you are on your own). Wordclay also asserts its right to withhold service if an author violates the terms of the agreement. It also reserves the right to change promotional offers and substitute offers of the same or greater value. And Wordclay does not promise that its site will be error free or even available. This is reasonable. The website availability language really means that if the site goes down for a while, you wouldn't have a cause of action against them.

The "Indemnification" section is basically more of the same and simply says that neither Wordclay nor its employees can be held liable for the author's work. If a lawsuit does arise as a result of an author's work, Wordplay can hold the author's royalties and stop publishing the book. Further, it will not refund any of the fees the author has paid. Again, this is reasonable.

The "Pricing and Royalty Agreements" section, namely 5.2, has some red flags buried in it. In fact, if I hadn't read it, I wouldn't believe it, so here is a direct quote cut and pasted from the actual document: "If your account is inactive or terminated and we are unable to contact you using the contact information provided, we may also, at our discretion, charge a termination fee equal to the amount of unpaid royalties to cover administrative costs."

Even worse is what comes later in section 5.2.: "We will remit payments to you on a quarterly basis (4 times a year) along with a report of sales in that reported quarter by electronic mail; provided, however, no payment shall be made to **unless and until the amount of the royalties is equal to or exceeds $20,000.**" (emphasis added)

If for example, you sell a slim volume of poetry for $9.64 a book, you'll have to sell 6,430 books on Wordclay or 31,250 books on Amazon.com before you see a penny of the profits. The odds of that are slim. So while an author may earn royalties, Wordclay gets to sit on the money until the author breaks $20,000 in sales. It's one of the great scams I've seen. This alone is a major reason not to use this publisher. Oh—and you are not allowed to alter the price of your book without Wordclay's permission.

The "Termination" section states that either party can terminate with 30 days notice but that authors will not be eligible for any kind of refund.

The "Force Majeure" section basically states that Wordclay is not responsible for acts of nature that might keep it from providing its services. If inclement weather or an act of war keeps it from providing said services for 90 days, the author can terminate his contract.

The "Governing Law" section simply says that any arbitration arising from this contract will take place in Bloomington, Indiana, which is fair but not advantageous to the author, unless he or she happens to live in Bloomington.

AUTHOR-FRIENDLY RATING: Wordclay is AuthorHouse's answer to Lulu and Amazon.com's CreateSpace. The fact that it's AuthorHouse in disguise should say it all. However, AuthorHouse has actually outdone itself here by pulling the ultimate royalty scam. It can essentially never pay out royalties except to the very few authors who exceed $20,000 in royalties.

If after reading everything in this review you're still considering Wordclay, one piece of good news is that the book setup was very easy to navigate and understand; however, it was incredibly limiting. There is no page formatting other than what you provide using Microsoft Word, and the cover templates are very limited. In fact, there are so few cover options available that browsing through the bookstore one sees two or three books on every page with the same exact cover, sometimes more.

If something goes wrong in the book setup, the help desk will simply tell you to start over; they appear not to be able to look at your account.

Similarly, once you have gone through the setup, there is no way to look back at what you've done. For example, you choose a book price and royalty during setup, but afterward there is nowhere to look that information up; nor can you look at your book. After setup, you'll simply have to wait for the book to go through production so you can buy a hardcopy.

The best thing I can say about Wordclay is that the website is easy to navigate and the live chat was friendly and available; I waited under a minute for someone to pop up. Still, the live-chat operator could offer to clean my house, and I still wouldn't use this company to publish my book.

XLIBRIS

http://www2.xlibris.com

FORMAT OF BOOKS: paperback and hardcover

GENRES ACCEPTED: all

PUBLISHING FEES: Xlibris offers seven black-and-white publishing packages. The publisher also offers six color packages, which will not be covered here, but can be found at http://www2.xlibris .com/pubservices/index.asp, along with a full description of the packages below.

Advantage Package: This package (http://www2.xlibris.com /pubservices/ps-advantage.asp) is $299 This package does not include distribution; books are sold on the Xlibris website only. It includes:

- Paperback version
- One copy of the book
- Choice of three cover templates for which the author supplies the image and author photo
- Choice of two interior templates
- ISBN
- UPC bar code
- Electronic galley proof: Xlibris will correct its own mistakes for free, but yours are $25.00 a set plus $2.00 a change
- Author webpage, which includes ordering and contact information, author biography, and an excerpt of the book
- Access to Xlibris's web-based sales monitoring system

Basic Package: This package (http://www.xlibris.com/pubservices /ps_Basic.asp) is $499 and includes everything in the Advantage Package, plus:

- Five copies of the book
- Choice of eight cover templates
- Choice of five interior templates
- Ability to supply your own complete cover and interior design
- One free paperback of your choice from the Xlibris bookstore
- Listing with online booksellers: Amazon.com, Borders.com, BarnesandNoble.com and more than 200 other online stores
- Distribution through Ingram
- R.R. Bowker's Books In Print registration
- Fifty bookmarks
- fifty business cards

Professional Package: This package (http://www.xlibris.com /pubservices/ps_professional.asp) is $899 and includes everything in the Basic Package, plus:

- Ten paperback copies of your book (total)
- Hardcover version for a $249 fee
- Choice of 18 cover templates, for which you can supply up to three images
- Choice of nine interior templates, including options for the head, foot, folio, and chapter heads; 20 images ($400 à la carte); and five tables ($200 à la carte)
- Registration with Google Book Search
- Five posters

Custom Package: This package (http://www.xlibris.com /pubservices/ps_custom.asp) costs $1,599 and includes everything in the Professional Package, plus:

- Five hardcover books
- Custom-designed cover, which includes consultation with cover and interior designers and, according to the Xlibris rep, as many comps as it takes to get the design right (this is not in the contract or on the website) You must supply artwork or up to fuve images.
- Thirty interior images and 10 tables
- A PDF review galley for both the hardcover and paperback books
- Fifty postcards
- Personal Starter website with domain, which includes three pages, up to two images, an e-mail account, and a choice of five templates. Xlibris owns the domain, but the site will remain live as long as you continue to pay the $89 annual fee. The à la carte cost is $349. This is outrageous. A domain costs $8–$10. And if you don't own the site, why should you pay the hosting fees? All that will happen here is that if you build up a fan base and your domain name becomes known, you will lose all that goodwill if you ever leave this publisher, since the domain is not yours.

Premium Package: This package (http://www2.xlibris.com /pubservices/ps_premium.asp) costs $2,999 and includes everything in the Custom Package, plus:

- Five hardback and 20 total paperback books

- Unlimited cover and interior photos
- Author alterations service, which includes two sets of galley proofs with no fee for your changes
- U.S. Copyright Office registration: The à la carte cost is $249
- Library of Congress Control Number (LCCN)
- Data entry service: Creates a digital file of your handwritten or typed manuscript; the à la carte cost is $2.50 a page.
- Copyediting service: Includes grammar, spelling, and syntax; the à la carte cost is $.01–$.012 per word.
- Citations: Includes formatting for endnotes and footnotes; the à la carte cost is $75 per 50 endnotes and $75 per 50 footnotes, plus $.50 for each footnote.
- Indexing: This service does not include the actual indexing, but only the formatting of the index; the à la carte cost is $100.
- CD archive: Includes a PDF of the cover and an unformatted copy of your corrected manuscript; the à la carte cost is $99(in terms of record keeping, you can scan the cover of your book yourself, and you'll get a PDF galley of the book during the proofing, not to mention your copy of the book. This archive will not be useful for printing a copy of the book because it is not formatted for a press. Although a rough text version of the book might save the author a little time if he/she ever wanted to print with another publisher, $99 is a lot to pay for what is essentially a Word document of your work)
- Professional book review campaign: This is not a campaign, but a set of tools with which you can do the campaigning. It includes five 8.5" x 11" printed galleys of the book (4 shipped to the media of your choice for your records), a cover page, and a press release written by an Xlibris publicist based on a questionnaire you fill out. Should any of these book reviews result in a favorable quote, Xlibris will revise the cover to include them for an additional $150.
- Press release campaign: Includes 100 media outlets. Xlibris publicists will write a press release, distribute it, send out requested review galleys (at no extra charge to you or the reviewer), and forward you any of the resulting interviews.

The à la carte cost is $349 (Note: If you were going to pay for one of these services, this may be the better deal. This service costs the same amount as the book review campaign, yet your press release goes out to a targeted list, and the service description states no limit on the number of bound review galleys. However, when I asked how Xlibris compiles its media list, the publisher's representative answered that the marketing team "has its resources, which I am not at liberty to discuss," so it's unclear what tools the company is using if any at all)

· Opt-in e-mail marketing campaign: Includes 200,000 recipients. This is simply an e-mail with a picture of your book and click-through ordering that goes out to a massive, untargeted list. Even if the publisher insists it isn't sending out spam, you can rest assured that 200,000 people did not sign up for e-mail alerts for books by unknown authors. The à la carte cost is $349.

Executive Package: This package (http://www2.xlibris.com /pubservices/ps_executive.asp) is $5,999 and includes everything in the Platinum Package, plus:

· Twenty-five hardcover and 75 paperback books (total)
· One edition in pigskin leather
· Ability to set your own price: Allows you to raise or lower the retail price of your book. Under the terms of the service, you agree to take a $1 royalty—no matter where your book sells—and the price of your 200-page book goes down to $15.99; each additional $1 of royalty raises the price of the book by $2. The à la carte cost is $249 (a company that charges you an extra $249 for the ability to set your own price is one that should make you go "Hmm.")
· Press release campaign: Includes 500 media outlets. Again, Xlibris declined to reveal what tools it uses to compile this list, so it is unclear if there really are 500 viable, interested editors out there or just 500 spam receptacles.
· Opt-in e-mail marketing campaign: Includes 1,000,000 recipients. If this isn't spam, I don't know what it is. However, the Xlibris representative insisted that each of these 1,000,000 people has individually contacted Xlibris asking

to be notified when the publisher releases books. If this is true and Xlibris can prove it, I'll fly to the publisher's offices and eat my book in front of all its employees.

· Personalized regular website with domain, including six pages, five images, three e-mail accounts, one animated image, and 10 templates. The à la carte cost is $549.
· 250 business cards

Platinum Package: The package (http://www2.xlibris.com /pubservices/ps_platinum.asp) costs $12,999 and includes everything in the Executive Package, plus:

· Twenty-five hardcover and 250 paperback books
· Five leather editions
· Ultimate customization: When asked how this level of customization was different from the Custom Package, the Xlibris representative had no specific answers, except to sputter that this was "the Rolls Royce of publishing and, for what you're paying, you will get a lot more attention, if you know what I mean."
· Bookstore return status: Your book is listed as returnable, which may increase the chance of booksellers stocking it. The à la carte cost is $699 annually.
· Ad in the New York Review of Books: Includes a miniature picture of your book cover on a page with many, many other miniature book covers. This is not an effective form of advertisement. The à la carte cost is $250. Do not confuse this with the New York Times Book Review.
· Press release to 1,000 media outlets: Again, since the Xlibris representative would not reveal what media tools the publisher's marketing department uses, it's unclear if this is really a targeted campaign or simply spam.
· Single targeted e-mail marketing campaign to 1,000,000 recipients: According to the Xlibris representative, "single targeted" means the e-mail is sent out only once to a list of 1,000,000 media contacts who have, on an individual basis, contacted Xlibris to express an interest in your specific genre of book. I'm laughing out loud as I reread this. Similarly, a million aliens interested in self-publishing

contacted me and expressed an interest in buying the new edition of this book.
- 300 each of business cards, bookmarks, and postcards, and 30 posters

RETURN OF DIGITAL COVER AND INTERIOR ART FILES: Xlibris states in its contract that it retains the rights to digital property and ownership related to all completed production and data files. When I asked the Xlibris representative why the authors, who pay for this service, do not own the files, too, she said: "You retain the rights to the book, but the files remain ours because we created them."

The production files are not even available for a fee. So the author's only recourse, according to the representative, is to buy Xlibris's CD archive, which for $100 includes a PDF of the cover and an unformatted rich-text version of the manuscript, neither of which will be of any real use in printing. Whether you want to publish the book yourself or move to a new publishing house, you will simply have to reformat the book. What is the point of going with a company that you pay to create files of your book, but then when you want them, you don't own them?

RETAIL PRICE OF AUTHOR'S BOOK: A detailed chart of Xlibris's book prices can be found at: http://www2.xlibris.com /bookpricing/chart2.pdf.

Number of pages	Retail price
108–199	$20.99
200–299	$21.99
300–399	$22.99
400–499	$24.99

Ridiculously high printing markups and pathetically low author royalties are two reasons why a 200-page book that costs at most $3.90 to create is retailing for $22.

AUTHOR PRICE FOR BOOKS: Xlibris bases the author's discount price on copies of his or her own book on the retail price and the number of books the author buys. For a 200-page, paperback book that retails for $21.99, the price per book the author pays is determined as follows:

Number of books	Author discount	Author price per book
1–9	40%	$13.19
25–49	49%	$11.21
500–999	63 %	$8.14

Here's another way to look at that math:

$21.99	retail price
– $8.80	40% author discount
– $3.90	printing cost

$9.29	Xlibris profit

Marking up the cost the author pays for books by close to 150% is a formula for disaster, unless of course you're the one marking up the book. Do you get how impossible this makes it for an author to actually make money selling his or her books? The retail price is inflated to an unrealistic level in order to accommodate an excessive printing markup of nearly 150% of the actual print costs. Remember, the author pays Xlibris $1,500 or more to publish your book. Now, every time you want to purchase a copy of the book, they make another $9.29? If you've ever seen the movie *Network*, this would be a good time to relive the famous scene: go to your window, open it, stick your head out, and scream as loud as you can, "I'm mad as hell, and I'm not going to take it anymore!"

ROYALTIES PAID TO AUTHOR: According to the Xlibris pricing chart (http://www1.xlibris.com/bookpricing/bookpricing_chart .pdf), paperback and hardcover royalties are 10% of the retail price sold through a bookseller or online retailer and 25% of the retail price sold on the Xlibris website. Here's what that looks like on the 200-page book mentioned previously:

$21.99	retail price
x .10	author royalty percentage

$2.20	author royalty

How much does Xlibris make on that same sale?

$21.99	retail price
– $3.90	printing cost
– $8.80	40% Amazon.com discount
– $2.20	author royalty

$7.09   Xlibris profit

For a book sold through the Xlibris online bookstore:

$21.99	retail price
x .25	author royalty percentage

$5.50   author royalty

On direct sales, Xlibris's profit is even more outrageous:

$21.99	retail price
– $3.90	printing cost
– $5.50	author royalty

$12.59   Xlibris profit

Repeat the scene in Network. This company makes 300% more profit on every sale through Amazon than its authors do and about 225% more on direct sales.

NOTABLE PROVISIONS OF THE PUBLISHING AGREE-MENT: The publishing agreement can be found at http://www.xlibris.com/pubservices/ps_author_agreement.asp.

The section titled "Your Work…Your Rights" states that Xlibris acquires no rights in the work and only provides services such as printing and book sales. This section also states that Xlibris has no obligation to review or correct the work and that the book will be printed as submitted.

The section titled "Term & Exclusivity" states that Xlibris retains all digital property and ownership related to all completed production data and files. Otherwise, the contract is nonexclusive, and the author can enter into other publishing agreements. If the author terminates the agreement before signing off on approval of work performed, all publishing fees will be refunded in full, which means that if you terminate before signing off on the final prof of your book, you're entitled to a refund. Otherwise, all bets are off. If Xlibris terminates at any time, all publishing fees will be returned or applied against outstanding amounts in the author's account. Publishing fees are those fees directly associated with online, disk, and paper manuscript submission.

Under the section "Law and Venue," the parties agree to arbitrate disputes. Should either party want equitable relief or need to enforce the arbitrator's judgment, the remedy must be found in the state or federal courts of Pennsylvania.

AUTHOR-FRIENDLY RATING: Xlibris is a bottomless well into which you will throw all of your publishing money. The publisher charges authors too much for its books and takes a huge royalty on retail sales, leaving authors holding nothing more than an overpriced book for which they make a tawdry royalty. While Xlibris offers some cheaper packages, if you don't pay to have a custom cover design, you are just wasting your money (this applies to any company, not just Xlibris). Taken at face value, the $1,599 Custom Package is decently priced, but the author website and the book's production files, which you pay for yet do not own, make that package not so great in the end.

And therein lays the rub: on their own, some of the packages aren't so bad, but when you add in the huge printing markups and incredibly low royalties, the positives wash away. The inflated printing costs cause the retail pricing to be ridiculous. Xlibris sells its books approximately $6.00 higher than what is commercially viable. Couple that with the fact that Xlibris makes double what the author does in royalties, and you've got a recipe for disaster.

If 250% printing markups and the publisher making twice your royalties don't bother you, just hang on—there's much, much more. Rounding out the hellish trifecta is the price you'll pay to purchase copies of your own book. That 200-page paperback can be purchased by the author for $13.99, a full $10.09 more than what it costs to print. At that price (plus postage, don't forget!), you'd need to sell it for $20 to make any money, and your book would have trouble competing in the marketplace.

And last, yet hardly least, for all that money, if you leave Xlibris you can't take your book's digital production files with you. You'll have to start all over with another publisher or pay a graphic artist another $500 to lay out the book and cover for you again.

On a customer service note, the publisher's operator seemed annoyed to receive my call and suggested I look for the answers to my question on the website. When further pressed, she forwarded me to a representative who would not answer any questions without taking down my address and phone number, seemed little versed in the company's offering, and tried to strong-arm me into committing to a package. She even promised that, if I just went ahead and locked into the package at the sales price, I could cancel the purchase if I changed my mind.

Yes, Random House Ventures, the investment subsidiary of Random House, owns a minority stake in Xlibris, but don't let that fool you into thinking you aren't getting played. If Random House actually knows what's going on and condones the way that Xlibris rips off authors, then it is the Michael Vick of publishing.

If what you read here isn't enough to convince you to stay away, then P.T. Barnum was right—there really is a sucker born every minute.

CONCLUSION

You Found a Publisher, Now What?

If you follow the advice in this book, you'll end up with a reputable, author-friendly publisher that doesn't gouge you by grossly inflating printing charges and taking steep royalties. That will put you in the best position to make a profit when you sell copies of your book. But, in order to make money selling your book, you need people to learn about it, find it and want to buy it.

Marketing your book and making it sell ultimately falls on you. Today's book publishing environment is not The Field of Dreams—there is no guarantee that if you publish it, anyone will buy it. New, unknown authors face the same challenges regardless of whether they were published by a traditional publishing house or by a self-publishing company. The first-time novelist fortunate enough to sign a contract with Random House and the first-time author who pays one of the publishers listed in this book start from much the same place. Sure, the other guy brags to his friends about his "publishing deal," but that's where the difference ends. Virtually all traditional publishers expect new authors to market and promote their own books with, in most cases, little or no monetary assistance from the publisher. These authors face the same uphill marketing battle that a self-published author like you faces.

If you don't invest your own time and some money in the promotion of your book, don't expect it to sell. Some self-publishing companies provide good marketing programs, but many still try to get authors to buy junk that does nothing for them, like bookmarks, posters, etc.

In some instances, especially with nonfiction books, traditional marketing techniques like hiring a publicist still work. However, when that publicist lands you a radio interview, the gap between the interview and a listener actually buying your book is a chasm. Not everyone listening to that radio program is going to be interested in your book. If some are, you'll have to depend on them to write down and/or remember your name or the title of your book, and then to actually go to a bookstore or online retailer to look up the book and buy it. The longer the interval of time between the radio appearance and the potential reader taking any steps to buy your book, the more the chance diminishes. Television ads, magazine ads, and articles in periodicals have the same problems—they rely on the person seeing them to get around to taking some action at some future point, and they aren't very targeted. For example, I don't advertise this book in Writer's Digest because even though readership is almost all writers, only a fraction of them are thinking about self-publishing, and even a smaller percentage are considering self-publishing companies. So, even though the magazine is targeted, it's not targeted enough for my advertising dollar.

The Internet changed the advertising and promotion landscape. It's possible to create websites that rank high for specific search terms. For example, go to Google and type in "self publishing companies." In the natural results (not the ads) you will see a description about the website for this book, www.book-publishers-compared.com, in the top few results. Why is that important? Because I know that most people who type that search term into a search engine (like Google, Yahoo, or MSN) are looking for information on self-publishing companies. Once that searcher clicks through the link, they are on my website. Now, this already qualified prospect (based on the search query he typed into a search engine) is presented an offer to buy my book on a topic that truly interests him. That is the kind of lead I want for my book—laser-targeted, not tire-kicking.

The same theory applies to purchasing online advertising. The difference between the natural results and the ads are that every time someone clicks on your ad, you pay an agreed upon fee to the search engine, whereas there is no charge if the person clicks on a link to a website in the natural results.

My entire company of more than 30 websites was built solely on two factors: knowing how to write websites that rank high on search engines, and understanding how to effectively advertise online. Selling books online is no different than selling any other product or service online; in order to be successful doing it, you need to spend your money wisely and put together an effective, targeted online campaign. The learning curve is a big one. I suggest hiring someone to help you, especially with the creation of an optimized website and an online advertising campaign. I became successful at this by learning the hard way.

Not every web strategy works for all types of books. Grassroots marketing of fiction on social networking sites is more effective than online advertising. The key to doing anything online is a solid, well-written, optimized website. When you market online, all roads lead back to your site, and you need a good one if you want potential readers/buyers to take you and your writing seriously.

The most effective book marketing techniques are the ones that involve traditional methods (e.g., sending out galley copies), a smart online strategy, and an author dedicated to hitting the pavement herself. If you can secure a real distributor for your book, that helps tremendously.

If you would like to learn more about how to create a targeted, cost-effective online marketing program for your book, e-mail me at mark@clickindustries.com. Put, "Hey, I actually read the conclusion" in the subject line, and in the body of the e-mail, tell me about your book. I'll e-mail you, and we'll set up a time to chat. Think of this as a little bonus for making it all the way to the end of this book.

Whatever you choose to do with your book, it's an accomplishment to have completed and published it. How many people do you know have a book inside of them that yet never find the time or courage to write it?

I wish you success with your book. I hope I've helped make the process, especially your decision about publishing options, easier and less stressful. Good luck and good writing.

Acknowledgments

Updating this book was a massive undertaking. I couldn't have done it alone. My thanks to the following people for their contributions:

Jenni Wheeler (Book cover design)

Susan Pagani (Editing and research)

Sarah Kolb (Editing)

MSB Media Group (Interior layout and editing)